GARMENT GODDESS

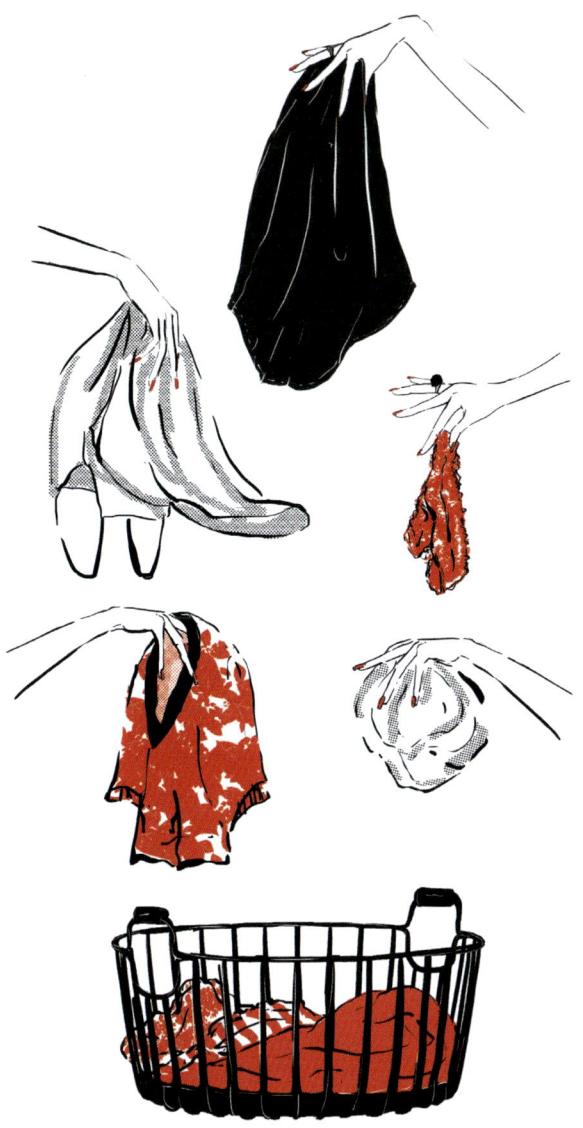

LAURA DE BARRA is a Cork-born property portfolio developer, author and illustrator. Prior to working in property, Laura studied for her degree in fashion at Edinburgh College of Art. She went on to work as a designer across both menswear and womenswear for a large high-street fashion supplier and high-street brands. Her previous books, *Gaff Goddess* and *Décor Galore*, were No. 1 bestsellers, with *Décor Galore* winning the An Post Lifestyle Book of the Year Award in 2021. She is a regular guest on RTÉ Radio 1, BBC Radio Scotland/London and *The Late Late Show*, and contributes to the *Irish Times*. Her Instagram and TikTok accounts (@lauradebarra) are packed with clever décor and fashion repairs, SHE-IY tips and how-tos.

Laura de Barra

GARMENT GODDESS

How to buy, care for and increase the lifetime of your clothing

GILL BOOKS

Gill Books
Hume Avenue
Park West
Dublin 12

www.gillbooks.ie

Gill Books is an imprint of M.H. Gill and Co.

© Laura de Barra 2023

978 07171 98788

Proofread by Ciara McNee
Printed and bound by Interak, Poland
This book is typeset in 11 on 14.5pt, Futura PT.

The paper used in this book comes from the wood pulp of sustainably managed forests.

To the best of our knowledge, this book complies in full with the requirements of the General Product Safety Regulation (GPSR). For further information and help with any safety queries, please contact us at productsafety@gill.ie.

All rights reserved.
No part of this publication may be copied, reproduced or transmitted in any form or by any means, without written permission of the publishers.

A CIP catalogue record for this book is available from the British Library.

5 4 3 2

This book is dedicated to Kieran,
forever missed.

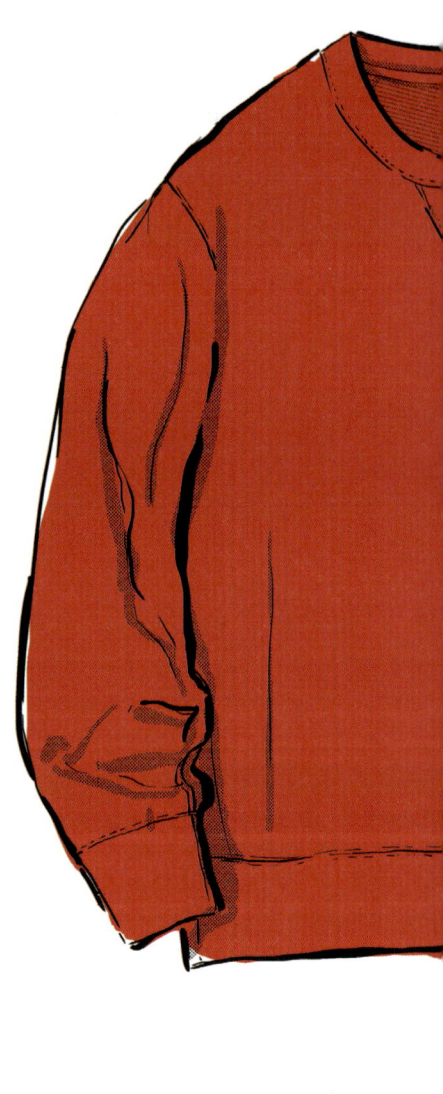

Contents

You'll Never See Clothes the Same Way Again   1

BUYING AND TRYING   7

1. Fabulous Fabric   10
2. The Art of Reading   49
3. Purchase Points   61
4. Virtually Speaking   131
5. The Changing Room   139

WEAR AND CARE   151

6. La-La-Laundry   155
7. She's Living   197
8. YIKES   216
9. Adieu   229

REPAIR AND A SPARE   243

10. Building a Sewing Kit   246
11. A Stitch in Time   266
12. Make Me Over   290

Acknowledgements   303
Index   304

You'll Never See Clothes the Same Way Again

WELCOME, welcome, welcome, welcome!

If you have found your way to *Garment Goddess* you are either starting, or are already enjoying, a long-term love affair with your clothing. I am simply delighted to have you here!

This book was created for anyone who would like to learn how to build a long-lasting wardrobe and make the clothing they already own live with them for longer. She is here to help you to learn how to shop for, care for and repair your wardrobe.

We will be delving into delights like fabric composition and manufacturing techniques. This will help you to quickly spot the signs of high and low quality, as well as to assess if garments are right for your wants and needs. There's a delicious section on laundry and garment care that will help you to ensure your routine is enhancing and not hampering the life of your clothing (I'm drooling even thinking about it). We round off with a section on the art (and the joy!) of mending and creating. After all, every Garment Goddess knows how to carry out an essential repair here and there or rustle up a little something for the weekend. 'C'est bon, c'est bon,' as de Lesseps would say.

You will quickly notice that this book is neither aimed at womenswear nor menswear; instead there will be a mix of refs throughout. This is because there is a chic, high-backed seat at the gothic, glossy dinner table for everyone when it comes to GG books. The tips and tricks cover all the most common garments we shop for on the high street, whichever department we find ourselves in. You will go away with enough knowledge under your Moschino belt to help you identify the garments that will play a significant role in your life, be fit for purpose and long-lasting – and avoid those that won't.

GENERATIONS PAST

As I was putting together this book and chatting about her with friends who have also worked in and studied fashion, we would always end up reminiscing so fondly on the care and time previous generations spent on their clothing. This, after all, was the generation that had taught many of us how to sew, how to mend and how to pattern-cut before we ever started in formal fashion education or careers. Their slow consumption of clothing and attention to fabrics and finishing have stayed with us all to this day. Their approach was gentle, it was considered and it was kinder to our world in so many ways. The generations before us wore their clothes for far longer than we do, shopped less than we do and made and mended more than we do.

During these conversations, it was often noted how stunning it would be to apply the previous generation's approach to our generation's consumption problem. However, in this era of fast fashion and poor quality, it is simply impossible to adopt the previous generations' ways in a bid to make our garments last longer. We are working with different lifestyles, fabrics and qualities.

Unlike the icons of the past, we are faced with issues they never had to contend with. Fabrics are often unfit for their purpose, production methods are chosen for speed instead of suitability, fastenings often fail, and many garments produced these days are created to be worn only a handful of times. We also care for our clothing in a much different way. Laundry, for example, has become less about the clothing and more about the scent afterwards. Machines are used in a more damaging way and we often over-launder.

The landscape of shopping for clothing changed faster than anyone could have anticipated and it has done so across many levels. From demand through to supply, every part of the process is different, with the end products often being unwearable and unrepairable after a few outings.

Older generations required, and could shop for, garments that would last for years, whereas those available to us can sometimes barely last a wash. Our battles on the shop floor are different now, so we need to arm ourselves with more than a needle and thread in our quest for a long-wear wardrobe.

HOW TO: DO YOU

As with my first book, *Gaff Goddess*, the reason I began passionately putting this book together is that I felt it could help us to take back control over something that plays an important role in daily life. We spend time and money on our clothing – from shopping to laundering to repairing. However, there is very little out there to tell us how to make sure we are doing it right without some kind of consumption push behind it.

There are many fabulous fashion 'how to' books out there. Most focus on style: such as how to dress like the French or get tailored suiting right. Others may be strictly about mending and repairs but can be so craft-focused and rarely include the basics or are not focused on modern clothing and style. You'll see some fashion books that will focus on storage and managing more stuff. And let's not forget the not-so-fabulous: how to dress for your body 'shape' and age. Thankfully the era of learning how to dress like a 42-year-old apple has dropped off the face of the Earth.

Drawing from my background in clothing construction and repairs, along with my passion for a great laundry routine for all, we will cover what you need to know to adapt the previous generations' ways to our current set-up. A sprinkle of long-wear mentality here, a tszuj to our laundry routine there and BING a stunning state of affairs.

THE DAWNING OF A NEW ERA

We are embarking on a change in fashion; the speed of consumption is (thank gawd!) set to slow down. This will largely be a reaction to poor quality and the customer wanting more from what they buy but also a change in more commercial style. Signs that we are simply fed up with buying badly made clothing have already started to creep in. You may have noticed many people you know or follow online choosing to create capsule wardrobes and opting for fewer

wear-once garments. You may see people talking about the difficulty of finding well-made clothing or being frustrated that something they love has fallen to bits.

What this book will hopefully teach you is that change is in our hands and our hands only. Production only responds to one thing and that is customer demand. When we slow down, they slow down. When we snub the poorly constructed and start to opt for quality, they start to supply more quality. To trigger change, we need to become more knowledgeable shoppers and know how to shop well for our own lives.

As it stands, there is very little out there that helps us to understand modern clothing and production techniques in a way that will help us to spot the good and avoid the bad. Having worked in a clothing supplier for years after I studied fashion, I saw first-hand how the design process changed in response to the shopper wanting faster, cheaper clothing. Practicality and quality were stripped. I will be able to help you see what has been taken out to deliver lower cost, what you should expect in some garments and what you should not accept.

The aim of this book is to arm you with enough knowledge that the shop floor, and your wardrobe, become less of a minefield and more of a pleasure.

All in all, she's a joyful ride and one I hope you enjoy,

BUYING AND TRYING

BEFORE WE can even think about dipping a well-manicured toe into the wear, repair and care of our clothes, we first need to master the art of ... great selection. Buying well is something anyone who wants to can conquer, and this is for one main reason: you, the wearer, hold all the answers. *sunbeam enters, cue angels singing* Glorious.

There are different elements to clothing that contribute to its longevity, suitability and sustainability. These elements must all be assessed to make sure we are making a wise purchase for ourselves and our wardrobe. After we have decided something is a lewk we like, it mainly boils down to:

WHAT SHE IS MADE OF:
Fabric composition, fastenings, threads.

HOW SHE IS MADE:
Production, construction, finishing, fit.

As well as being Mother when it comes to your true aesthetic, you, my dear, are also the most qualified person for selecting garments that will tick the right boxes and work in harmony with your lifestyle. Nobody else will be more aware of the journey that your garments will take from hanger to hamper than you. You know the body positions, body temperature, storage, comfort requirements, areas of stress, washing routines ... I could go on.

Bottom line, you've got the answers to the questions that we should be asking ourselves prior to every purchase. This section, Buying and Trying, is going to help you unlock exactly what these key questions are. Understanding what we should all be querying when we review new items for our wardrobes is key to matching new garments to our intentions for them. You will learn how to scan clothing for signs that they will suit you, the wearer and carer, and build a wardrobe meant to last and, most of all, be loved for a long time.

Buckle up, bebe, the first stop on our journey is the wonderful world of fabrics and fibres. Choo, choo.

1 Fabulous Fabric

ONE OF THE most important pieces of information a garment tag can tell you is the fibres that make up its fabric composition. Why is this such vital information? Think of fibres as the raw material for fabric. These raw materials determine the garment's cost, how it performs when worn, how it responds to your body, how it makes the garment fit, how it feels, how it wears and, of course, how it will fare once discarded.

The characteristics of fibres can differ massively. Even when two fabrics look and feel the same, they can both perform in very different ways if different fibres are present. That is why it is super-important to be aware of the fibres you're buying and to understand their characteristics.

This knowledge will help us to commit to purchases confidently, avoid disappointment and make more planet-conscious purchases. It will also give us reliability and trust in purchases that will help to slow us down beautifully and enjoy a long-lasting wardrobe that suits our needs from head to toe.

A CHANGE IN PACE

A visit to any preloved store will show you everyday items whose fabric is still fit for purpose after 15 years. So how exactly did we get to a place of such poor fabric quality? Before the emergence of fast fashion, clothing manufacturing for the high street was a more thorough process, mainly because most shoppers wanted their clothing to last for a long time and their price expectations reflected this.

This gave space, time and budget for producers to match the fabric to the wear-and-tear potential of the garment. Everything from the way the garment fell to how it made the wearer feel, to how it performed when it was worn, was considered prior to production. After all, the producer would make enough of a margin to warrant it. Stunning!

Then along came the rise in demand for cheaper, faster clothing and all that changed. Over a very short time (cast your mind back to when clothing hauls started to take off online), correct fabric consideration was swiftly dropped in a bid to respond to the customers' changing demands. Instead of using more costly but more suitable fabrics, producers were left with little choice but to go for something unsuitable to create the desired aesthetic very cheaply. This new demand has led to us no longer being able to rely on the fabrics chosen for high-street garments being as fit for purpose as we did before. Even with higher-priced brands, we cannot assume that the fabric will match the function.

This means that we are often bringing home clothing that is destined to fail, despite our best efforts and best intentions, and a lot of it is down to it being in a fabric that doesn't suit the use of the garment.

WHAT'S A GAL TO DO?

For something that is in our daily lives since birth, we know very little about fabric. So, trying to shop these days can be more than frustrating as so many brands seem to be at these low-quality shenanigans. Learning the basics of fabric, even if you seldom shop, is incredibly useful as it helps you to understand more of what you already own as well as be able to purchase new bits properly. No one needs to become a fabric expert to shop for their wardrobe so we won't overwhelm and will mainly cover the basics. Having these basics under your belt will cover 90 per cent of what you're going to see in-store these days and give you enough knowledge to help you cast critical eyes over anything else you encounter.

WHAT IS FABRIC?

The basics start a little something like this:

NATURAL FIBRES come from plants and animals. Synthetic fibres are made from synthesised polymers (chemicals).

YARN is created by twisting raw fibres together, or created from scratch using synthetic materials

FABRIC is essentially yarn woven together to create cloth.

Now we know that it's all about the fibres, let's kick things off by getting to know the two categories of fibres a little better ...

NATURAL GALS

The Naturals are derived from plants or animals and insects. As you can imagine, these have much less of a negative impact on our planet than synthetic fibres but they also have the massive advantage of having a less negative impact on you, too.

It is always a great move to opt for natural fabrics where they suit your needs, as they not only feel and last better but their production and damage to the planet, post-wear, is nowhere near as harsh as synthetics. Some natural fibres have a less-than-desirable environmental impact during the makeover into yarn – but we will get into that later on. The main takeaway is that, although they are less damaging as a whole, we cannot assume that all natural fibres are eco queens.

POPULAR NATURALS
Here are the more common natural fibres you will encounter on the high street and where they come from. Note here: if they are plant-derived, they will be made from cellulose and if they come from an animal, they will be protein queens. If you don't wish to shop for animal-derived products, this is handy to get to know, as it will help you see what has animal protein and what does not.

CELLULOSE-DERIVED
COTTON: Made from bolls of the cotton plant.
FLAX (THINK LINEN): Stalks of the flax plant.
HEMP: Stalks of the *Cannabis sativa* plant.

PROTEIN QUEENS

WOOL: The protein here is keratin (the same as our hair).
SILK: Made from the cocoons of silkworms.
CASHMERE: From the underbelly of specific breeds of goat.

WHAT THE NATURALS OFFER

Here are the main things you need to know about natural fibres when it comes to the wearer.

BREATHABILITY: You'll never get overheated in a natural as they are so breathable. They can keep us cool in summer but also warm in winter with no risk of overheating. This is down to them being more permeable, which means body temperature can be more easily regulated.

COMFORT: There are qualities in each natural fibre that will contribute to them being very comfortable to wear. Some of the softest fabrics you can buy are made from natural fibres. Think silk and cashmere.

ALLERGIES: They won't irritate the skin or respiratory system like synthetics can. This is down to the fact that many are naturally hypoallergenic and that they are not created from harsh chemicals.

ABSORBENT: The naturally high absorbency makes them a stunning match for things like tees, shirting, bedding, towels and anything else that sits close to the body. This is because they happily wick sweat away from the body by absorbing it but also, most importantly, can release it quickly. This keeps you feeling fresh and prevents odour build-up.

DURABLE: Many high-quality natural fibres used in day-to-day clothing, like cotton, are durable and long-wearing. This means they can survive washing cycles much better and will wear out a lot slower.

Our own needs aside, natural fabrics are also better for our planet:

RENEWABLE: We are not eating into limited resources when we create natural fibres. They come from living things that are renewable sources.

SUSTAINABLE: It is much easier to find sustainable and organic versions of natural fibres than synthetic, so conscious shopping is a lot more achievable.

BIODEGRADABLE: They can break down naturally in landfill (when strong chemicals have not been used) and will not live to haunt the earth for decades as a synthetic can.

MINIMAL LAUNDRY IMPACT: Washing natural fibres does not release harmful microplastics during each wash, which means their environmental impact during their lifetime is not as heavy.

And finally, there are factors that influence the producer, both good and bad:

EASE OF PRODUCTION: Although more labour-intensive than synthetics, The Naturals can be produced with less modern, costly machinery. This means the producer isn't stuck in a cycle of expensive machinery updates and having to compete with wealthier countries or companies.

HIGH-QUALITY CONNOTATIONS: The Naturals can be more expensive to produce but have an affiliation with quality so a higher price can be sought. This allows the producer to have a better margin and deliver a higher quality product.

EASE: Natural fibres can hack a lot of heat and so they can be treated in ways synthetics can't, which makes them less intense and harmful to work with. They also take dye extremely well due to how coarse the fibres are.

DEMAND: Although they can be the more suitable option for a garment, they are not always chosen. The fast-fashion customer is constantly seeking lower prices in trend-led items which is leading to traditionally natural garments needing to be made in cheaper synthetics. This affects producers massively as their place in the market can be threatened.

GOING GREEN: It is easier to branch into the growing market for sustainable and organic garments when you are set up for natural fabric production. For many types of fabrics, certification can be gained by removing toxic chemicals and altering production processes so it allows the producer to move easily into a growing sustainable market where synthetics cannot. This benefits not only the surrounding environment but the people working with the fibres too.

MANUFACTURED MADAMS

Synthetic or manufactured fibres are those made from inorganically created polymers, which are basically synthesised chemicals. To put it bluntly, synthetic fibres are mainly created from petrochemicals. For example, polyester is usually derived from petroleum. Doesn't sound too stunning ... because it isn't.

To create a yarn, the most common method, simplified, is that the chemicals are formed into a liquid matter which is then pushed through a sieve-like structure that results in thin strands of plastic. These strands have the characteristics of yarn and can then be woven to create fabric.

This fabric can appear so much like a natural fabric that sometimes only a burn test will show if it is the real deal. This is because when intense heat is applied to synthetics, they will melt back into a plastic-like substance. Think about when you burn the edges of a ribbon, you may have noticed it hardens and you may see a hard drip-like shape form. This is plastic melting. On the other hand, when you burn a natural fibre, it is like burning anything you can go outside and pick up from the garden. It's a clean burn that doesn't melt back into a gloopy mess.

POPULAR SYNTHETICS

Below are some of the most common synthetics we buy today. As most of them were created to do something a natural couldn't, their damage to the planet was not considered. At their debut, they were simply innovative and a solution to a problem.

NYLON: She was first found as an alternative to silk hosiery. The durability and affordability she offered saw her rise so much in popularity that stockings were soon called nylons.

POLYESTER: This gal gained notoriety due to her anti-wrinkle and easy-care qualities. She boomed for decades but started to decline as wearers realised she was not as comfortable to wear.

ACRYLIC: Due to being able to deliver a wool look at a low cost, acrylic solved a cost issue. This is why most high street knits are made from her. She may be cheap, but she is one of the least breathable fabrics and very hard to care for.

SPANDEX: You'll also hear this called elastane or the trademarked Lycra. Did you know Spandex is an anagram for expands?

This is famed for its ability to stretch and still retain its shape. This is why it is often combined with naturals to give shape or hold to the body, like in underwear.

CHARACTERISTICS
What can you, the wearer, expect from synthetics?

OVERHEATING: Most synthetics are not naturally breathable, which means they encourage excessive sweating. (Do you have a top that makes you sweat no matter what? Check her ingredients!)

NOT TRULY ABSORBENT: When sweat cannot be absorbed or released properly, it has nowhere to go and sits between the fabric and your skin during wear.

ODOURS: This trapped sweat cannot evaporate properly and this can cause a strong odour to gradually form on a piece.

CHEAPER: The low production costs mean a style can be cheaper to purchase in-store than its natural competitors.

COMFORT: They are low in comfort due to the lack of ventilation.

IRRITATING: As they are made from harsh chemicals and go through such extreme processes, these fabrics can often irritate wearers with sensitive skin.

WEAK: As they are often poor quality, they can weaken and degrade quickly through wear and washing.

WATER RESISTANT: They can keep us dry when needed but, to truly benefit from full water resistance, seaming and fastenings must also be resistant. These come with a high price.

LESS LIKELY TO WRINKLE: As you can imagine based on the way the fibres are made, synthetics have a memory that prevents them from wrinkling badly.

There is also a much greater planetary impact:

PRODUCTION IMPACT: There is heavy impact through the production stages due to the machinery, chemicals and processes used. Now you know the journey from machine to mannequin, you can see why fast fashion has such a harsh impact on the environment.

MICROPLASTICS: Each time a garment made with synthetic fibres is washed, it releases microfibres into our ecosystem.

NON-DEGRADABLE: They do not break down and so will live alongside us pretty much for lifetimes. This means they are contributing to a large percentage of landfill due to their popularity.

Finally, the factors affecting the producer:

COST: It is cheaper to produce on-trend styles quickly so higher margins can be made. However, fast fashion has created such a poor opinion of synthetics, some cheaper producers are having to take costly measures to improve their quality.

EASE: Larger quantities are faster and easier to make as there is less labour required due to the use of expensive machinery.

DESIGN: Dyes will wear out slower and synthetics can be manipulated more easily than naturals when it comes to things like laser cutting and pleating. This means there is always demand for fashion styles.

HARMFUL: Many of the chemicals used are harmful to those working with them and to the planet. This is a growing issue for producers that could once allow this harm to go unnoticed as demand for transparent and sustainable practices is now higher than ever.

SEMI-SYNTHETICS

We cannot mention synthetics without touching on rayon. Rayon starts her life as a natural fibre. Where she meets her synthetic fate is when she is processed using chemicals to be turned into a solution. Then, as happens with synthetics, this is extruded to form a yarn and not spun as a natural fibre would be.

When the natural fibres used come from cellulose, the finished product is rayon. Rayon can come from trees, plants or bamboo.

The reason rayon in clothing became so popular is that it has some qualities of naturals – such as breathability and moisture wicking – but it could be produced more cheaply and more quickly.

As these fibres come from renewable sources such as wood and plants, many people assume they are in some way sustainable. This is why you might see some rayons described as natural fibres. However, the chemical processes used and the fact the fabric is not spun cements the fact that it is not truly a natural fibre. Also, their production is often involved in deforestation and the chemicals used are extremely harmful to those involved.

As there is such a heavy environmental load with rayon, adding it to your wardrobe should be done with the same consideration you would give synthetics. It is good to be aware of on its pros and cons.

MICROPLASTICS

Plastic destroying our oceans and other ecosystems is nothing new. We are all too aware of the damage single-use plastic – including bottles, straws, bags and so on – have done to the planet over time.

Less obvious to the eye are microplastics, defined as plastic less than 5mm in size. Small but certainly as, if not more, deadly. As well as appearing on our beaches and in our oceans, they are now in our water and seafood.

Microplastics are broken into two categories: primary and secondary. Secondary are fragments of larger plastic items, such as bottles, that have broken down over time.

For the context of this book, we need to focus on primary microplastics, which are caused by cosmetics and, you guessed it, ... synthetic textiles.

These are released during manufacturing, laundry (more on this later!) and, of course, dumping. This is mainly in synthetics but some naturals with heavy chemicals and dyes can also be an issue.

CHARACTERISTICS OF POPULAR FABRICS

Now that you know a little more about the main difference between The Naturals and synthetics, how can you apply this when buying new clothes? How can you make sure you are matching up the fabrics to the intentions for the garment and buying something that can stand the test of time and deserve its place in your wardrobe? Let's take a look at the most commonly used fibres and how to spot good quality.

COTTON

We are going to spend a little more time on cotton than other natural gals. This is because she is required more in day-to-day clothing and a simply stunning addition to a long-lasting wardrobe if bought correctly.

Great cotton was once a no-brainer for certain garments, but she was greatly affected by the influx of fast fashion and a lower price expectation from customers. This meant that good cotton was constantly replaced with cheaper synthetics or cheaper low-quality cottons.

You will always pay a little more for good cotton upfront, but its stunning characteristics will mean it is cheaper to own long-term. This is why having some cotton knowledge under your belt will help you massively in terms of selecting garments that can last.

A re-emergence in demand for great cotton and long-lasting daily wear clothing has meant that customers see her value and brands are starting to react, so your choice of good cottons will be abundant in the near future.

This demand does mean, however, that some low-quality cottons are sneaking into the higher price levels. To help you avoid the trap and shop well, we will dip into cotton qualities. High-quality cotton is quite easy to spot with a little know-how so let's get into it!

WHO IS SHE?

Cotton fibres come from the *Gossypium* genus (a stunning drag name if you ask me) or, as it is more commonly known, the cotton plant. The white fibres that you see on a cotton plant are there to protect the seed pods on the plant and are what is used to make cotton fabric. Divine!

WHAT IS SHE GOOD FOR?

Cotton is simply superb for anything that will be sitting close to your body. Her natural qualities will keep you cool in summer and warm in winter, she is soft, she will wick sweat away from your skin with ease and she won't trap odours.

Don't forget, garments that sit close to our skin will always need to be washed more, so the durability of cotton makes it ideal for these! As it is such a tough fabric, it can hack the warmer temperatures needed to completely remove the sweat and oils it will encounter during wear. Ever notice that no matter what your knickers are made of there will be a cotton gusset? This is exactly the reason why.

From a long-term use point of view, it is easy to care for cotton. She is one of the more durable fabrics we can choose and can be much easier to repair than others. This is why she is used in denim jeans and many outerwear items.

In short, the day-to-day garments that are ideal to have a fabulous cotton composition are:

- Underwear and socks.
- Tailoring.
- Garments you wear against the skin, especially the pits.
- Anything you need to be breathable, like summer garments or work shirts.
- Outerwear and workwear.

GETTING IT RIGHT

You would be forgiven for thinking all cotton is the same but there are different qualities of cotton used in clothing. The quality of cotton and how long-lasting and comfortable it is, is usually down to where the cotton is grown as better soil and regions produce a more stunning cotton fibre than others; premium cotton is always long-staple cotton.

WHY DOES STAPLE MATTER?

What exactly determines high-quality cotton? Well, all cotton quality comes down to its 'staple'. Staple means the length of the cotton fibres that are then spun into a yarn. The longer the staple, the better the cotton, to put it simply. You'll have heard of Egyptian cotton, I'm sure. She's a long-staple queen.

A great cotton with a long staple will live in harmony with you as long as she is cared for correctly and so is always worth the little extra you'll pay for her. Why? A longer staple means a stronger yarn. The longer the staple, the thinner the yarn.

Thinner yarns are superior for the following reasons:

DENSITY

Thinner yarns mean you can have a much denser weave, which means there is less stress on the yarns when worn and they can be better for temperature regulation.

DURABILITY

When we have thin yarn, we can achieve a much more durable fabric as the yarns are more compact and secure. Short staple can snap easily.

PILLING

Longer staple will sit stunningly in place, whereas short staple is more likely to loosen and create bobbling.

TOUCH

Short staple has far more exposed ends which leads to a coarser handfeel. Long staple will always feel smoother to the touch and better to wear.

HOW TO SPOT LONG-STAPLE COTTON

As a consumer, there are some pretty easy ways to spot a long-staple cotton:

PRICE POINT: You cannot get great cotton at a really low price unless it is on sale or preowned, so price is usually the first give away. Do be aware that if the piece is expensive and the boxes below aren't getting ticked, it's probably just cheap cotton at a high price.

NOTED

Brands LOVE to tell you if they use long-staple cotton as it means they can justify a higher price point. Look out for these popular long-staple cotton types if the price is high:

ELS: Extra-long staple.

PIMA: A hard-wearing but ultra-soft cotton. Renowned for its durability and long-lasting qualities.

EGYPTIAN COTTON: Used in many higher-price shirts as it is said to not pill/bobble and is super breathable.

SUPIMA: Literally superior Pima, this is an extraaaaa-long staple. This is one of the most popular ELS cottons as it has a traceable supply chain due to being trademarked cotton so you'll see great brands opting for this

SEA ISLAND: This is said to be the most luxurious cotton so it is more expensive. It is famed for its silk-like handfeel. Expect very high price basics to be in this.

If a cotton garment is pricey, look for justifications like these. Usually, it's a swing ticket or sticker on the

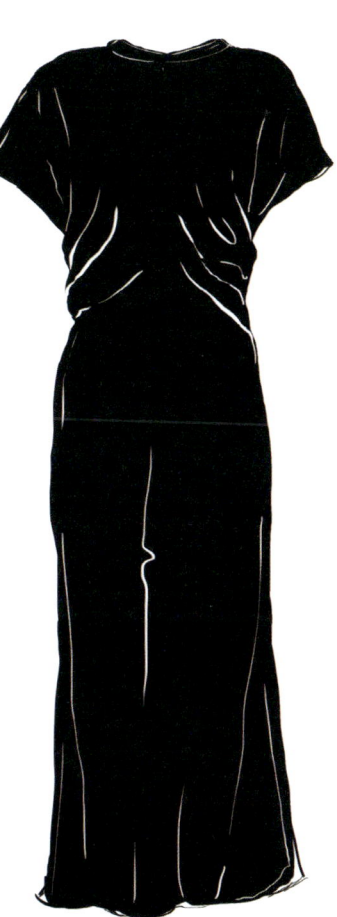

garment or a spiel in the online description. If you don't see adequate reasoning or notes on the fabric, it is usually safe to assume that the garment has a higher price to make a margin or for branding reasons and it's not down to just the fabric.

WHAT TO LOOK FOR IN-STORE

TOUCH: Put one hand up inside and rub the fabric on both the inside and outside. Great-quality cotton will feel gorgeous and almost cold to the touch. With good-quality cotton, you won't get a coarseness to the fibres or feel small inconsistencies. Some poor-quality cottons will have a coating on the outside to present better before the first wash and stop it from pilling in-store. Rub it between your fingers to check; if there is a coating, you won't be able to feel the weave of the fabric properly and it may have an odour.

APPEARANCE: When you examine closely, lower-staple cottons will have an irregularity to them due to having chunkier, shorter fibres. Long staple on the other hand provides long, sleek yarns and allows the fabric to be evenly woven, with a uniform and clean finish. If you see little irregularities or patches where the yarns look lightly pilled, this is low quality. Rub your thumb over a small area and see how the fabric reacts. If you see fibres lifting or the weave opening the price should reflect this. Long-lasting cottons have a lovely dense appearance and feel compact no matter how thin the fabric is and rubbing between your thumb and finger will not alter a long staple in any way. Density is vital for long-lasting clothes as it protects the fibres during wearing and washing.

GAPS: These will never be obvious on the hanger. Always hold cotton up to the light (or when super-expensive, I use my phone's torch on the inside) to see if there are irregular gaps or small holes in the fabric's weave.

When you see gaps in the weave of a fabric, it is down to inferior yarn as it can be bulky in places and upset how tight the weave can be. Even if a cotton is super-lightweight, you shouldn't be able to see gaps in the fabric.

PILLING: Really cheap, short-staple cottons won't be able to avoid some pilling by the time it gets to the store. If it looks like fibres are loosening on the shop floor or you rub it and you can see bobbles already, she's not going to last well.

TRIMS: Make sure you also look at the cuffs and collar of cottons, especially if they are ribbed. Some brands will scrimp on cost by using these in a lower quality but it will be very obvious if you examine the piece. A very slight difference in colour will also give it away.

SUSTAINABLY SPEAKING

It would not be right to only sing her praises and not highlight the cost to the planet in some instances of cotton creation. This will help you to see why cottons that have sustainable accreditation and more planet-friendly processes can be worth their higher price level.

WATER USAGE: First up is the amount of water used in cotton production. She is one thirsty gal and it is widely known that one kilo of cotton can take up to 20,000 litres of water to cultivate. Not so stunning in areas where there is not a massive amount of rainfall and local sources are exploited. Once cotton has been grown, the spinning, prepping and dyeing processes are also thirsty work, with even more litres being used to create cotton fabric.

CHEMICALS: Cotton was once a wild-growing shrub but grew to be heavily farmed. This meant a lot of pesticides and chemicals were being used to keep harvests strong and regular. This depleted the land in many areas and polluted waterways and soils which, in turn, led to producers having to exploit surrounding areas. The use of these chemicals can also heavily impact the people involved in the process.

HUMAN IMPACT: Many cheaper cotton varieties come with a long chain of exploitation attached to them. This is another reason to try to avoid them. Historically, cotton is manufactured in very poor countries where the people involved — from the picking right through to the spinning and weaving stages — are extremely underpaid and overworked, causing generational poverty and a reliance on the exploitative trade in these areas.

If you are buying something new in cotton and are keen to make sure that the cotton you choose has a minimal environmental and human impact, there are some simple steps to help you do this. The main thing to look for is whether the cotton used is organic or sustainable.

Organic cotton is grown by standards that are certified as organic:

- There are no harmful chemicals or pesticides used.
- The cotton seeds are not GMO.
- Soils are not depleted in a way that creates exploitation of surrounding areas.
- Dyes will be water-based or natural.

As you can imagine, such softer methods will mean organic cotton is great. With less interaction with harmful chemicals, she can last a lot longer. Sometimes if you hold up a brand's organic and regular cotton tees, the organic version can look a little less perfect but this is because it hasn't had the same amount of chemicals applied rather than a quality issue.

To be sure something is organic, look for certification. Global Organic Textile Standard (GOTS) is one of the strictest on the high street and the garment must have a minimum of 95 per cent certified organic fibres. Some brands will state that their products are organic but when you investigate the certification or percentage it's not what it seems, so certification is always key to look out for.

LINEN

While cotton is derived from the bolls of the plant, linen is made from the cellulose inside the stalks of this plant. The flax plant to be precise.

WHO IS SHE?

She shares many characteristics with cotton but uses less water and harsh chemicals during cultivation. This is why many conscious shoppers love her.

Linen is one of those fabrics that you can buy a piece in and keep for years and years and years. This is mainly because linen looks better the more it is worn. Over time it becomes more silky and appealing to the eye as well as the hand.

WHAT IS SHE GOOD FOR?

Linen is not a fabric that is usually worn all year, which adds to her longevity. She is instead best suited to warmer months as her qualities are impeccable at keeping you cool. She is better than cotton for more humid months and something like a neutral linen shirt can be pulled out and depended on year after year.

The reason you will see linen in looser silhouettes and not in a lot of intense tailoring, drapes or slim fits is down to its lack of elasticity. This means it is super-susceptible to wrinkling so a looser shape will allow less creasing during wear. If it's a summer garment you want to last for a long time, go linen. Trousers, jackets, skirts, shirts – you name it. Just be sure to store her hanging as she can wear down along creases and so folding can be hard on her.

If the creasing gets to you, do as the chic do and wear long line tops over linen bottoms to cover crotch creases, opt for simple wider silhouettes and try to remember that only real linen creases so easily, so it's actually a good thing.

GETTING IT RIGHT

HANDFEEL: Yes, linen is not as smooth as, say, cotton but it should not feel really coarse. Although it will be drier, it should not feel like it will be uncomfortable against your skin. Wrap a piece of the garment around your forearm; if it is scratchy, then shorter, inferior fibres have been used and it will not last as long a good-quality linen.

IMPURITIES: These are good. There is a natural slub to most good quality, reasonably priced linen. Slub is like a little bump in the thread and adds an irregular look to the weave. Only the most fine, high-quality linen threads will have zero slub (usually in occasion wear and suiting) and their price will reflect their refined manufacturing. Imposter linens will be completely smooth, zero slub and of a low price.

SCRUNCH TEST: There is no elasticity to linen. Scrunch a bit in your hand gently and it should crease. If it springs back, it is not a great quality or it is mixed with a synthetic. This is a great test if you are looking at vintage and it has no label.

DYES: Spread the garment out so you can see if the dyes are even. Poor-quality linen clothing can appear blotchy in areas. Lift arms and check front and back to make sure the garment took to dyes well.

SUSTAINABLY SPEAKING

Linen is stunning in its natural, undyed form with almost an oatmeal appearance colour-wise and lots of undertones; it can look great in any garment. For this reason, you can opt for less heavily dyed or treated linen and go for the natural look. Linen has natural sustainable qualities but be sure to look for pure linen if you are looking to be more eco-conscious. On the high street, it can often be mixed with viscose or polyester, which will only counteract her splendour. If it's a mix, make sure it's a natural.

Wool

WHO IS SHE?

Wool comes from wool-bearing animals – most commonly sheep. It can also come from goats, camels, rabbits and other animals. As we have been using wool in clothing forever, we have developed so many ways to take advantage of its stunning characteristics.

WHAT IS SHE GOOD FOR?

Wool can retain heat, has natural waterproofing, is breathable, durable and, of course, very easy to work with and repair.

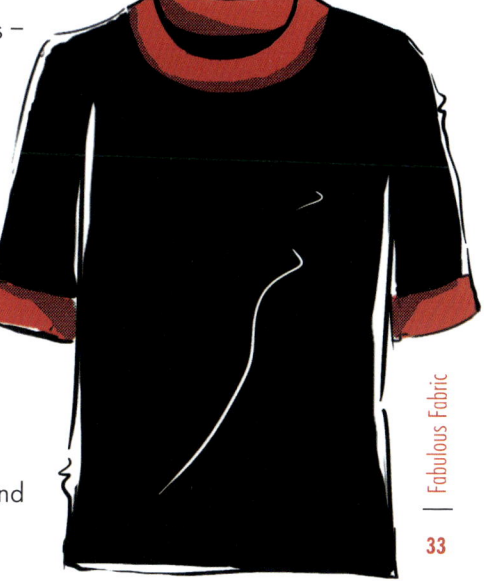

Jumpers, coats, cardis, base layers and winter tops are ideal in wool but don't write her off for summer! Some lighter weights can be a serve in warmer months. Wool is also crease-resistant and holds tailoring really well, so it is fantastic for suiting, skirting and trousers. The drape you get with wool is divine; think Vivienne Westwood's iconique (cruelty-free, of course!) wool pieces. Stunning.

TYPES OF WOOL

The reason wool can do it all is because there are many different types and each has its own delicious qualities, care guidelines and price points!

SHEEP'S WOOL

The most common type of wool you will see on the shop floor is sheep's wool. This is a wonderful natural fibre that we use in so many ways and it can be a stunning addition to a wardrobe as it is lovely to wear, easy to care for and super-durable.

She is very versatile and can be woven into so many weights and textures. Combined with her heat-retaining and comfort qualities, this means she can appear many times in one wardrobe but in completely different ways, from coats to skirts to suiting.

Her versatility is down to the difference in how her staples present:

WORSTED, LONG-STAPLE WOOL: When we have a long-staple wool we can make a much sleeker and flatter fabric. This means we can use it to make super-soft suiting and outerwear. Because the fibres are longer, they are more durable and can go through a few extra steps to make a smooth and super-strong, fine yarn. These tend to be more expensive garments that wear and last well.

WOOLLEN, SHORT-STAPLE WOOL: When a wool is short-staple it is used for fluffier, cosier garments. Woollens are ideal for jumpers, jackets and cardis. The shorter fibres cannot hack as much processing and combing and so have a rougher and fuzzier appeal. For this reason, woollens are advised to be worn and washed less vigorously. They are also usually lined or worn with something underneath to avoid feeling scratchy.

LAMBS' WOOL

This, as you can gather, is from the first sheer, also called virgin wool, so you'll have a much softer wool which is also quite expensive due to its rarity. This is great for something that you will have against your skin, like a sweater or top. If I see lambswool in a vintage or second-hand piece I am adding her to try-ons immediately as she usually comes with a much lower price tag preloved.

MERINO WOOL

People rave about merino and it's no surprise. It's a joy to wear as well as care

for, but mainly it's a luxury that doesn't have to come at a huge cost. This wool comes from the merino sheep and is super-fine so you'll most likely see it in fine-gauge knits and it is also really popular for suiting. Merino is most famed for being super-soft and comfortable but repeat purchases will usually be down to how well it performs. It can keep you warm without causing you to overheat; it has great elasticity so doesn't wrinkle badly; and is also said to be stronger than cotton. These characteristics mean it's a reliable purchase and one you won't see degrade or lose integrity quickly.

On the high street, she is commonly used in a lot of basics and base layers due to how much warmth can be gained from such a thin garment but you will also see merino in lightweight formal wear. Don't, however, sleep on merino for summer! Her breathability and moisture-wicking qualities can make her ideal for warmer months.

If you are adding merino to your wardrobe, start with a simple jumper or tee and you'll be able to see how well she performs compared to others. Merino mixes can also be divine and brilliant for garments that need a bit of durability to keep them lasting longer. Merino and silk, for example? An outrageous state of affairs.

GETTING IT RIGHT

When shopping for wool, good quality can be quite obvious if you know what to look for.

QUALITY: The quality of the yarns is important. Examine the yarn and how uniform the rows look. If the yarn is inferior quality, it will look shoddy, even in-store. You'll see the knit looks like it won't be able to recover well after washing.

PILLING: A major downside to wool is pilling. It happens. To assess if the garment is very likely to pill, before you buy, look under the arms and other areas the garment would be likely to wear. If you can see pilling already, you'll have a good idea of how it will fare in your wardrobe. If you want to avoid pilling entirely, look for smooth, densely woven knits and fine yarns as these need to be long staple to be pulled off and will be of higher quality. Wearing wools with care and washing them gently will reduce the risk of pilling massively.

WATERPROOF: The wool will only usually be waterproof if it is untreated. Treatments and dyes can wipe out the waterproof realness of lanolin and instead, companies will use a chemical to add back in the waterproof characteristic. You may not be up for this so keep it in mind and suss why a wool garment is saying it is waterproof.

LUXURY WOOLS

There are many 'luxury' wools out there – such as alpaca, mohair and angora – but no wool dupes us as much as cashmere. This is why we will have a little meauxment to shine a light on when you should be parting with your cash for a cardi.

CASHMERE

Cashmere is soft and super-lightweight without being scratchy like wool and instead feels incredibly soft. This makes it ideal for anything worn against the skin. It also has great recovery so can keep its shape for years and years.

The goats that grow cashmere grow two layers of wool to protect them from harsh climates, usually in place of fat as they live in arid conditions and are lean as a result. The outer layer is coarse and the inner, protected layer is extremely soft. The reason cashmere is so sought after is that it comes from that underlayer.

However, don't be fooled into thinking the high price is down to quality alone; there are a few other reasons. It takes a lot of goats and a long time to create cashmere, so its high price is also down to how hard it is to supply in comparison to other yarns. It may be famed for being so fine, but it is this characteristic that can also drive up the price as it has to be handled extremely carefully during each of its production stages. All in all, it's a more time-consuming and delicate process to get to a cashmere garment and the price will always reflect this.

Having cashmere pieces in your wardrobe is often recommended due to their softness and long-wear capabilities (if worn and taken care of properly!) and its marketing has everyone assuming that no matter what cashmere you buy, it is worth a high price tag. However, there is a lot of poor-quality cashmere out there and it is good to know how to spot the good if you would like to invest in some.

GRADE: Look for grade A. Cashmere fibres are graded A, B and C, with C being the lowest in quality. A has lovely long yarns, making it more durable and, of course, softer.

LABEL: Some brands will have signage saying 'Grade A Cashmere' or 'All Cashmere' and when you read the label you find that the piece is actually a blend of cashmere and something else. If it includes another fibre, think of its characteristics and why it is there. Wool will add more warmth, silk will give it a more luxurious lewk and so on. If it's something purely there to reduce the cost, it may not be worth it.

HANDFEEL: The next step is how soft the piece feels: high-quality cashmere will be extremely soft. If it is a preloved piece or there is little info available, feel it all over inside and out.

PILLING: Always rub your finger over a patch of the cashmere to see if it pills. By nature, it will be a garment that pills over time but if it does it after a simple rub in-store? Not a great sign.

DYEING: When cashmere is dyed it can affect the handfeel and so only really premium cashmere is dyed to intense shades. This is why you will see a lot of cheaper cashmere in lighter colours. If she is a bright or dark garment, not mixed with a synthetic and of a good handfeel, she is usually a premium quality. Always check the labels on brights and darks, however, as these can also be blends mimicking high quality.

SUSTAINABLY SPEAKING

With some fabrics, bright dyes can mean toxic chemicals but wool is different. Because it is made of a different protein from other fibres, it can be dyed using much milder and simpler dyes. It also takes well to dye so that is why you will see wool in so many colours and strong hues.

That said, with the rise of cheap clothing, this is another fibre that has been impacted. The quality of wool is pretty much related to the treatment of the animal involved. In new garments, look for certifications that the wool is from a trusted source to guarantee that you are investing in a piece that will last. The better the life of the animal, the better the product. Buying cheap wool from animals that were treated badly is not great for obvious reasons but it will cost you more in the long run as it simply won't last.

Polyester

WHO IS SHE?
Polyester, formally known as polyethylene terephthalate, is one of the most popular synthetic fibres. Although she started out as a miracle fabric and something designers loved to use to push the boundaries of clothing production, polyester started to decline in the 70s. This was mainly due to people not thinking that her anti-wrinkle, easy-care characteristics were worth the discomfort when worn.

These days polyester is the darling of fast fashion and landfill after seeing a massive boom in popularity. When wear-once culture started to kick off, her low price and quick production speed meant that many brands turned to her in place of more suitable natural fibres.

The main problem with this rise in popularity is that poly is harmful to the planet and people both before and after she is a garment. Her production methods involve a lot of harmful methods and chemicals, and she does not break down in landfill. Once she's here, she is here to stay. So, although we will speak about some benefits of polyester, this is more for you to understand where it shouldn't be used rather than to promote it. This will, in turn, hopefully help us to reduce our dependence on such a toxic gal.

WHAT IS SHE GOOD FOR?
Throwing shade in regard to something being polyester is a little dated, as you will find many designer and performance garments in poly these days. The true tea with polyester is that, as she is basically a plastic, she can be used in ways a natural cannot. Working with polyester correctly means only using it if a natural cannot do the same job and not as a substitute for a suitable natural fibre to reduce costs. Polyester may be able to do things

The Naturals can't do but it's also rare that she can do what they can.

PERFORMANCE

In good-quality form, polyester can be a reliable performance fabric. As it is strong and can take treatments well, it is often a good option for outdoor brands that need weatherproof, waterproof and UV-proof fabrics. This means performance gear can often last decades if bought in a durable, high-quality polyester.

You'd think polyester is great for all sportswear but it's a little tricky. Because polyester is not absorbent like a natural fibre, it can be ideal for a gym kit as it won't get weighed down with sweat. However, although polyester may not absorb liquids, she does hold on to body oils and bacteria easily. Over time, this can lead to strong odours and gym clothes that just don't ever feel fully washed. For this reason, avoid polyester workout clothing for heavier workouts or for items that are not washed on the same day that you work out.

AESTHETIC

You will often hear someone curse a luxury item in polyester, but to understand if it should be there, we need to look a little deeper.

The way polyester reacts to heat and dyes means that higher-end brands will use it in some of their more intricate styles to be able to achieve the aesthetic they are after. This is why you will often see high-end pleated suits or laser-cut dresses only in poly.

In this case, as polyester is not being used as a cost-saving measure, it will usually be a great quality of polyester that is made to last. This, sadly, is not the same for lower-priced garments as the polyester will be of poor quality and most cheaper polys will degrade quickly.

As you can see, polyester can have a place in the market and there are uses for it. However, these types of garments usually require quality construction and durability and are rarely created to be bought in a throw-away manner.

Should you be buying polyester? It is best to take a moment to consider if it is something that will suit the wear you have in mind and if your wear will justify its purchase. If it does, there are some steps to making sure it is the kind of quality that will last.

GETTING IT RIGHT

LONGEVITY: When you see a polyester garment, think about the function and design of the garment. If it is obvious that the polyester is there purely as a cost-saving measure and to mimic a natural fibre, it is not going to last. If the brand didn't want to spend on a natural to do the job right, it will have used the cheapest poly possible.

FUNCTION: If the polyester is in a performance garment, go in-depth on sussing the construction to make sure it is a durable piece. High-quality performance wear will be constructed immaculately and, in turn, it will use good polyester.

OVERHEATING: Think of when you will be wearing the garment and how hot you will get. As polyester will not allow your temperature to regulate, you may overheat, causing strong odours on the fabric as well as discomfort. Bear this in mind for t-shirts, shirts, dresses, linings and so on.

APPEARANCE: If there is an almost whitish-grey sheen to the polyester, it is one of the cheapest versions and will most likely be made badly too. Look for depth of colour and as non-plastic an appearance as possible.

TOUCH: Poorer-quality polyesters will be obvious by the handfeel. They will feel a little sticky and uncomfortable on the skin.

SMELL: if there is a chemical odour from the fabric, you do not want it on your body. The same goes for any coatings or dyes that seem to be rubbing off as you examine them.

REPAIRS: Polyester can be much harder to repair than a natural fibre so this should always be kept in mind for anything you want to stick around for a long time.

SUSTAINABLY SPEAKING

The manufacture of polyester is awful for the environment due to the harsh chemicals used and melted, the gases emitted, and the water needed for cooling and other stages. But her harm isn't just pre-purchase. When you wash a polyester garment, you shed microplastics and when you discard the piece, it probably won't be breaking down in your lifetime. It will simply take up space on this planet for a long, long, long time after it has served its purpose, which is why much more consideration should be used when purchasing products that include polyester.

Polyester's advantages may soon be matched by something that is kinder to the planet as new technologies are constantly leading to advancements in fabric manufacture. In the meantime, recycled polyester is how many brands are trying to be more eco-conscious in their need for using it. As with anything sustainable, the brand will shout about it from the rooftops if they are using recycled options so do be sure to look for a note on it. It is much easier for brands to do this now for a reasonable price so it won't be hard to get your hands on.

Rayon

As rayon can have such a heavy environmental impact while it is being created, it is important to be aware of what it is good for and what to avoid when adding it to your wardrobe.

WHO IS SHE?
These are the most common types of rayon that you will encounter when shopping.

VISCOSE
This is also often called rayon. Hailed as faux silk as it was first created to emulate it, this early rayon has one of the worst impacts on the environment due to the way it is produced.

Viscose is the most common type of rayon you will encounter and is used in a LOT of fast fashion due to her drape-ability, price and 'party' fabric characteristics. The main issue with viscose is that she can lose shape quickly. This usually happens when wet so laundering can be detrimental and even wear can damage her. If you want a long-lasting garment that needs a lot of wear and washing, viscose is not a serve.

If you are buying occasion wear or rarely worns in viscose, sustainable alternatives are on the rise and a great option. Look for certification and trademarks rather than greenwashing descriptions. Be very careful when washing and wearing and don't expect it to be the most durable item you own. I would even say to keep it to something that seldom needs to be washed and doesn't incur a lot of strain when worn.

MODAL

This is the younger, chicer sister of viscose. Her development was done with the user in mind.

Simply put, the handfeel is better, it's more breathable, the similarity to silk can be easier to achieve and the life is longer. She is more durable as she doesn't become misshapen when wet and looks far nicer.

While there are still chemicals involved, it has a kinder processing method than viscose. There is a lower use of harsh solvents and they are reused in what is known as a 'closed-loop' system. While not perfect, it is far more eco-conscious than flushing them into the world after one use.

Unlike viscose, modal will live with you longer and is far more breathable. Look for modal that comes from certified brands like Tencel™, where they are not involved in deforestation and use sustainably sourced wood. As she can withstand washing, day-to-day, drapier items that you want to wear and wash more can suit modal.

LYOCELL

Up another level is lyocell, whose development considered the user and the environmental impact far more.

This can be even more breathable, durable, soft and silky. This is a newer rayon and so has been created using far fewer harmful techniques. Here the solvents are organic and a closed-loop system is also employed. Tencel™ also does lyocell, which gives you a more sustainable option.

She's more expensive than other rayons but can be stunning to pick up in sales if you want to make her a wardrobe addition for less cost.

SUSTAINABLY SPEAKING

The greenwashing with rayon is intense. As you can see, you can't really call rayon fully sustainable unless it is from a certified source but what you can say about her is that she is biodegradable. Studies have proven that she breaks down as a natural would, which makes her a far superior option to polyester.

Blends

Then there are blends ... you may come across naturals mixed with synthetics and this can leave you wondering what to do. The best way to think about mixes is to look at the percentage. There shouldn't be a mix of a lot of fibres as blends are only really meant to add something to make the garment better, not cheaper. A good example of a blend that works well is when elastane is added to cotton, say in denim, to give it a stretch that allows a tighter fit in specific areas. A bad example is when a cotton work shirt is mixed with two synthetics to reduce the price but you just end up sweating more. Examine the blends and think why those gals are hanging out together to be sure it's the right garment for you.

A CONSCIOUS QUEEN

It is important to note that natural vs synthetic is not always the only decision for everyone. There can be a lack of accessibility to more sustainable or natural choices for many reasons – from sizing to budget to location – so it is not something people should be made to feel guilty for doing if lack of availability is an issue. Also, you could just want to buy a stunning A-line mini skirt in a synthetic fabric but know you will wear it for decades and will care for it well.

Instead, it is wiser to first think about consumption itself before you start delving into what exactly is being consumed. Buying less is far more sustainable than buying a lot of sustainable things. Remember, if you are looking for more planet-friendly versions of fabrics, it is easiest to think like this:

RECYCLED

There are two types of recycled fibres:

PRE-CONSUMER: This is waste from the production stage being used. Think of offcuts, yarns, rejects and so on.

POST-CONSUMER: This is when garments get used again instead of going to landfill.

The argument you will hear here is that for some larger mass producers, pre-consumer

recycled clothing isn't true recycling and that some bend the truth. Post-consumer is always seen as better as it has a direct impact by preventing clothes from going into landfill and new clothing being produced.
In most high-street garments you may see pre- and post-consumer mixed but the bottom line is, it's better than non-recycled, innit?

RESPONSIBLE
This is usually on fabrics derived from animals and The Naturals that can be produced in harmful ways. When you see brands talk about responsibility accreditation, it will be in relation to the animals, land and people involved in and affected by the production of the garment.

ORGANIC
This only really applies to natural gals and it means no harmful pesticides and fertilisers in the growing stage, no harmful chemicals in the production stage and no harmful processes at either stage. They are better for the planet and people involved before, during and after production as well as for the wearer.

Right! Next stop, a little bit of reading ...

2 The Art of Reading

BEFORE WE GET into learning how to read the garment itself, there are some other pitstops that can help us assess the quality, suitability and durability of a garment, from the price and the care label to the signage and sizing. These little pops of text can give so much info that helps us to find our match, yet they often go unnoticed.

PRICING

As a general rule of thumb, if she seems too good to be true price-wise, baby, she is. If something is brand new and for sale at a knockdown price, someone or something has suffered to get it on that hanger. There is no such thing as a free mani-pedi, so *caveat emptor* to the max when it comes to low-priced fashion.

The same goes for the other direction. If something has a higher cost than you would associate it with, do some digging. Are there certifications, declarations or trademarks for high-quality fabrics? Is there some intricate detailing or embellishment? Can you see the reasoning for the higher price?

Often brands will do a small line of something super-on-trend and, due to the low quantities, not achieve the economy of scale they get with more commercial styles. This can mean it will naturally have a higher ticket price based on the brand's margin and nothing to do with quality or durability. The same goes for small fast-fashion brands that cannot reach the higher quantities that achieve bigger discounts. Check out the details, fabric and finish. It's not enough to think 'Oh she's expensive, she must be great.'

SALE SPIN

When it comes to sale prices, some can make your head spin and seem like a must-buy. A dress for the price of a coffee?! Listen, certain things are a bargain and others are not. I am hoping by the end of this section, you'll be a curious, chic shopper with an eye for detail and finish. You'll know a must-grab sale item when you see one. Look for great fibres and finish in sales rather than super-low prices. It's only a bargain if you're getting value for a lower price than the norm.

Not all sale items are created equal, you see. In the past, sale items were unsold stock from that season and there wouldn't be a tonne of it. It would be a great way for a store to free up the floor and stockroom ahead of their new season's arrivals and not have to incur costs of transport or disposal. The quality wouldn't deviate from the usual stock so it was a good time to snap up a great discount.

These days *sigh*, alongside the bits nearing end of season, we have sale rails packed with clothing that is simply unwearable. These items either were not developed with the necessary time and care to make a successful, well-fitting and usable garment or they were overproduced to deliver a fad and soon fall out of favour.

CARE LABELS

Funnily enough, care labels are not legally required in many places but the reason you see them on every garment is that, technically, the customer can be reimbursed if they damage the garment through washing. Get to know what exactly the labels mean on page 116 so you can establish what is a non-negotiable for you care-wise.

Each garment must state the fibre content, although in UK guidelines, for example, this does not have to be sewn into the garment but can actually be in the form of a hanging tag or swing ticket, on the packaging if applicable, and so on.

However, if you think about a production line, it would be cheaper to sew in a small one-colour printed tag when you are sewing in care labels rather than having to produce separate packaging or add a stage for applying swing tags and ensuring they are always there on a shop floor.

When it comes to statements like '100 per cent' or 'pure', these cannot be messed around with. There are some allowances: for example, if you have some embellishment or smaller elements attached to the garment that is not 100 per cent of the main garment's composition, you can still use 100 per cent/pure on the label.

When it comes to mixes, the label, like food labelling, must put the content in descending order. So, you could see a big deal made over a department store's cashmere jumpers, with lots of signage and exterior tags, only to see cashmere as the last fibre. This is where people are easily misled and can think something is a steal. To avoid disappointment, always double-check the inner tag.

SIZING

Speaking of labels, another label that is not a legal requirement everywhere is sizing. Imagine! Nor is there a standard for it. Sizing is tricky as it doesn't really have any reliability these days. This can be a good thing as brands can adapt to what they think their core customer is looking for in the size. But it can also be negative as it can mean sizes aren't 'true', so it can be difficult to know what size to buy where. Some brands will scale down purely from a cost point of view so, all in all, it can be a bit of a minefield.

The best advice when it comes to shopping is rather than think of yourself as a size, match the garment to your biggest measurement. Whether this is your stomach, hips or chest, take your widest measurement and compare this to the same spot on the garment. If you want to avoid taking an armload to the dressing room, measure on the shop floor. This doesn't have to be with a measuring tape. A trick I used when looking for true sizes for sampling was using a pre-cut ribbon to swiftly decipher if the garment was going to be the size I needed.

1. Measure your widest point top and bottom. This varies, so trial a few areas if you are not sure.

---

2. Once you have both of these measurements, divide them in half. When we measure a body it's best to go the whole way round but a quick garment measurement can be taken 'on the flat'.

---

3. Cut a piece of ribbon a little longer than the widest measurement. Singe the ends with a lighter (safely please) to avoid it fraying.

---

4. Grab your measuring tape again and mark and label both measurements on it.

---

5. When you are looking through a rack, all you'll need to do is slip out the ribbon and hold it at the part that will sit at the widest measurement. It's far easier than having to figure out if the sizing is well done or bringing lots of different sizes to the dressing room. It's also less obvious than a measuring tape, which I loved when secret comp shopping.

GRADING

Another thing to look out for size-wise while the garment is on the hanger is how different the sizes are from each other.

If a garment is of good quality, it will be graded well and so the difference in dimensions will be obvious, and it will also be uniform. There won't be massive jumps between sizes, but enough to be obvious at a glance. Have a look at the rail. Is there a noticeable difference in lengths and shoulder widths? This is usually a good sign that a garment's sizing is done well. When there are only one or two differences, it can mean that the garment was only slightly tweaked and there could be fit issues. Take a few to the changing room.

FIT MODELS

This brings us to a 'good to know' point. Fit models are something most brands use to establish the fit of their garments. Carole Radziwill was a fit model for Jordache jeans, remember? Most brands work with fit models to ensure continuity and accuracy in their sizing and fit. Fit models are involved in the tweaks made to samples before they are put into production and really enhance the overall process.

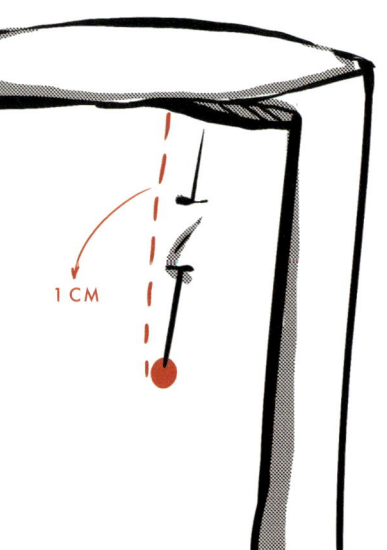

Usually, brands will break their shoppers into categories and edit differently for each one; most high-street brands have around six categories. Each category will have a different style and so there will be a fit model per category. The models traditionally would be what the brand considered a medium or size 12.

The reason a size 12 is used is that it is the size all pattern-cutting basic blocks were in and essentially is the original to which everything else is worked either up or down. Thankfully, this is changing as more brands are opting to use their most popular size as their fit or use a mix of sizes in order to get it right for their range of customers. This makes more sense to me having seen it first-hand.

The piece you see in-store will have been fitted on a fit model many times to make sure the look is within the branding – such as where the customer will expect details, armholes, hems and neckline – but also so that the overall design is executed well and will sell. After the fit model stage, the garment is also examined on a hanger, so it looks good in-store. The last sample that is made will be the 'gold seal sample', the one that everyone from the brand to the factory agrees is what all production will match.

WHEN IT GOES AWRY

You can probably see now why fit models and this process works for keeping sizing uniform. But what happens when some of this is skipped? When there is a lack of adequate sampling and not enough consideration of the fit or the range of customer sizes, you will see it on the shop floor, in sizing and in the changing room. I am sure you have tried something on and thought how on earth did this even make it to production? This is unfortunately a direct result of fast fashion wanting to supply trends at the speed of light and so, skip vital fit stages.

Some brands will sign off a sample based purely on the measurements of a shopping sample, which can go awry very quickly. Others may leave the sizing up to the supplier who can have a totally different size chart. This can lead to us being frustrated and confused when trying to purchase from them.

FIT ISSUES

Hopefully, we are in a space where we can see that sizing can be wack these days and not a reflection on us having a good or bad body but more indicative of a good or a bad producer. The main thing to remember is to consider the fit rather than the tag; this can be difficult when sizing has been so drilled into us. For ease of selection, choose a garment based on your widest point rather than what you think your size should be to find the piece that is good for you.

When a garment fits right, there is no stress on areas that cannot hack it, for example, a chest that is too tight will pull at the armhole and can result in holes or worn fabric.

If it is an option, go up a size and see if there is still some kind of issue. Sometimes this resolves the problem and you can take in other areas if needed.

If the issues are minimal, look at nearby seams and if they could be let out by a tailor. But always bear in mind, the bad fit is usually down to the garment not being well made so a pull across the crotch could be a sign all is not well in other places or that the fabric is not a match. We get enough grief over our bodies, so it's good to keep in mind that we are in an era of poor quality. If a garment fits well, it may render the size irrelevant.

HOW TO MEASURE

Knowing how to measure yourself is extremely useful these days as sizing can be so all over the place. You also may be new to buying womenswear or menswear. There is an art to measuring and getting it right and this is how it's done.

When it comes to measuring, there is a lot out there about your navel being X from your bust, etc. but every body is different so this can feel a little outdated. Instead, it is better to measure with clothing grading and size charts in mind.

TIPS WHEN MEASURING:
- Don't suck in for these measurements or hold the tape too tight. The tape needs to feel comfortable in order to lead to a comfortable garment.
- Keep the tape as straight as possible when wrapped around you and try to work in front of a mirror to check it is not dropping at the back or front.
- If you find it easier to read the tape when it is off you, use some masking tape to mark the spot and jot that down after removing the tape.

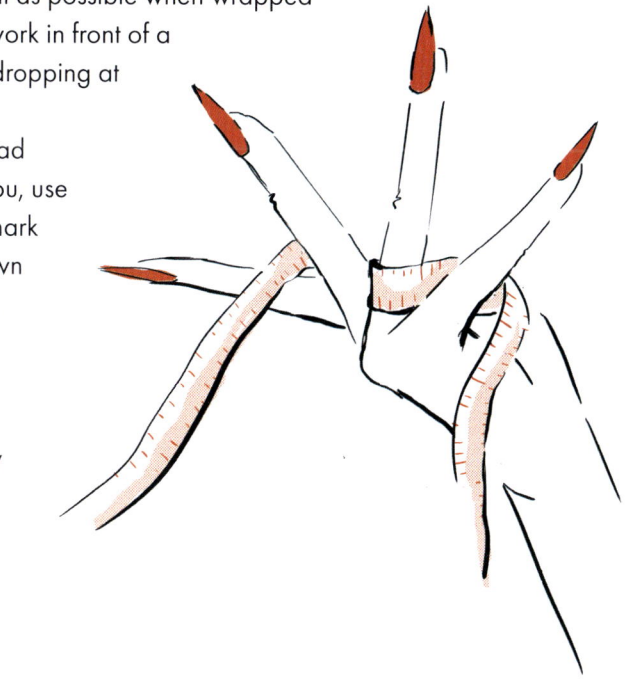

Let's run through the most common measurements in high street size charts. They will usually be noting the widest and narrowest measurements on garments and it is good to know the best way to get yours spot on.

WOMENSWEAR:

BUST: This should be the widest part of your bust. If you are buying for a certain occasion or routine, don't forget to wear anything you may be intending to wear underneath, be it a bra, top, harness, whatever.

Holding your tape like a feather boa as if you're about to shimmy, pull it across your back, under your arms and over your chest. It should be sitting straight across at the widest point of your bust.

WAIST: The true waist is at the bottom of your rib cage. When taking this, breathe in and out deeply and set the tape where it feels most comfortable.

HIP: Go for the widest part of your hip area the whole way around, making sure the tape is straight. The hip measurement on these charts is the lower hip, this is also called your seat. Raise your leg at a 45-degree angle and feel the joint – that's your lower hip. It's not always the widest part of everyone's body but it's usually the widest part of the garment for the producer. Matching yours and theirs will help ensure that it can be tailored a lot easier if needed.

MENSWEAR:

Menswear can differ because there is so much tailoring and to be honest a lot more tends to go into the construction. When I moved to a menswear design dept I could not get over the difference in the attention to detail in comparison to womenswear, but that is for another time. In short, you'll probably see more measurements:

CHEST, WAIST, HIP: These are pretty similar to those used in womenswear with going for your widest point.

SHOULDER: Think of a set-in sleeve (page 94). Imagine the seam where the sleeve meets the garment is on your body; the shoulder measurement is from seam to seam basically.

COLLAR: Annoyingly many shirts are sized by collar and then base the rest of your measurements on this. I would check out all measurements to be on the safe side but as the collar is the hardest element to alter (so many parts!) make this your priority as other seams can be adjusted. Simply sit the tape around your neck where the collar would sit, and make sure that you can fit two fingers underneath to allow for comfort and movement. Then take the measurement.

SLEEVE LENGTH: This will be from the shoulder seam to the end of the cuff.

NOTE ON FLAT MEASURING

Measuring 'on the flat' is how most preloved garments are done. This is where the garment is laid out and measured on one side. This allows you to then double widths to match to your measurement. This can be great for some garments but for others – for example, jeans – you may need to compare them to some you already have or ask for more measurements from the seller.

Online, a great brand will have a note on sizing next to the garment if there is something they feel is vital for you to know about the fit. The length of the garment should be given as a standard in the description but it is sadly not the always the case.

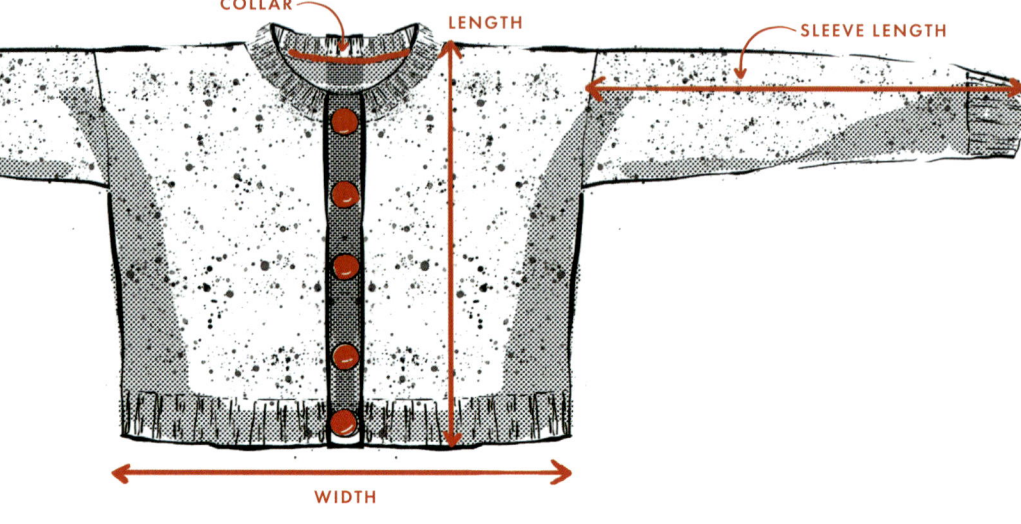

IN SUMMARY

If you find that there is little info on sizing or other elements in an online description, there is often a reason. It's not hard to add relevant information to a garment's page so omissions are always a little suss to me.

Many great brands will have stunning customer service and happily shine more light on areas where you need it. Often a lack of info or clarity on how to get more info is not a good sign.

Speaking of red flags, it is time to click-clack to our next section, one of the juiciest in this book ...

3 PURCHASE POINTS

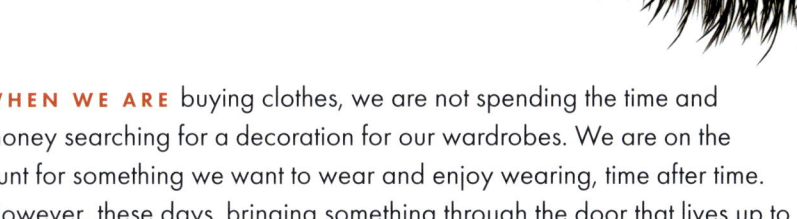

WHEN WE ARE buying clothes, we are not spending the time and money searching for a decoration for our wardrobes. We are on the hunt for something we want to wear and enjoy wearing, time after time. However, these days, bringing something through the door that lives up to these expectations, wear after wear, is proving trickier than ever.

THE ERA OF POOR QUALITY

As fashion has changed and the landscape of the high street has altered, I am sure that you have noticed that the garments on offer aren't the same as before. A level of mistrust in what we once expected as the fundamental qualities of a garment has developed and true quality for a reasonable price feels like a thing of the past. What started as the high street reducing details on trendy items to deliver the faster fashion that the consumer craved, has now led to a reduced quality across the board. Even the most common of garments, such as a simple t-shirt or pair of jeans, have not escaped cost-cutting through detail and quality dropping.

We can no longer rely on seaming, lining, finishes or even fabric qualities to be as they were, and it can often lead to us being unhappy with what we buy. Even worse, we can find something we absolutely adore that appears to have the quality we desire but it falls to bits quickly. Sadly, in today's market there is no longer a guarantee that a piece of knitwear will keep a certain weight or handfeel or that a work shirt won't make you feel hot and sweaty or that a zip won't fail after a few wears.

SHOPPING LIKE A PRO

So, how do we get it right in a store full of wrongs? To truly understand what we are buying and how it will fare, we need to channel the energy of industry experts. *Thworps*

THE DRESSMAKER

When you start to pattern-cut clothes, the first things you learn are the basic blocks. The skirt, shirt, jacket and so on. This not only gives you a great handle on how to draft the most common elements of garments and where in a garment the crucial parts are for fit, but it also shows you what practical details are vital in terms of a body wearing it. For example, when drafting a skirt, you learn that a pleat or split/vent may be needed when you add length to facilitate walking or sitting. You'll also learn what height it should be and

how it should be finished to withstand the wear it will endure.

After dressmakers have the knowledge of basic blocks under their belt, they start to learn how to exaggerate them and manipulate them into their desired aesthetic. In pattern cutting, you will almost always work from an original block as your starting point and edit, edit, edit. This means that when dressmakers pattern cut, they are more likely to get it right for the wearer whilst still achieving their own design. A dressmaker will know by just looking at a garment if functional elements have been skipped or underdone and whether that will affect wear. They will also always know if the fabric is a good match for the function.

If you observe older generations clothes shopping, you will see that they examine the garment in much more detail than the younger generation does. This, you may guess, is down to the shopping culture, but I would argue that it is more due to the fact that those generations were more likely to pattern cut and or make their own garments and so know what to look for in terms of weight, quality, stretch and so on.

To truly become a savvy shopper, being aware of the details that cater to fit, form and function, in the way a dressmaker would, is key. The latter part of this chapter will take us through what the basic blocks are like and why certain elements are a must if you wish the garment to live for a long time. Once we understand these, it will allow us to be able to assess more trend-led items on a case-by-case basis and see if that item will truly suit its prized position in our wardrobe.

THE MASS-PRODUCTION DESIGNER

Another expert we can channel when shopping is someone involved in mass production design. When they are researching for upcoming seasons, they will carry out some form of 'comp shopping' and also trend analysis in stores. This method is ideal for sussing out quality. The latter is usually done overseas, in search of the latest techniques, styles and silhouettes to bring back and work into their own range so they can offer their customers the next hot trend or fabric before a competitor.

Comp shopping, on the other hand, is looking directly at your competitors and seeing where you can improve, what you're missing out on, how they are doing their bits and what seems to be popular for them. I LOVED comp shopping as a designer. There is no way one design team can be on top of every single advancement or improvement in the industry so it was super to see what else was going on. Also, there were times you didn't want to be the first to jump on a trend as you were never sure how it would fare. When you comp shop, you can see what newness has been tried and where it failed or did well. It is a more cost-effective way of seeing outcomes without having to sample or trial in-house.

After aesthetics, the mass-production designer will look at cost. They will be aware of the margins most brands work to on the high street and will be looking for new techniques or fabrics that have helped the brand achieve those margins with new trends. The mass-production designer is not always an in-house brand designer – they are more likely to be a designer for a supplier or producer. This is a designer that works as part of a company that will design and produce garments for brands. Even brands with in-house design teams use suppliers and these are the fastest-moving designers as they cater to multiple brands all season. They are always in competition with other suppliers to get designs in at a lower cost to get brands to place orders and so they comp shop like no one else. I should know, I was one and comp shopping was one of the key things that helped us when designing.

In a comp shop, the designer will be looking deeper than anyone else at garments, especially at finishings. They will be trying to see where the brand was able to cut corners to achieve a trend or use of fabric or finishing. The weight of the fabric, how it was finished and the techniques used will all be run through. They will also examine the whole garment in detail from front to back and from the outside in.

Being able to examine a garment in the same way this designer does can help you to distinguish the good from the bad in minutes.

SHE'S A PRO

Although the outcomes of their store research visits will differ, both the dressmaker and the designer examine and critique garments in a very similar fashion. They will rub, pull, hold up, hold down, scrunch, stretch and scratch in their mission to understand the garment better. Even now when I walk through a store, I can spot a comp/research shopper immediately. When I do, I always think how much would change if we all shopped with this level of detail and interest when considering a garment to take home. What is stopping us? As with most things, it's knowledge and know-how.

In this section, we will be learning how we can use the methods of these two pros to assess garments for our wants and needs. We will get familiar with red flags, high-quality indicators and signs of durability. These will come under four main headings:

FINISH

The first port of call in garment assessment is the finish. This is both from a hanger appeal point of view and the construction.

In this section, we look at the outside and the inside of garments. The interior plays a major role in the garment's fit, comfort and durability. Until recent times, it was the norm for garments to look just as good on the inside as they did on the outside. It was a sign of good quality, reflected a lengthy production time and implied that the garment could be worn for years. Nowadays this is more likely in high-end or hand-made only. This is mainly down to the cost and speed at which many fashion customers demand new clothing, which has resulted in the finishing stages suffering badly.

Garments that are finished well will always look good on both the hanger and the body, even when you turn them inside out. This is because technically, more time should be spent on the interior; it's kind of like under the bonnet of a car. So, bear this in mind when looking at finishing: a lot of important information can be hidden from view but it can tell you the most about a piece.

BATCH CHECK!

A wee note on assessing finish. If you love a piece but find a flaw, be sure to suss out the rest of the garments on the rack to see if these flaws are repeated. From the start to the end of a production line, things can go awry: a loose button here, an over-pressed shoulder there. For this reason, an extra 10 per cent (usually) is produced to make up for errors and to ensure the brand gets the amount they ordered. To deliver a full order that matches the gold-sealed garment, each piece is checked many times through the run and, last of all, at the main quality check before packing. For this reason, seeing loose threads, uneven hems or seams on many means it's probably the standard for the batch and that it is not a garment that has been well made or intended to be worn a lot. When multiple garments are flashing the same red flags? Let her go.

STITCHING

Stitching is a massive giveaway of the durability of a garment as it is a key indicator of the strength of the seams and finish and how the garment will react when worn over and over.

When we see shoddy stitch work, loose threads, puckering and so on, it is a massive red flag that the production was rushed to achieve a lower price. Sewing is the most labour-intensive part of many high-street garments, so this is where corners can get cut when they need to speed up. Fast-fashion producers are also notorious for using unskilled teams – usually very badly paid with little or no training – in a bid to pay less overall. The chances are, if the product looks badly made, its profit is going to a company like this.

STITCH LENGTH

As well as stitch appearance, stitch length can be a massive giveaway as regards the quality of a garment. Generally speaking, even though the correct stitch length for a garment is vital, more stitches take more time and fewer stitches speeds up production. It is also easier to sew cheaper fabrics with fewer and longer stitches so producers can then use less-experienced machinists in order to cut costs.

SPI

SPI (stitch per inch) is something that clothing producers use in their production specifications to indicate the length of the stitch to be used. SPI is chosen based on many things, from fabric to the garment's function. When the SPI is correct, it ensures that the seams of the garment look great and are strong enough to wear well. For example, a garment that endures a lot of stress – like denim or shirting – will need more stitches per inch to withstand the movement. A stretch garment will have lower SPI as too many small stitches mean the fabric can tear during wear.

However, these days, there is an increased use of low SPIs on many high-street garments regardless of the intended use. This is to reduce sewing time and use of thread and it is causing garments to fail during both wear and washing.

Thankfully you don't need to learn the ins and outs of SPI in great depth. And besides, counting stitches to gauge if the SPI is correct would be an impossible task for someone who is not industry trained.

STITCH INVESTIGATION

There is a simple way you can gauge if the stitching will enhance or hinder the life of the garment.

When looking at seams, make sure you look at all the stitching. Start with the side seams and gently pull the fabric to expose the stitch work and consider the following problems throughout.

GAPS: Are the gaps between the stitches reasonable or does it seem like the stitch length is too long? If pulling forms obvious gaps between stitches, this garment won't stand the test of time, and this may also affect how the garment fits.

UNIFORMITY: Are the stitches uniform? If the tension of the machine or the chosen SPI is incorrect, stitches will not be neat and uniform. Instead, they will appear tight in some areas and loose in others, with varying stitch lengths. Uniformity in stitches is a key indicator of quality. Uniform stitching won't cause stress or the garment to rip during wear.

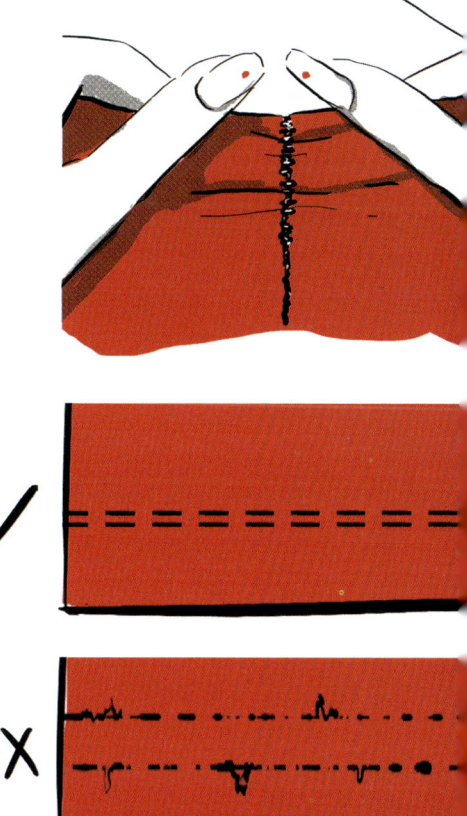

ERRORS: Are there areas where the stitch line looks like it's been run over a few times? This can be a machinist going over an error to save time instead of unpicking and resewing the full stitch line. This will usually end up creating further damage down the line.

PUCKERING: Is there puckering around the seam? This can be when an SPI, tension or speed of fabric being fed through the sewing machine is incorrect. Puckering can lead to the garment looking cheap and wearing badly.

LOOSE THREADS: Are there loose threads at the end of stitch lines? This is a major red flag finish-wise. On a high-end garment, the threads will be pulled through and secured by knotting so they cannot come loose and cause the stitch line to unravel over time. In most high-street items, a back stitch is done by machine, which anchors the last few stitches and prevents them from coming loose later. You can see that this has been done when the last stitches look doubled. However, in the era of high-speed for low cost, stitch lines are not being anchored and loose threads are left. This can lead to splitting seams, holes and dropped hems.

Loose threads after an anchored stitch can also be a sign of rushed production. This is when time has been saved by not inspecting and snipping close to the fabric. This can happen in a cheaper garment but if you see it on a garment with a higher price tag, question it.

WHAT'S A GAL TO DO?

You may have found a piece that ticks a lot of boxes for fabric, fit and function but the stitching is off.

If you love the piece and want to wear it for a long time, consider having key areas restitched by a tailor.

Sometimes it can also be a case of rushed workmanship. The stitching looks okay but hasn't been cut close enough to the fabric so you have some loose threads? Simply thread the end through a needle and pull it back into the interior of the garment. Too short? Start with the needle already in the garment and then pull it through. This is always safer than snipping on the outside of the garment.

PUCKERING

If you see random folding, little pleats or puckering at the armholes or other seams in the garment, investigate. This shouldn't be the case on a hanger as there is nothing inside the garment to cause it. This will instead be down to low quality and lack of adequate quality control.

SHOULDERS

When you see puckering around an armhole, it is usually down to poor fit editing or too much heat or steam applied during construction. The latter is quite common in blazers, for example. From a construction point of view, a sleeve will always be slightly too big for an armhole; it requires precision, time and skill to manipulate it to fit into the armhole as you sew. This is done so the wearer has some ease of movement.

However, when a garment is rushed, the armhole can end up warped. If you see puckering and love the garment, check the fabric composition. Some natural fabrics can be spritzed with water, re-steamed and rubbed with your finger to remove these little pleats, but a synthetic usually cannot be saved.

SIDE SEAMS

When there is puckering or warping along the body of a garment or from the side seams, this can be due to the fabric not being cut in the best way. The fabric has a grain to it; if you look closely you will see yarns that are vertical and horizontal. The fabric should always be cut so that these are perfectly level on the garment. This accuracy can lead to some waste fabric. To reduce cost and waste, a low-quality producer can cut against the flow of the grain and you will see the fabric react badly. The result is that the garment looks like it's twisting when on the hanger.

Warping and puckering are not only visually hindering the garment, but they can also cause stress on parts of the garments where there should be none, which affects the fall. This is common in high-street blazers, low-priced tees, party dresses and so on.

To spot puckering, hold the hanger from the top and spin the garment around slowly, the light with catch the puckers and twists if any are present. Pay special attention to the shoulders and side seams.

NOT ALL IS AS IT SEAMS

A seam is a stitch line (or lines) that holds two, or more, pieces of fabric together. Seam finishing is how the raw edges of a garment are treated to preserve them. This prevents them from fraying and bothering the wearer and can help in making the seam itself more durable.

Understanding seams and seam finishings will help you to spot long-wear items quickly and also to have a greater understanding of a garment's quality and the time spent making it. Seams are a massive giveaway in terms of how good a garment is.

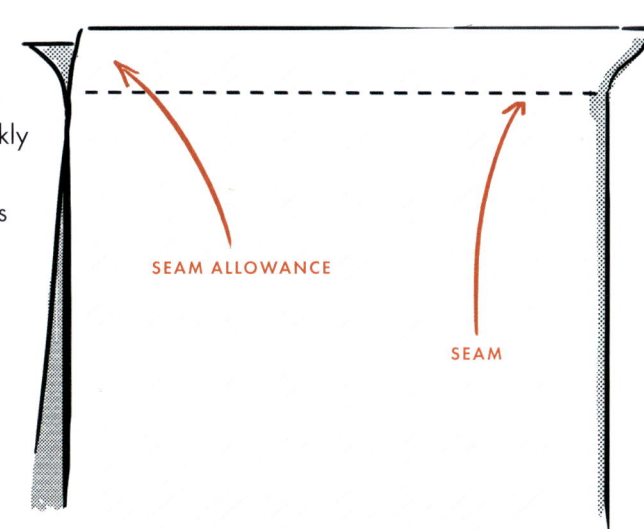

THE IMPORTANCE OF GREAT SEAMS

Seams and their finishes are vital to the integrity and longevity of a garment. Not only do they impact hanger appeal, but their main performance responsibilities are in how they behave during wear.

- They should be secure enough that they do not unravel easily – or at all, frankly.
- They should be neat and appropriately done so as not to bother the wearer or the eye.
- During wear and movement, they should provide enough give that the fabric does not tear but be strong enough that the seam itself does not snap.

When even one of these characteristics is not present, our seam and its finishings are at risk of failure.

When analysing a garment, designers will inspect the seams and their finishes in great detail as it gives such a good indicator of how well made the piece is. They can then consider if the price tag is reflecting the quality. As you can imagine, the more time spent on a garment's seams, the more expensive it will be. Dropping the workmanship of a seam down a few levels can cut the production cost, which a lot of fast-fashion producers opt to do to be able to charge less for a garment. Even if it means the garment's longevity is reduced dramatically.

Grrrrrreat clothing producers will vary their seam type at different parts of the garment to ensure that the seam is working with the garment, both on the body and on the hanger. Producers of inferior-quality garments will apply the cheapest (most efficient use of thread and labour) seams all over a garment with little consideration.

Learning about the stitches, seams and finishing in relation to garment production can get extremely technical and can also differ greatly in high-end and high-street clothing as well as from piece to piece. There are many categories and classifications but this is more for clear communication between factory and designer than for the customer to worry about. For this reason, we will only focus on the bits that are relevant to us, the shopper.

OPEN SEAMS
RAW EDGE

The only time you should ever really see one line of stitching and the raw edge of the fabric is if the garment is fully lined and/or the fabric doesn't fray. Even if it is the latter, the seam allowance should still be treated in some way so that it is encouraged to sit flat and not bother the wearer. For example, leather may be topstitched into place.

I would never encourage buying a garment with a raw interior seam allowance. If you see one, run.

OVERLOCKED AND SERGED

An overlocked (or serged) finish is where the edge of the fabric is protected by being encased in looped thread. It's the one you'll see the most.

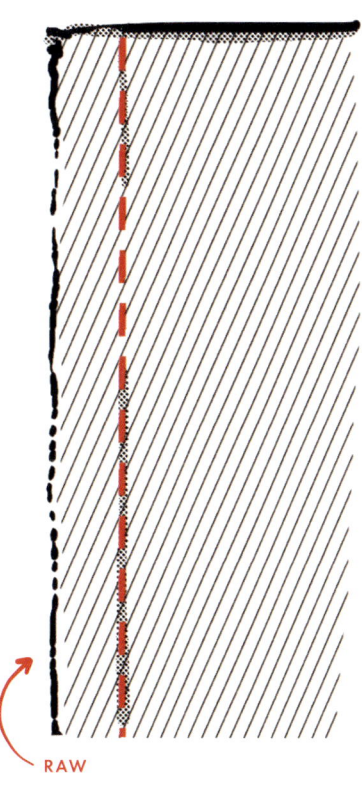
RAW

OVERLOCKED

Traditionally, this would be used on woven (non-stretch) fabrics. The pieces are overlocked separately first and then sewn together. In a non-stretch, this should only be used in looser garments, in areas where the seams need to sit flat or in areas where other techniques could be too bulky. You shouldn't be seeing it in the side seams of good shirting, for example, or in higher-priced trousers, as there are much more durable seams out there that will help the garment live longer and look far better. If it is present, the price should reflect it and it should be done extremely well.

SERGED

Stretch garments are usually overlocked and seamed in one go as per image B. If you are wearing a tee right now, have a look at your inside seam and it will be B. This allows the garment to stretch and move without threads snapping. It is also far easier to construct the garment. It gives flexibility to the seam and is lightweight so suits stretch garments wonderfully.

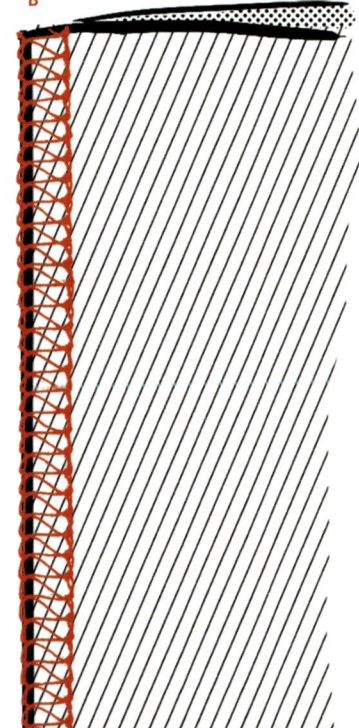

THE FAST-FASHION APPROACH

As B is cheaper to do than overlocking, pressing and then sewing, it has become the fast-fashion seam. These days it's even used on non-stretch garments or areas that are truly unsuitable. Cripes! Although it uses more thread, its speed helps reduce the overall cost because you can trim, sew and finish an edge in one move with no pressing needed in between. The major downside is how bulky and weak it can make a seam. It means it can wear down faster and feel more uncomfortable to wear.

To execute this finish well, time is needed. The machine needs to be set up perfectly for the fabric and it cannot be forced through the machine too quickly. When it is rushed or steps are skipped, as is the case in a lot of fast fashion, you will be able to see it.

When you see an overlocked edge, inspect it. Run your nail over it to see if the loops are secure and well done. If they are loose and not uniform, they will further unravel during wear and washing. I massage it slightly between my fingers to see how sturdy it is. This seam will be rubbing against your skin or other garments and it needs to last but it will also show you if it feels too rough to be comfortable.

HANGER APPEAL

Another note on this type of seam finish: if it is visible when the garment is hung, such as along the back neckline, it is an indicator of lower quality and cost-cutting. Looped stitching like this is usually covered to improve hanger appeal and also to reduce wear and tear. It's a small move that pays off so seeing it dropped is a major red flag. When you see it on a garment, it's a sure sign there are more red flags to come.

WELT SEAM

The welt seam was originally used for heavier fabrics where the seam needed to be more durable while the seam allowance needed to be less bulky. You can also trim down one side of the seam allowance and tuck it inside, resulting in an even flatter seam.

WELT SEAM

Sometimes it is called the mock flat felled seam due to its appearance. Once you can confirm that the raw edge is finished well, it's a good seam to have as it is so durable. It is often found in denim and work wear.

HOW: After a plain seam, the seam allowance is pressed to one side and top stitched to the garment. People will argue whether this is open or closed as the seam allowance is stitched down. However, the edges are still exposed. This is great to add more durability to seams and flatten seam allowance where needed.

DOUBLE STITCHED

This seam strengthens high stress areas but also allows seam allowance to sit more smoothly and comfortably. It works well on garments where the seam allowance needs to be as flat as possible to avoid irritation to the wearer or bulk to the silhouette.

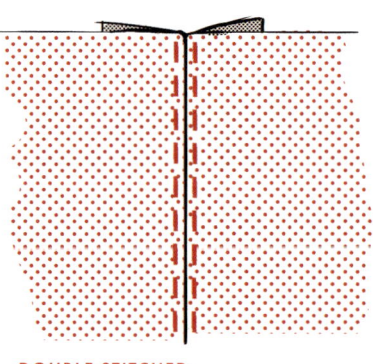

DOUBLE STITCHED

HOW: A plain seam is sewn and the seam allowance pressed open. Then two stitch lines are sewn either side to anchor the seam allowance to the garment.

CLOSED SEAMS

While the last seams are classed as 'open seams', another more costly type are closed seams. As these contain the raw edge, they are much more durable and are ideal for garments that endure a lot during wear, fabrics that fray easily and the seams of a garment that undergo the most stress.

To complete these finishes, one seam will pass through the machine many times, often with pressing in between. The time taken, skill needed and thread used will drive up the price but the durability is far, far greater. This is down to the edges never being disturbed and super-strong seams.

BOUND SEAMS

This is mainly used where the seam finish will be exposed to the eye or irritate the wearer and it is almost always used somewhere on a handmade garment to show attention to detail. This is far more costly than open seams as you are paying for even more fabric and labour. Look for them on:

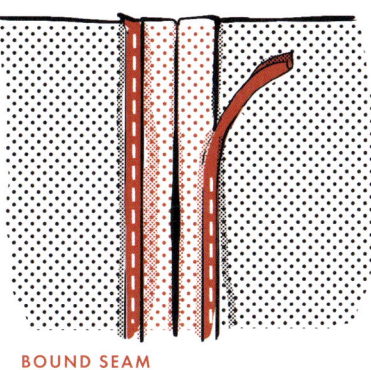

BOUND SEAM

- Unlined tailored items like a summer blazer or trench coat.
- The neckline of tees and sweats and other garments that have a neckline seam.
- Curved edges on well-made wovens, like armholes.

- Well-made trousers will feature these around the pockets and seams that rub most against the skin.

HOW: Bound seams have a trim that encases the raw edge. It is a more expensive and time-consuming type of seam finish. The fabric must be suitable, usually cut on the bias, and also before sewing. This usually involves a lot of folding and pressing.

FRENCH SEAMS

This gives a super neat finish and it is great for light fabric where over locking will spoil the lewk, like sheers. These are great for a super-strong seam. You should find them on:

- Great quality sheers and lightweight woven, thin summer garments.
- Shirting sides and sleeves.
- Areas where a lot of stress will occur.
- Higher-priced woven (non-stretch) garments.

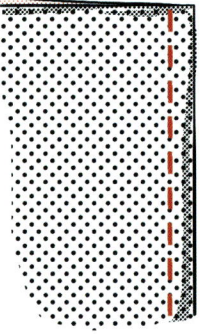

STAGE 1 OF FRENCH SEAM

HOW: The wrong sides are placed together first and a seam is sewn. Then the right sides are placed together and sewn again. This results in the seam allowance becoming hidden in the seam and, so, completely concealed and protected.

STAGE 2 OF FRENCH SEAM

FLAT FELLED SEAMS

She is one durable queen. In fact, she is probably the most durable seam there is and this is why you will see her in hard-wearing garments.

Popular in everyday clothing, this classic seam is super for denim and garments like workwear

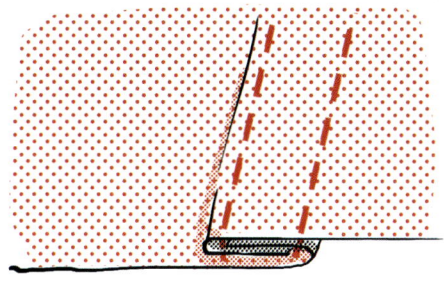

FLAT FELLED

jackets. That guy you dated with the beard and his flat keys on a carabiner clip even though he's only ever climbed the stairs? – he's covered in flat felled seams.

Flat felled seams keep the edges enclosed but also stitch the seam allowance on the fabric and secure it with a stitch visible to the outside. Look for this in:

- Heavier fabric, like denim.
- Workwear styles.
- Areas where there is a lot of pulling and wear.

HOW: A plain seam is sewn and then the seam allowance is pressed and folded or 'locked' together and topstitched down. It creates long lasting, glorious seams.

Over all, great seams may take longer but will stand the test of time and feel sooo much better to wear than an overlocked edge. High-end brands also tend to favour them, as they give a much more high-quality and hand-made look. As it is impossible to execute them in a rush they will always come with a higher price. But do bear in mind, these garments may cost more but will be cheaper to own in the long run as they will last longer and wash far better.

HEMS

Hems play a huge role in the look of a garment. They not only prevent the fabric from fraying, but they can reduce wear and tear by reinforcing ends and also allow even weight that gives the piece a better fall.

Hems can be finished in a few different ways. Here is when and where they are best used and when you'll be able to see your non-negotiables.

VISIBLE HEM STITCHES
TURN AND STITCH

This is when the garment is overlocked to prevent fraying, and the hem is turned up once and stitched into place. This hem is usually thin in width and is frequently used in mass-produced clothing.

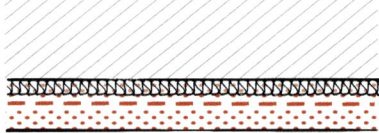

TURN AND STITCH

Not only is this hem a red flag in terms of rushed and cheap production, but it is also not a durable hem in the slightest. The overlocked stitches are exposed, which will cause unravelling and fraying. They can also irritate the wearer and, of course, it's hard to edit this hemline effectively as the hem allowance is so small.

DOUBLE FOLD

Pretty similar to the previous hem but she will be turned twice before sewing and so is not as cheap but is much nicer for the wearer. The hem is also more durable as the overlocking is protected inside and won't be rubbed against in wearing and washing. You'll often see this in denim and some workwear styles. It is also popular in some shirting where a thin hem helps to prevent the end of the shirt from being bulky and visible through the trouser.

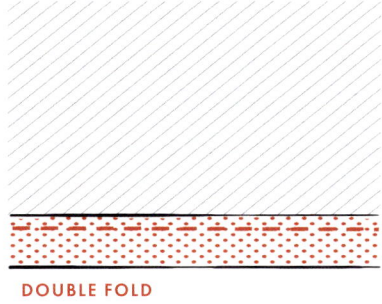
DOUBLE FOLD

INVISIBLE HEM STITCHES
BOUND HEM

These are most common in high quality clothing as they are a lot of work. They can be common in mass-produced clothing as a styling point or if the hem is so curved a traditional fold-up won't work. When you see these, examine them in detail as bad-quality binding can come apart easily. Look for areas where it is not stitched into place.

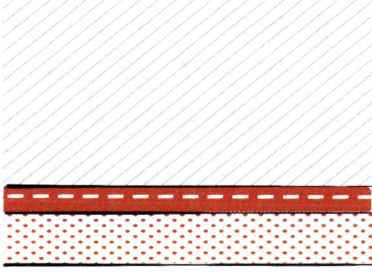
BOUND HEM

BLIND/INVISIBLE

These are stunning hems that are completely invisible from the outside. They are also more expensive to do as they have to either be done by hand or on a special machine. Because they have a minimal effect on the outer layer of the garment, they are really popular in well-made bottoms like trousers, skirts and dresses. You can remove the stitching and take the hem up or down as required with little to no evidence there was originally another hemline. These hems also allow the hem allowance to be much wider, which is great in well-made clothing. It adds weight and also means you can edit the piece further down the line. In mass production, these blind

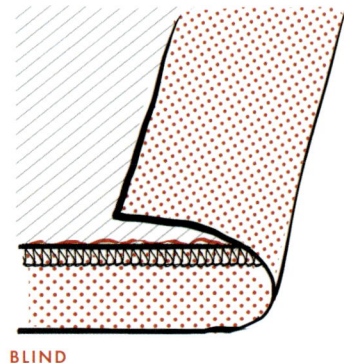

BLIND

hems are the first thing to go. When in store, if you cannot see an exterior stitch line on the hem, fold over and look inside. There should be no unravelling on the shop floor or loose threads in a well-made garment. If the piece is ideal otherwise, you can always redo the blind hem yourself; there's a tutorial on page 278.

Form

Form is a massive selling point in a garment. It's all about the shape of the garment and how it fits and wears.

Form is something that has been used rather negatively, in my opinion, for years. The main learning around 'form' has been how to identify elements of garments that can help us conform to feminine/masculine beauty standards. Creating smaller waists or broader shoulders, enhancing or hiding your body type … you get the idea.

Let's pop all of that in the bin where it belongs and get acquainted with understanding how we can use form to help us achieve the wardrobe we want.

WEIGHT

The weight of a fabric plays a massive part in the form a garment takes on. Think about the wonderful silhouettes of dense wool coats or the divine drape you can get in a lightweight jersey (Kylie in a Grecian dress appearing for anyone else?). The correct weight will always ensure that the garment responds to the design brief immaculately.

However, weight also plays a big role in the price. Fabric is sold in GSM (grams per square metre). It is not necessary to weigh an entire roll, though, as a kit is used which cuts an industry standard size circle in the fabric and this is weighed and then you calculate from there.

To reduce the price of a garment you can first reduce the weight of the fabric. This method was used a lot for on-trend items on the high street as it meant a look that has many bells and whistles can still have a healthy margin as the fabric is made cheaper by literally removing the number of threads in it.

Now, however, it is being done on garments that it just shouldn't be. Who wants a jumper in winter that cannot keep you warm? Or a pair of work trousers that become worn at the seat in weeks?

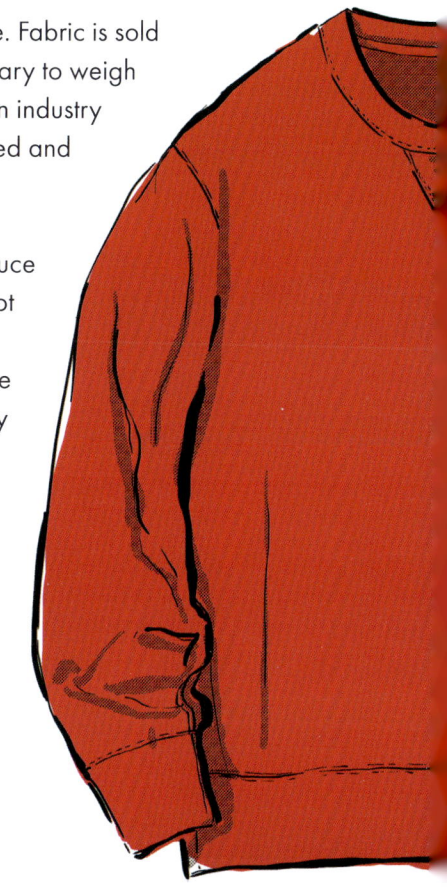

ASSESSING THE WEIGHT OF THE FABRIC

Take in the fall of the garment. If the correct weight does not exist in the fabric, it may not fall as it should, thus affecting the overall look. Simply holding up the hanger and viewing the front and the back will help you to see if the fabric is a good weight for the design and finishing.

Suss how see-through the fabric is. There are not many garments that benefit from its fabric being see-through when you hold it up to the light. Unless it is an organza or extremely lightweight garment in which the design lends itself to transparency, it will be a weaker fabric that will not last a long time. Rub the fabric between your index finger and thumb; if it feels like it should be thicker for the function of the garment, it may have had its weight reduced to keep down cost. The fabric, even if lightweight, should feel densely woven and durable. Don't forget that if you see light coming through little holes in the fabric when you hold it up, this is most likely a poor-quality yarn that is creating gaps.

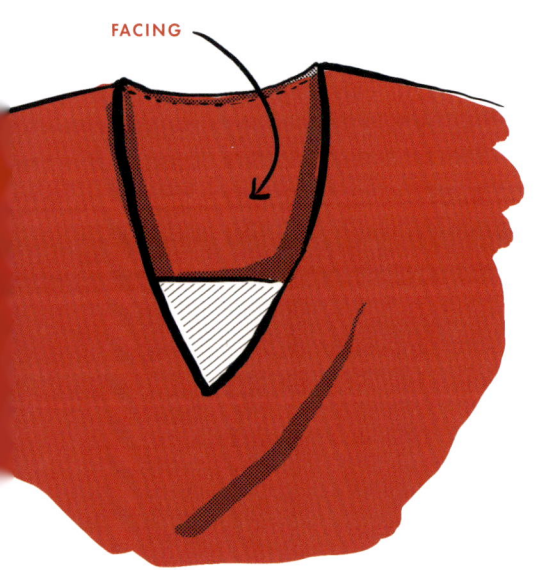

FACING

Another beaut you will see without having to take the garment off the hanger is if it has adequate facing. This is a major issue with higher-priced high-street items. I can almost understand a fast-fashion brand skipping it as the integrity isn't there. But when I see an expensive high-street dress with scrimping as regards facing, I am always shocked.

Facing, simply put, is a layer of the fabric on the inside of the garment with the right side shown. You will see facing on openings like a collarless neckline, armholes with no sleeves attached, openings of jackets and coats and so on. It is used for many reasons:

FINISH: Facing allows you to finish the garment beautifully by hiding the raw edge inside a seam without showing any seam finishing.

SHAPE: Applying a facing can help openings keep their shape. Without facing, a neckline or jacket front can flap open whereas a facing will help it to stay in place.

STREAMLINE: There's no visible stitch line on the outside of the garment when a facing is in place so a cleaner finish is achieved.

PRINTS: When a garment's interior is drastically different to its exterior – such as a printed dress – facing the openings will mean there is no flashing of the interior unprinted side when the wearer moves. Due to many cheaper modern printing techniques, the inside fabric can appear almost grey and facing helps prevent this from being seen.

REINFORCE: Facing can add strength. In a sleeveless top, for example, facing most of the bodice can help it to sit better on the body but also to be stronger and endure more movement.

HANGER APPEAL: Having adequate facing on a garment like this will also massively increase the hanger appeal in-store and make the garment look much more expensive, yet it is constantly skimped on these days.

As you can imagine, facing costs money and its application is time-consuming. This is why many producers will either incorrectly install it or will use a cheaper method.

WHEN SHOPPING

Look for signs that the facing has been done incorrectly. Is it too short, finished badly or is waving due to being cut from scrap fabric and not in accordance with the direction of the weave of the fabric? These issues will often result in the facing peeking out during wear. Not great.

BACK NECK TAPE

When there is no facing, consider why. Instead of using facing or another finish on the raw edges of a neckline, binding is sometimes used. This will create a visible stitch line around the opening, which only works in some garments and it has to be well done to look good. When looking at a collarless or trimless neckline, consider if the facing was skipped as part of the design or if it was a cost-saving exercise.

JACKETS AND COATS

Sometimes brands will go to all the effort of facing but skip the last stage. This stage is vital for ensuring that the facing sits well. After you insert a facing, a little discreet stitch line is applied to the facing to anchor it to the seam allowance. This not only stops the seam allowance from bunching but also makes the facing stay as it should. When this stitch line is missing, as you will nearly always see in fast fashion, you start to see the facing 'roll' out and be visible on the exterior of the garment. It can be pressed into place before each wear with a neckline but on something like a blazer, it can be hard to save unless you take it to be tailored.

In summary, you will be able to tell if facing is adequate on a jacket or coat if it is enhancing the look of the garment and not hindering it. Necklines and openings will not be warping on the hanger, they will be holding shape and extremely neat.

Don't be afraid to turn the garment inside out to inspect the facing. You are mainly checking for:

FABRIC: Is the facing the same fabric as the garment or a cheaper version to save costs?

HOW DOES IT SIT?: Is it following the garment or is it warping?

ENHANCING: Is it enhancing the garment or is it causing it to contort because it is too small or too tight?

HOW IS IT FINISHED?: You want it to be flat and neat so it doesn't show through the fabric on the outside as a bulky line. Speaking of, does it end in a place that doesn't look great?

HOW IS IT ANCHORED?: The bottom of the facing should be anchored to a seam allowance and not the main part of the garment. If it is the latter, movement could cause a hole. If it's not anchored at all, it's a sign of lower quality and can mean it will come out during wear.

STITCHING LINE: Is there a stitch line on the facing that is stopping it from rolling and peeking out? This will be a lovely discreet stitch line on the facing itself.

You will also see that lined garments have their lining attached to the facing, which takes us to our next point.

LINING

Lining is used for many reasons but in recent years its quality has gone seriously downhill on the high street. This has led to otherwise functional garments – like coats, dresses and skirts – being discarded due to disintegrating or uncomfortable lining. The lining has many duties.

FOR THE GARMENT

DURABILITY: It keeps the seams, hems and anything else inside the garment intact by keeping them out of harm's way. A heel or bracelet is not at risk of snagging the seams or finishes. This is vital in a tailored piece as the construction is so detailed.

WEIGHT: It adds weight, which helps the garment to fall better and keep its shape.

LONGEVITY: It protects the most expensive outer shell from the wearer. It acts as a

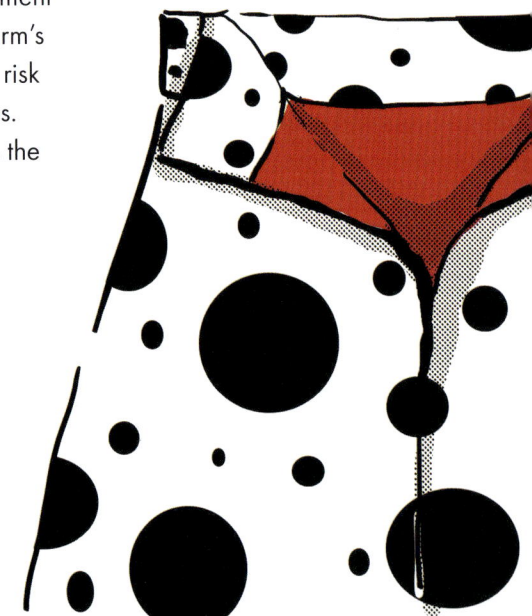

barrier between your sweat, skin particles, lotions, potions and so on. This adds longevity to the piece as lining, if it is in the right fabric, can easily expel odours, sweat and so on in a way outer fabric may not.

LESS STRESS: The lining reduces stress on the outer layer by taking on most of the pulling and straining during wear. This is why someone may only need to replace a lining in a suit jacket after, say, ten years while the outer layer is still intact.

FOR THE WEARER

WARMTH: This can be added if needed, which is why summer garments may not always be lined. Instead, the main fabric will be of breathable, natural qualities and the inside seams will be finished wonderfully.

COMFORT: It offers comfort to the wearer by not exposing skin to seams or finishes which can irritate and tickle.

IRRITATION: It protects the wearer's skin by providing a gentle layer between the main fabric and the wearer. A lot of tailored garments are made from wool or scratchy fabrics and other garments can be made of fabrics with a coarse underside. A soft lining in between can offer the wearer the benefits of a coarse fabric such as structure, fit and durability, without the risk of chafing or discomfort.

POLYESTER LINING: Seeing a polyester lining on an expensive coat or dress is always extremely frustrating as it means only the outside is going to be fit for purpose. Inside, you basically have a layer of plastic sitting right against your body that is trapping odours, increasing body heat and sweat and will break down quicker than the outer fabric.

If someone researching in-store thinks, 'Gah! How did they get that coat into the price point?', opening the garment and assessing the lining and finish inside will often tell them why.

WHAT TO LOOK FOR WHEN ASSESSING LINING

COMPOSITION: What is it made from? You want a fabric that is suited to how you intend to wear the garment.

DURABILITY AND COMFORT: Does it feel strong, durable and comfortable on the skin?

CARE LABEL: Does the care label state that the lining and the outer fabric can be treated similarly? If it cannot be washed, this can shorten the garment's life.

MOVEMENT: Is the lining restrictive? Some poorly made clothes won't have correct lining and it will make the garment feel too tight in places. If there are pleats in the garment to allow the wearer to move – such as in the centre back of a coat – this should also be in the lining.

FINISH: Is the hem sitting badly due to the lining? This again is due to bad quality. Your lining should allow the hem to sit comfortably.

Linings are not a must for all garments, for example, summer coats, but there are times when I will walk away from an unlined garment as I know it's a cost-saving measure:

- **Winter coats.** No-brainer.
- **Wools** work best when lined, be it a skirt, jacket or coat. This is mainly down to comfort but it also stops them from wearing out quickly.

- **Suiting, dress trousers** and **tailored items** should always be lined and finished immaculately to ensure a long life.

DARTS

Darts are used to help give a garment its desired silhouette. They are essentially a triangle that is sewn out of the garment to give it shape. However, your personal style may mean you never wear a garment with one. They are mainly for a tailored or fitted look and left off boxier, wider styles completely.

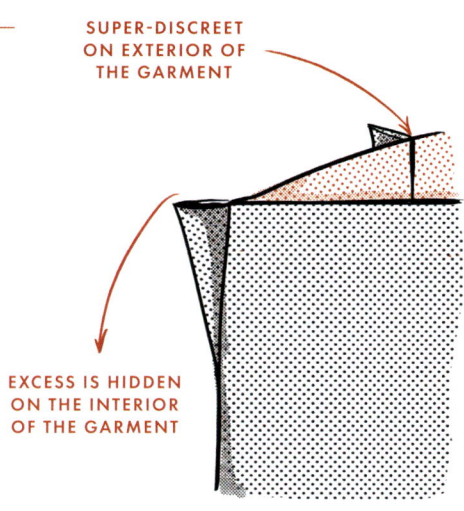

SUPER-DISCREET ON EXTERIOR OF THE GARMENT

EXCESS IS HIDDEN ON THE INTERIOR OF THE GARMENT

Should you see darts in a garment, you can soon tell if they were part of a rushed production line or made to last.

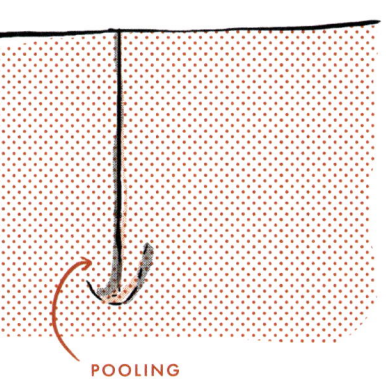

POOLING

POOLING: Does the dart end in a perfect point and disappear into the fabric effortlessly? Darts should be immaculately finished. Suitable fabric and gentle production speed allow this. A dart can indicate poor quality when it pools.

When this occurs it will hint that the garment's production was most likely rushed.

SYMMETRY: Are the darts the same length on both sides? Again, lack of symmetry will give a big indicator of rushed production.

PLACEMENT: Is the placement correct? When garment sizing is done correctly, the darts are moved properly to suit the size better. If the dart seems in an odd place, due diligence has not been done.

Not all garments need darting. Their design or fabric can lend itself to a dart-free life. Then we also have garments that are called 'easy fitting'. These have no darts to provide a baggier look which is ideal for workwear, for example. Where this goes awry is when fast fashion drops darting to drop the price. So, when you are sussing a piece, think about the lack of darts as well as the darts that are there.

SLEEVES

Something we should mention here is sleeves. Not many people know about sleeve variations yet will have a preference without realising it. If you want a sleeved garment to last, consider the type of sleeve you are buying.

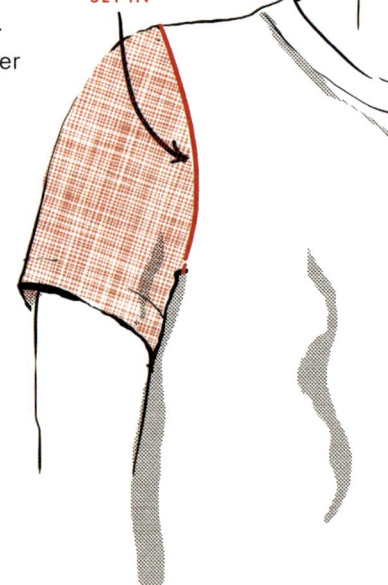

SET-IN SLEEVES

These are the traditional sleeves you see in many garments. They will fit to the body and are ideal for shirts, some styles of coats and fitted tops. When you have a set-in sleeve, there will be stress on the armhole during certain movements so look for ways in which the garment is reinforced to help with this. It could be stitching or pleats along the back of the garment.

Set-in sleeves can be either one-piece or two-piece sleeves.

The two-piece sleeve always suits a garment that will be worn a lot like a coat, jacket or some shirting. This is because it can take a lot more stress and movement due to its additional seaming. This is also ideal for tailored garments as you can get a stunning silhouette. They are pattern cut to follow the shape of the arm in a relaxed position (slightly bent) so you don't get a pucker at the elbow. As well as not looking great, this puckering can often cause wear to the fabric. The additional seam is also favoured by many as it means you have more opportunity to let the sleeve in or out to suit you.

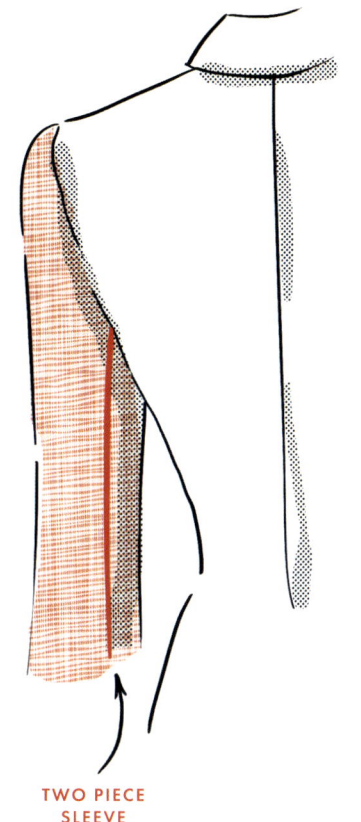

TWO PIECE SLEEVE

RAGLAN SLEEVES

I LOVE a raglan sleeve. These were often most used in sportswear as traditional set-in sleeves didn't give the desired range of motion. They are more expensive to produce but I find they last longer as the stress on the seam is in a different location.

There are other bonuses of a raglan sleeve besides the fact you could vogue for hours

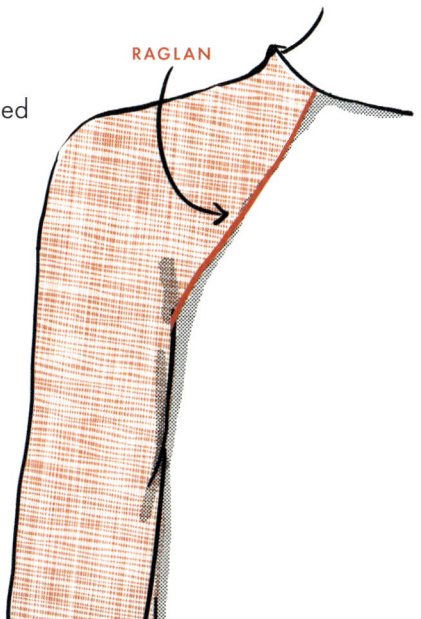

RAGLAN

in one. The top of the arm is usually cut wider so many people find this sleeve much more comfortable than a set-in, which can feel quite high cut.

Raglans also give everything a slightly casual edge so are delicious in formalwear, jackets and dresses.

The set-in sleeve can look slightly off if the shoulder seam is not in the exact place it needs to be. Raglans don't have this problem, so people that find shoulders on garments are either too big or too small on them tend to adore a raglan as it doesn't matter where the natural shoulder is.

DROP SLEEVE

A drop sleeve is as you would imagine. It sits on the upper arm as if the armhole has been dropped. They leave you loads of room during wear. I find them great in garments I know I will be quite hot in as they give me some room to breathe. A drop sleeve again, gives a much more casual look to a garment and also adds a far boxier shape. Often you'll hear people selling clothing online and saying they have 'sized up' to get a boxier look for their top. All they had to do was look for a drop sleeve as this is what gives a true boxy look.

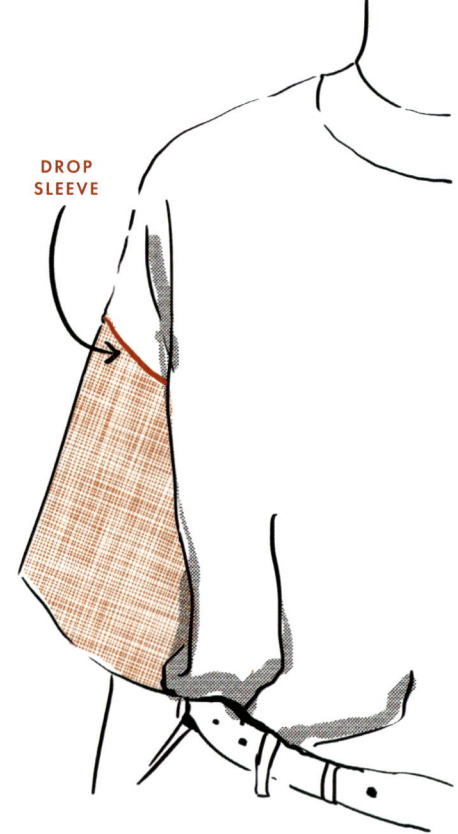

DROP SLEEVE

Function

POCKETS

Each season there are a variety of pocket trends. In some garments, the pocket alone is the focus and the only 'fashion' element. Some years it's zipped pockets, others it's combatesque and all over the place, or it could be minimal in seam pockets and so on. Regardless of the styling, pockets mean more labour and more labour is more cost.

One way to cut the cost of a pocket is to cut its functionality. Pockets require an opening to be made and finished, as well as a pocket bag, which involves extra fabric and finishing. This is why you will often see faux pockets on high-street garments. If the price is high, do not stand for non-functional pockets. They will be there for trend purposes which means you'll be able to find a similar style with better quality elsewhere as most trends hit all brands in some way through the season.

SEWN-UP POCKETS

Don't forget it is common on well-made garments to sew up the pockets before sending them to the store to ensure the garment keeps its shape. How stunning. For this reason, check inside the garment to see if there is a pocket bag; this will let you know the pocket is functional and that it's just sewn up for transport. You also don't need to open them once you purchase. Many people will leave them shut on the back pockets of a trouser, for example, if they don't carry a wallet and want to keep the back of the trouser as immaculate as possible.

If you are in search of long-term wears, look out for the signs of a good pocket:

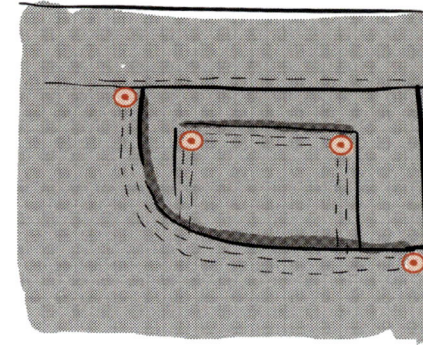

- Slide your hand in and out of the pocket to see if it is well made. You are looking for a tough pocket bag and adequate room inside. Don't be shy in inspecting the stitching around the pockets.
- Is it well done and nicely finished so it doesn't feel uncomfortable when you wear the garment?
- Look out for indicators that the pocket opening is reinforced to make it more durable, either with stitching or rivets.
- Pockets on the lower part of the body, especially, should always be able to fit your hand and be deep enough that what goes in does not fall out during wear.

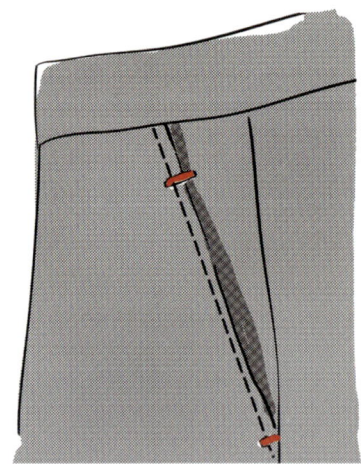

- Pockets on the top half are fine not to fit a hand, take a 'ticket pocket', for example, on old-school jackets to hold your train ticket. They just need to be well-sewn.

BUTTONS AND BUTTONHOLES

When it comes to anything buttoned, inspect not only the buttons themselves but also the buttonholes. These will get more wear than the button in their lifetime and it's hard to fix a badly done set. Different buttoned garments will have different elements (think of a coat versus a shirt, for example) but all will need the same once over when shopping.

Check that the stitching around the buttonholes is neat, uniform and secure.

HAND-SEWN buttonholes are cut first, then the edges are bound with thread.

MACHINE buttonholes are sewn first, like a window frame, and then a slit is cut into the pane afterwards. For this reason, lots of thread is used so it is tight and the fabric won't fray.

POOR-QUALITY buttonholes are like the above but often sewn too quickly with too little thread. They look weak and frayed on the shop floor.

Also note:

- Does the fabric around the buttonholes and buttons feel strong enough to withstand movement during wear? These are usually double-layered or reinforced to add strength. Cheaper garments will feature neither.
- Unbutton and rebutton the garment fully to ensure that all buttonholes and buttons work as they should. I mean it. When production lines are sped up to get a batch out quickly, the functionality of fastenings can often be the thing to go unnoticed.
- Inspect buttonholes and the button to ensure that the threads are secure and well-sewn and that no button is loose. If they loosen or show wear after one go, imagine what they will be like after a few wears.
- Are the buttons sewn in a straight line and evenly spaced? I have seen too many garments with buttons off position and it affects the entire garment.
- Pull the button gently and look for any loose threads that will cause the button to come off.

I hate to add this as I can't believe we have got here but ... in a shirt, your button should never be wider than the button stand and placket (the fabric panels that the buttons live on). If it is, it is a cost-cutting measure. Most likely a stock button has been used and the placket is reduced to save on costs. A button stand should be double the button width so when it is sitting in the centre, half its width is on either side.

HORIZONTAL AND VERTICAL BUTTONHOLES

Another way to spot cost cutting is buttonhole direction. Have you ever noticed that shirting will have vertical buttonholes on the body, but the collar's will be horizontal? This is to accommodate movement and increase comfort and it is a must!

When there is a lot of movement during wear at the button's location, the buttonhole being horizontal will allow movement of the button without it being able to slip out of the hole. This means the area can expand with ease as the button can slide from side to side. This is common on collars, waistbands and coats.

You will also note that the above are garments that don't have a placket (as a shirt would) and horizontal buttonholes suit the fabric better in this case. However, as it is easier to sew vertical buttonholes, fast fashion will often opt for these, even when there is no placket, and that's how you know a corner has been cut.

Verticals allow the button to stay in place all wear and usually run along fitted garments like shirts as there is nothing underneath and you don't want movement of the buttons.

In more expensive shirting, you will find the bottom buttonhole as well as the collar is horizontal to allow for ease of movement with tucking in and wearing.

On some fast fashion shirts, you will note that the button direction doesn't change at the top and this can make it harder to wear as well as to open and close.

ZIPS

Quality zips are a must, no matter what price level you are buying at. If a brand is pricing correctly and committed to producing garments that last, it will have great zips. As a consumer, it can be hard to establish what makes a good zip in-store but there is a shortcut.

One thing most people who know clothing will look for is the zip brand. Clothing brands outsource zips for their garments. Considering the time and money it would take to create their own zip each season, it would be insanity to even go there. The cost of the machinery alone would be exorbitant. This means it is easier to buy them in.

The most renowned zip brand is Japanese producer YKK. YKK stands for Yoshida Kōgyō Kabushiki and they are said to produce over half the zips in the world. The reason they became so popular and grew so large is down to their reputation for always creating reliable zips. Another reason is that they produce these reliable zips at many price points. This means every brand has the potential to use YKK, from lower price high-street through to designer.

How YKK maintains market dominance is down to the fact they run the whole chain themselves. Every component used is created by them, which allows them to be sure of quality and hit every price point. It also means they can develop in-house, which is why they are so advanced when it comes to innovation on the market, like waterproof or performance zips.

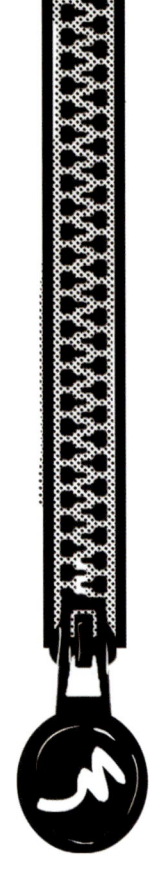

This in-house development is down to the fact that they have created their own machinery and methods, which is a stunning state of affairs. Their set-up allows them to always be steps ahead when it comes to new techniques and they can achieve lower prices than others due to their scale of production.

There are other high-quality zip brands, such as SBS, which you can find on the high street, mainly in higher-priced activewear and outdoor brands. Some high-end designers like to develop their own zips with a supplier. All in all, not all good zips are YKK, but no bad zip is YKK.

Due to their massive catalogue and range of prices, there is not much reason, other than wanting to sell the garment at a super-low price, that a brand will skip a YKK zip. They are a sure-fire way to build trust with customers and become a reliable brand yourself by creating garments that will function well for a long time.

How would you know if something is YKK or SBS? It's all right there on the zip. Some of the more basic styles will have lettering on the zip pull which will stand out. If the zip pull has the clothing brand's name or logo on it, the YKK will be in other locations, like the zip stop or the back of the head. Some non-negotiables for me in terms of a non-brand zip are jeans and fitted dresses. I once had a dress split in the middle of a wedding ceremony, right past my underwear, and had to be cut out of it in the car park before the reception, over a car bonnet. Never again. Now if I find something that is otherwise okay but with a questionable zip, I'll just replace it for peace of mind.

HERE IS WHAT TO LOOK FOR WHEN SHOPPING:
- **Test** the zip both on the hanger and on the body.
- Check if the zip sits **flat**. If it bulges, it's not right for the garment or the garment's fabric isn't right for a zip.
- Check to see if the teeth are **metal**; metal will always last longer and won't get damaged through heat or ironing. This metal can be coated so give it a tap with your nail.
- Is the zip **sitting nicely** when closed or are there gaps at the top and bottom?
- Is there something at the top of the zip that **holds** the fabric together? On trousers it will be a button, on dresses and tops, it's usually a hook and eye. Not all garments will need this kind of fastening, but be sure that it won't be encouraged to open during wear if its missing.
- Examine the **stitching** and seaming alongside the zip, it should be even and well done.
- Is there a proper **stop** at the top of the garment or is it a stitch line? Some cheaper garments will cut standard zips to fit instead of having the expense of a perfectly fitting one in place. This can mean that if the seam at the top loosens, the head of the zip can come off.

Fashion

PRINTS, PATTERNS AND STRIPES
Perilous at best these days! Getting prints, patterns and stripes right costs money and it is often skimped on in rushed or low-quality production.

PRINT MATCHING

First things first and that is matching up seams.

When lining up the production of a garment, producers will look at the cutting stage carefully. First, they must make sure that garment pieces are cut in the right direction, following the weave and print of the fabric correctly. As they do this, they also make sure they can fit the pattern in a way that creates as little waste as possible. This work is called a lay plan and even when dressmaking you would always do this.

When executing the lay plan for a printed garment, one would always make sure the side seams match. This is especially important for stripes and plaids as it is glaringly obvious when it is not done right. With some prints, it may not be possible to continue the exact point of the pattern, but it should be executed in a considered manner. Large patterns being cut off in a way that makes the garment look bad is easily avoided.

Always look at all seams; sometimes the back of a jacket can be a tell-tale sign of rushed production. As some seams curve, the stripe or pattern may not match the whole way along but it will be obvious if effort has been made on the main focus areas. This is why some shirts or t-shirts will have their pocket running in the opposite direction completely to the main body, as a perfect match of stripe or print would be far too costly.

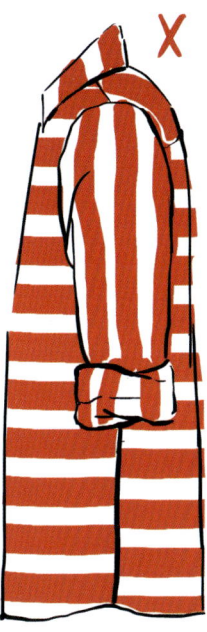

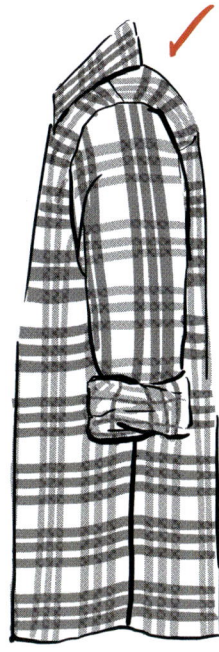

UNPRINTED AREAS

When buying anything printed, the inside is often ignored as we assume that once a body is inside it will not be seen. Unfortunately, this may not be the case: a side split, a collar or a vent in the sleeve can all flash the underside of the fabric. Make sure you investigate what is seen that is unprinted on a printed garment. It could make a big difference to how the quality of the garment comes across and how often you will wear it. Prints can often mask a lot of poor quality and rushed production so be mindful to investigate them thoroughly!

STRIPES

Back to stripes. These are usually woven into fabric. You'll know as the stripes are visible on both sides. When it comes to fast fashion, the pattern can sometimes be printed on cheaper fabric to save costs rather than opting for a more costly woven stripe. While visually it can appear the same, the issue with this is that on something like a shirt, elements of the inside will be able to be seen and it can affect how it looks on the body. As true stripes are easy to execute, it is a massive quality lapse if a garment has printed stripes when the inside will be seen during wear. For this reason, always examine.

That pretty much sums up how industry experts will examine garments on a shop floor to determine quality. These tips and tricks should help you establish what is right to take home, but that is not all there is to learn ...

BACK TO BASICS

Going back to the basics of garment design is where the dressmaker in us all comes in! Divine! Dressmakers and small-brand designers are usually well versed in pattern cutting so they will develop their own 'blocks'.

Blocks are the blueprint pattern for the garment. If she's not bang on and has all she needs to help the garment function properly, it's not good.

After they have sketched out their design, dressmakers will then think about the pattern needed to create this look. As they develop it, they will ensure that everything in the garment is adding to its wear, comfort and longevity. There will be elements in place for a good fit, movement and durability.

In mass production, it can unfortunately be the opposite. Details are dropped as they cost money. To round off your buying-and-trying knowledge, it is great to get to grips with some details that simply must exist in certain garments if you want them to feel good and last a long time. Let's run through some of the most common items we buy and things we need to consider.

SKIRTS

In general, a skirt should feel like the weight is fit for purpose and that you can move easily in it. The details in skirting make a massive difference as skirts endure a lot during wear.

LINING
Is there adequate lining? You will want some skirts to be lined for comfort but also because unlined means the skirt contours your legs, which doesn't always add to the lewk you want.

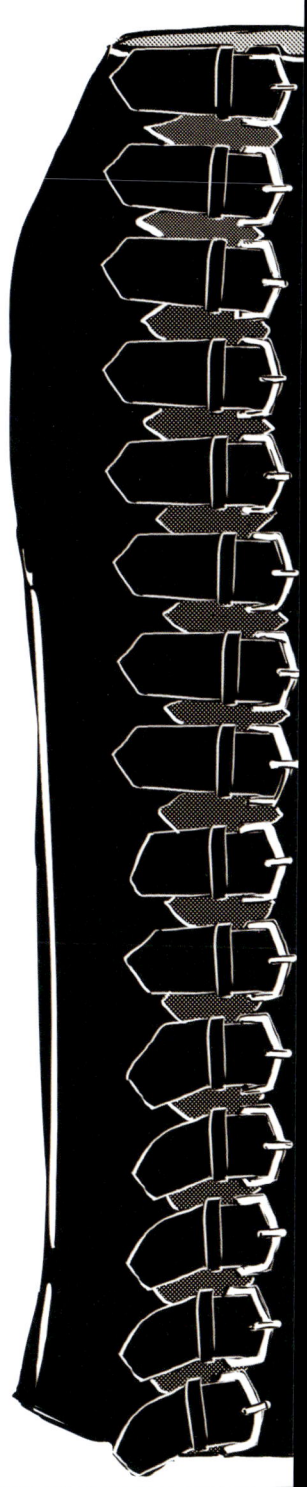

DARTS

Are these enhancing the garment? Skirts are one of the easiest garments to develop; there's a reason why it's always the first garment we learn to make. If the darting is bad ... it's not good news.

ZIPS

If you'll be wearing a top that meets or is tucked into the skirt, consider the teeth and top of the zip to avoid snags. Also, look for a hook and eye at the top as skirts move and zippers can slip open. There should always be some kind of fastening above the zip in high movement areas.

SPLITS AND VENT PLEATS

These are usually in the garment for ease of movement. For example, a vent pleat can be added at the back of a pencil skirt so you can walk. Or it could be a little slit on the thigh of a mini (*j'adore*). Look closely at this element; it should be reinforced as it is a key stress point of the garment and will be tugged at frequently as you move. Look for additional sewing techniques that help it survive wear and tear.

If a skirt has a split, it should come out of a seam. This means if the spilt threads do come undone as you get up to no good, it will only be the seam and not the fabric ripping. Trust me on this one. *winks*

SHIRTS

We are often told that a great white shirt is a vital part of any wardrobe but rarely taught how to buy one.

COLLAR AND CUFFS

These should be stunningly executed and finished but also have another key element. There should always be two layers and in certain styles interfacing/interlining is a must.

You'll be able to tell if the shirt has interfacing if you rub your thumb and index finger over two layers of the body of the garment and then the cuff or collar. If the cuff and collar feel stiffer, they are interfaced/interlined.

This extra layer is either fused on with heat to one side of the fabric or it is sewn in and 'floating'. The latter is usually in more high-end shirting.

CUFF PLACKET

Speaking of cuffs, there will always be a placket above the cuff. This is basically the finish of the slit that allows your hand to fit through the end of the sleeve as well as allowing you to roll up the sleeves. A great shirt will have a longer placket to fit all hands and roll

up nicely. It will also have a button mid-way to stop it gaping when rolled down.

If this addition feels very coarse but weak, it is a cheap version that will break down easily over time. It should feel soft and strong.

FINISH

Seams and hems should be extremely well done in a shirt. As the bottom usually gets tucked, the hem should have a closed finish and the same for the interior seams. Avoid visible overlocked edges as these will not last.

Stitching you can see should be tight and small. If you see long stitches, she'll literally come apart at the seams. Armholes and yokes should be reinforced and the plackets you see should be immaculate. Fabrics suited to quality shirting press and sew easily. If there are wonky seams and edges, it's a massive sign of poor quality or production.

BUTTONS

These are usually the main detail on a shirt and you need to make sure they are done well. You'll know if there are spare buttons that the shirt is made to be worn numerous times. Look at buttonholes closely and test buttons well. If the shirt is in a packet, ask for a sample.

Shirt buttons are important as they will go through a lot. Many producers will cut costs and use cheaper buttons, such as plastic, but these can fail pretty early on. They cannot take the heat of an iron, for example, or can fade in washes. The best shirt-makers will use mother-of-pearl buttons; these allow for long life and also feel and look a lot more expensive. If the shirt does not have great buttons, these are always replaceable!

YOKE

High-quality shirts will always have a yoke. A yoke is a panel at the top of a shirt's front and back to ensure that it doesn't wear out quickly. These should be double-layered and should be sewn in immaculately.

Bonus points if the back yoke is split (has a seam in the middle). This allows the yoke to move in one direction without added stress on the other.

Some pleats come from this yoke to enhance movement. I love a back pleat in a shirt as it gives a better range of motion.

HANGER LOOPS

These are rarely used as they were intended (first for sailors with little hanging space, then known as the locker room loop) and are more a sign that the brand is willing to take on the cost of a traditional detail. I personally love them. Dotey.

TROUSERS

Trousers endure a lot during wear, from when we move to when we sit to being opened and closed frequently. For this reason, attention to detail is important when looking for a long-lasting pair of trousers.

INTERIOR

The interior of a well-made pair of trousers is a sight to

behold. If they are unlined, the pockets, waistband and seam will all be finished in a way that won't bother you but will withstand a lot of contact and rubbing. This includes pocket bags.

FIT DETAILS

If I am spending more on a pair of trousers, I will always look for something either inside or out that allows me to adjust the waist when I need to. It's a sign of a well-considered trouser. The same goes for the hem, I will ensure it is substantial enough to allow for tailoring over the years should I want to alter it slightly.

POCKETS

Pockets are often overlooked. They are a stunning asset to any trouser but you need to investigate them a little further than how they look. Are they big enough for your hands and do they feel comfortable to use?
Look for additional measures taken to reinforce the pocket opening. It will usually be stitching that will help it to take some wear.

FABRIC RECOVERY

You don't want the knees and the seat of trousers to warp each wear so have a look at the fabric recovery. Pull the fabric gently and let go. If it goes back into shape easily, it's less likely you'll get warped knees during wear.

HEMS
A blind stitch is a must unless a topstitch is a styling element. Often people will purchase a pair of trousers with the intention of taking them up or down and not check if the hem and hem allowance will allow them to do so. Blind hems will move with the garment wonderfully and allow change over time.

PLEATS, PLEASE
Pleated trousers should be cut in a way that allows for a great fall, even during movement and use of the trouser. This usually involves adding more fabric than normal to other areas. Some fast fashion brands will add pleats to the hips, for example, and nothing extra, so the back is pulled and the pleats look warped. Always look for this. You should be able to pop your hands in your pockets and the trousers should still look nice if the pleats have been developed properly.

DRESSES

The dresses you wear most will probably have little dedication to shape and be more free-flowing. Less-tailored garments can be more comfortable and feel better overall for day-to-day wear.

INTERIOR
Free-flowing dresses will usually give peeks of the interior of the fabric so be sure to check that it looks good. When there

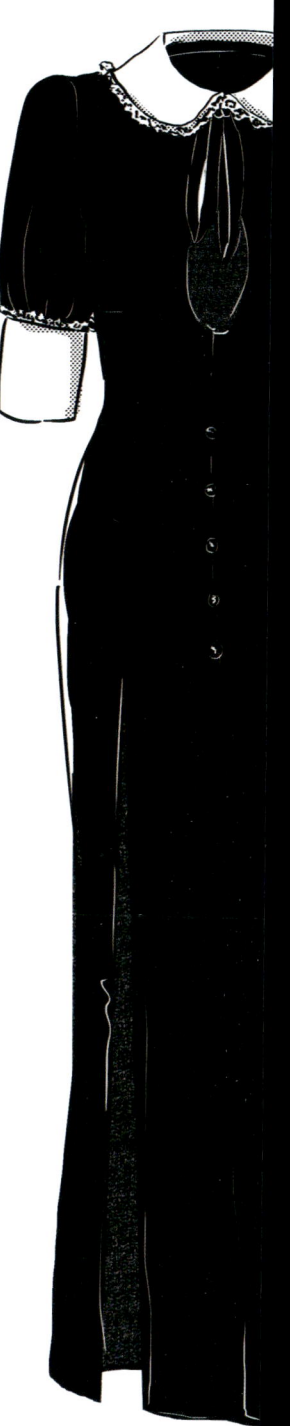

are side splits or high-to-low hems, which is common in more oversized dresses, the interior of the fabric becomes part of the exterior.

If there is a massive difference to the exterior, for example, if it's cheaply printed and white is flashing, you won't love this for long.

ZIPS AND FASTENING
An exposed zip is cheaper to do. Unless it is part of the design, the zip should be covered with fabric or be a concealed zip.

DARTS
If I am going to buy a fitted dress that I want to last a long time, I will look for seams or darts on the waist and hips. This allows an easy edit to the shape to fit me better or be changed over time. When there is minimal seaming, especially on a non-stretch, it can be harder for a tailor to pick a point to take in or out the garment without affecting its fall or fit overall.

COATS AND JACKETS

Oh, baby. How these girls have suffered in the era of poor quality. To keep this brief but effective, I am going to focus more on buying a coat or jacket that is less for shovelling snow and Arctic expeditions and more on the day-to-day side.

SLEEVES
A two-piece sleeve here is key if there is a high price. Unless the design lends itself to a one-piece boxier shape, that extra seam is a serve. It also is a good sign that the production time has been substantial. Two-piece sleeves have an almost L shape to them, which means you won't get a saggy elbow as well, which is always a tell-tale sign of poor quality.

CENTRE BACK SEAM

Vital. This will give shape and endurance. It also allows you another place to edit and tailor if you like. Without a back seam, not only is there no correct shaping, which helps with movement, but you also risk the fabric splitting. A seam will be more heavy-duty. I am always baffled when I see a blazer or coat with no centre-back seam.

FASTENINGS

Some low-quality coat fastenings can be bothersome for other pieces you wear. For example, Velcro can be a nightmare if you wear tights or knitwear a lot and cheap pop fasteners cannot remain closed during wear. Consider the wear of the garment when looking at the fastenings as well as what you wear with it.

POCKETS

Always look for some interior breast pockets. The best coats will have some form of pocket on the left and right and their bag will sit inside the lining and not bother you. As a *ciotóg*, I love the option of a pocket on both sides as there is often only one placed for right-handers. These will usually have a button to allow you to keep valuables safe.

When it comes to the external pockets, look for one that has the pocket bag sitting between the fabric and the lining. A patch pocket can get quite worn. A flap pocket is usually the most durable and safest

for what you pop in there. The bags themselves, on well-made coats, can differ from the lining as they need to be more durable. Keys or other hard items can cut into a soft, slinky lining material so often a tough cotton is used.

I will also always look for reinforcement around external pockets here as we rest our hands in these a lot more than with other garments.

LINING
Try to avoid polyester lining at all costs. It's just not suitable for a coat or jacket from both a comfort and long wear point of view. In winter, we want to keep warm but not overheat. This means our linings need to be breathable. Cheaper coats will use polyester lining and pocket bags and will disintegrate over the course of one winter. Also, check that the lining doesn't restrict movement or you will end up with torn armholes.

Speaking of fabric, you know best what warmth and weight you want but do look for wool. It has natural qualities that will enhance wear and comfort but is also much easier to repair than other fabrics. I love a wool coat. They can be harder to pick up these days as wool quality just isn't the same on the high street, so look at vintage where wool can be plentiful.

A LITTLE NOTE ON COATS AND JACKETS
Before the factory packs up garments for shipping, they will often apply a few stitches to coats and jackets to keep their shape during travel. This will be to the back vents and pockets. For many years this was a very obvious stitch as a tailor would use a basting stitch, which is a

contrasting colour and thickness to the fine tailoring stitch and is much easier to pull out. Now in the era of speed and low cost, the same thread will be used, and people will assume it is part of the coat's construction.

Free yourself up and snip these once you have the coat home to allow proper movement when the piece is on.

T-SHIRTS

I love a good basic tee and these are something that can be hard to get right.

FABRIC

Cotton all the way. If it's super-fitted, you may also see that the shape you like has some elastane. If you want to kick things up a notch, look into merino. A merino tee can look and feel simply stunning. Don't even get me started when it's got a silk blend.

Hold the fabric up to the light. It may not be super-heavy, but it shouldn't be see-through. The fabric should also be really uniform. If you see little holes or blocks of cloudy patches, this is a low-quality yarn. A great cotton will give a stunning, almost cold handfeel when you gather the body in your hand.

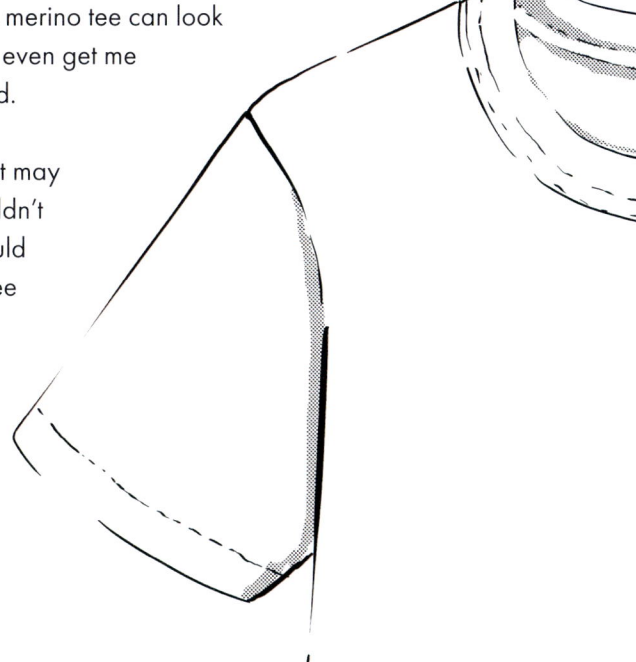

REINFORCEMENT

First off, look at the neckline. This should be in a ribbed band. Not only does this hold the shape of the neckline and stop any gaping, but it also recovers well after you put it on and take it off. Sometimes tees will have the neckband in the same fabric as the tee and it will become misshapen over time, giving an almost rippled effect. This band, in a high-quality tee, will have a neck tape of some sort to protect the seam attaching the rib and the body from ravelling; it also looks better on the hanger.

- Look at the **inside seams**; they will usually be overlocked due to the nature of the fabric and wear of the garment but should be substantial. If you compare a cheap and mid-range t-shirt, the latter will always have more seam allowance and a nice, tight overlocked finish. Cheaper tees will have very, very little seam allowance and stitching with poor recovery.
- The hems on both the bottom of the garment and the cuffs should be **double-stitched** in a clean and uniform way. Their stitching will have a lower SPI so it can stretch but nothing too loose. Older vintage tees will have a single stitch and it's quite a cult thing to have so if you ever see one …
- For a long-lasting tee that you can wear for a long time, look for reinforcement at the **shoulders** and along the **armholes**. This is more for casual styles. More dressy tees will have less visual enforcement as they are not going to be worn in the same way.
- Don't forget to consider your favoured **sleeve type**. Drop shoulders and raglans are so much easier to wear. Drop shoulders are also easier to keep cool in as the armhole is much lower from your pit. It can be stunning to mix these 'sportier' armholes with a more tailored or dressed-up bottom BTW. A drop tee tucked into tailored trousers? Divine.

SWEATERS

I wear a crew neck sweat almost every day and think they are a wonderful addition to any wardrobe no matter what your style. With the rise of loungewear clothing, this is one garment that has taken a massive blow in terms of quality. Here is what I look for in a sweat.

FIBRES

Long-staple cotton again all the way here but I will look for reference to the rib of the neck and cuff having a blend to allow a stretch. However, this HAS to be minimal. If the body of the garment and the cuff, hem or neckline has more than 20 per cent of another fibre they will wash differently and over time they will be different colours. Sometimes this can even happen after two washes.

FABRICS

You'll usually have two choices of fabric: loopback and brushed loopback. I personally prefer loopback in summer as it keeps me cooler and then brushed for winter.

One thing you will notice with these is that brushed has an airy plumper look and loopback has a more draped look. You can usually tell without looking inside.

Either way, look at the loops. They can take on different appearances at different

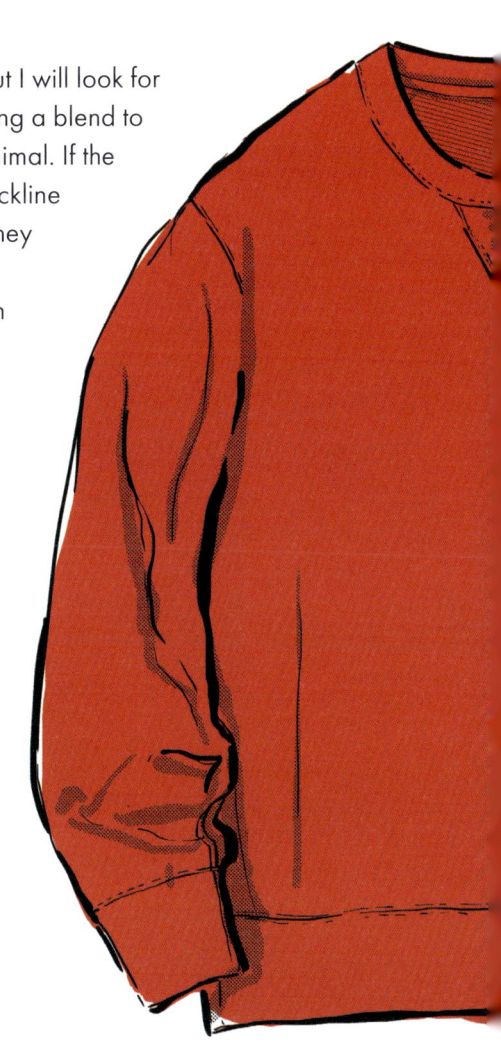

brands but should be uniform and have a good handfeel. For brushed, always hold up to the light with the brushed side facing you to see if it appears dense or cloudy. Cloudy is bad quality as it is showing patches of uneven or rushed brushing.

FINISHINGS
Look for reinforced stitching around cuffs, hem and neckline to show durability.

Speaking of the neckline, a long-lasting crew neck will have not just a triangle of stitching but it will be a double layer. Some brands have it wrong-side out for a styling note. This reinforces the neck so it can last the pulling and tugging as you dress and undress as well as wear.

DENIM JEANS

Denim is a subject where you can go as in-depth as you wish. There are denim fanatics out there who will tell you they never wash them, only buy Japanese brands, only wear selvedge and so on. For the sake of this being broader advice for all, let's go through the basics.

APPEARANCE
If you look closely at denim you will see that it has a diagonal pattern to the weave. This is a twill weave,

which is essentially a warp-facing weave so you can see the weft sit underneath it and it gives this ridged effect.

WARP AND WEFT

Woven fabric is essentially a series of yarns interlaced at right angles. The horizontal yarns are the weft and the vertical are the warp. Most woven (non-stretch) fabrics will be in a plain weave, in the same tone and woven one over, one under, like this to give a flat smooth appearance

However, in denim, a 'twill' weave is used. This is where the weft passes under two or more warps in a way that creates a diagonal, ribbed appearance. It is also the strongest and most durable weave due to how tightly it can be woven.

What makes denim so gorgeous is that the warp is usually dyed indigo first, while the weft is left undyed or will have been bleached. It is most commonly the weft passing under three dyed warp yarns and that is what gives its famous aesthetic.

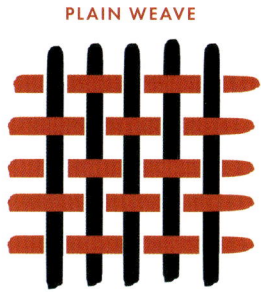

PLAIN WEAVE

TWILL AND DENIM WEAVE

FIND YOUR PERFECT MATCH

If you want to really match your denim to you, take in the direction of the diagonal. There are right-hand twills, left-hand twills ... and broken twills. Levi's famously uses the right-hand twill (RHT), which sees the diagonal run lower left to upper right. Lee on the other hand use LHT. Wrangler then started to use a mix of the two called broken twill to prevent legs from twisting. This takes on a more zig-zag appearance. This direction choice is why some brands appear to have always had a certain look to their denim. But these also come with different characteristics. It is said that LHT wears in quicker and you get a smoother denim over time. If you like that almost fluffy feeling of denim and one that contours your body during wear, this is good for you. RHT can give a more structured and drier-looking denim for longer so you don't have to wash it to get it back into shape. This suits a gal that enjoys a boxier look to denim.

COLOUR
Natural indigo is notoriously hard to get right so we now use synthetic indigo which is expensive to pull off. When it's done well, it gives a more distinguished colour than something dyed to look like indigo. Usually, you can see it on the shop floor and easily spot what is just a regular blue dye, as indigo is pretty hard to fake. It also takes more time to have two yarn colours so often cheaper denim is all one colour.

FIBRE
True denim is cotton, but many fast-fashion jeans will be polyester these days. This is because they cannot afford to use cheaper cotton due to the intense workmanship in the production of a pair. If you see polyester in a higher priced pair of jeans it will be better for durability and usually a higher quality cotton and poly together. Most denim will go through a 'wash' phase after it is made, and this is where cheap cotton can start to show signs of wear. Poly can endure more heat, but you are wearing something that isn't great for body heat, washing or other factors.
If you want denim with a stretch, look for something mixed with your cotton, like Lycra or Spandex, but make sure the stretch addition is very, very minimal; under 2 per cent is what many experts recommend. This is because it will wear out quicker and can ruin the shape of the garment.

DURABILITY

Chain stitch, double stitching, rivets, reinforcement in pockets, crotch and inseam are all vital elements of a good pair of jeans. Weaker fabric cannot take as much detail as it will tear easily so you know the denim is good if there is a lot of workmanship. You also know that a lot of time has been spent on it. Tap the rivets and buttons with your nail to ensure that they are metal rather than plastic.

HANDFEEL

Great denim always feels almost coarse to begin with and then, as you wear it, the garment starts to mould to your body a bit more.

KNITWEAR

Knits are a tricky one as they can come in so many varieties.

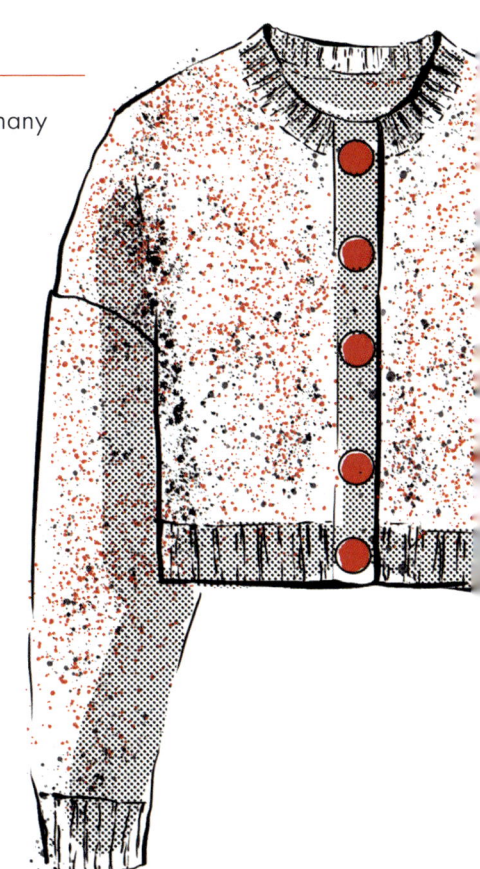

FIBRE

WOOL: Remember, the longer the staple the less scratchy. Wool is a great natural fibre but is best worn over a layer for comfort. She's naturally warm and cosy and will last for years.

ACRYLIC: Think of her as polyester's cousin, production-wise. Pretty much a plastique yarn that is made the same way from the same stuff. This is what most cheaper brands will use for their knits. You will see sooo much acrylic knitwear on the high street these days as it can emulate wool's appearance in many ways. It's easy to design with, takes on dye really well and the customer rarely notices that it is not a stunning set-up until it's worn. Acrylic can feel limp and starts to wear and bobble quickly. As it is a synthetic fabric, it can also hold a lot of bacteria and does not truly wash as well as natural does.

MERINO: This is super-fine and soft and gorgeous but less about keeping you super-warm and cosy unless it's blended with something else. A fave blend of mine is linen and merino. It gives a lovely dry handfeel that can pretty much work all year round and washes quite well.

COTTON: Cotton knits are great as they can wear well and, if good quality, don't pill. Cotton can be a great option if you overheat quickly in wool.

CONSTRUCTION

Knitted garments that are high quality will be made from pieces that are knitted to the exact shape and size needed and then 'linked' together on a special machine. There will be zero cutting of a knitted panel to make the final piece. This is a true knit.

Then we have cut and sew, which became super-popular during the fast-fashion explosion. A run of true knitwear takes far longer than a run of something like a t-shirt as the shapes need to be knitted individually whereas other garments are cut from long rolls of fabric.

'Cut and sew' or faux knit (it has many different names depending on where you are and who you work for) was born out of trying to reduce production time to reduce overall costs. This is where large rolls of knitted fabric are made and then the pattern pieces of the garment are cut from this instead of knitted and shaped one by one. The result is a much speedier production time although the durability just isn't there. This is due to the way the garment's pieces are joined together. It is usually the same as a t-shirt or stretch garment and is overlocked. Overlocking something that is knitted is not a long-lasting solution to finishing its raw edge. This can fall apart over time.

You can also get a true knit and cut and sew mix. This is where most of the garment is knitted in pieces but trickier and more time-consuming areas like armholes are shaped using an overlock during assembly.

These two methods are why it is vital to turn a knitted garment fully inside out and to inspect the seams. All the seams.

Another sign of true knit is to look at the cuffs and hem. These should all be part of the garment and not attached using an overlocker as cheaper production does. In true knitwear, the machine will simply change its settings to create the hem and cuffs and keep on knitting, then cast off. Good quality will have a lovely stretch and when you pull it in-store, it will recover wonderfully.

If you are committed to having knitwear you can wear year after year, look at knitwear specialist

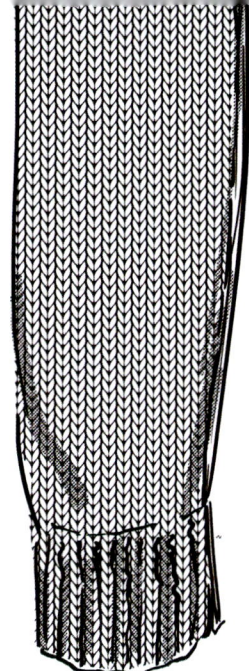

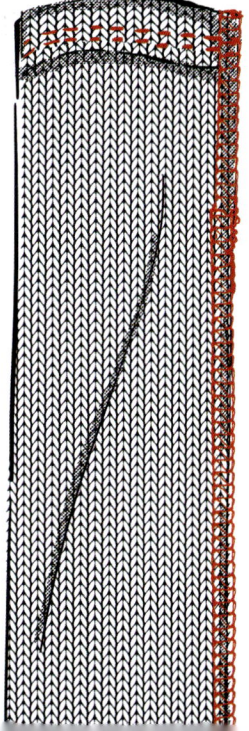

brands; brands that have long statements about their blends, fibres and construction. Check these out during sale seasons and search their name in preloved apps and you will almost always find an amazing bargain.

Vintage and preloved

Preloved clothing of any age can always be a great option as you are shopping from what is already out in the world. If something can be resold after use, it is usually a great sign of quality and how the garment can stand up to wear. As some used clothing can be so low priced, due diligence can sometimes drop or people can over-shop as it doesn't feel the same as shopping for new clothing. However, this is where shopping for used clothing goes awry. It's still consuming and so you should have the same approach.

EVERYDAY ITEMS

As most used clothing will be cheaper, this is a great way to pick up everyday items that are of superior quality. A new trend that is emerging is brands having a used section on their site where customers can resell their barely-worns. Divine. Before this kicks off fully, consider searching online for a brand beyond your budget before you buy your next t-shirt or basic everyday item. It is a stunning way to add amazing quality to your wardrobe for a low cost.

OCCASION

Sizing can make occasion wear an absolute melter to shop for. If you are looking for something for a wedding, for example, there is also the risk that you and others in the same outfit form another set of bridesmaids. For this reason, preloved occasion wear is ideal.

You don't have to take the risk of vintage. Vintage can need more tailoring and it also isn't always available in a range of sizing. Instead, browse your usual shopping sites (and ones higher than you want to spend!) and use my favourite trick. Copy and paste the description of anything you love into preloved selling sites. As the item is still online, sellers will usually copy the description right off the site for their ad so it will be super-easy to find. This is how I will buy most of my more modern clothing. The items are usually barely worn or unworn as they are so new to the store and so the lower price is delicious.

OUTERWEAR

Great items to shop for are preowned coats and jackets, mainly because they tend to last a lot longer and so the condition of them is better but also because the current quality of these is so bad. One rule I would have when it comes to outerwear is to stick to what you can afford. Avoid buying these for low prices in charity shops or somewhere where you are taking a very practical item from the hands of someone with a lower budget. I use this rule for anything that is worn for warmth and suiting. Shopping preloved is an excellent way to be sustainable but when you are buying stock that is cutting off accessibility to someone else due to price, it is best to be mindful. Charity shops, of course, need sales to thrive but there is an etiquette to charity shopping in a conscious way and it is to mainly reach for the less practical.

NEW PLACES
Relying on a Google search to give you all you need won't work. Some of the best used clothing out there is with small sellers who are not using SEO and other marketing tools. They are on apps. If you ever find a brand you really, really love and that caters to all your needs, seek them out on preloved sites and socials. This always leads me to independent stores and sellers that stock the styles and sizes I'm after.

BEFORE YOU BUY
When looking at vintage or preloved pieces, you want to give everything a once over as you would when buying something new. It can be amazing to find something that looks different and is one of a kind, but she should get the same scan that new clothing goes through. For preloved items, you need to add a few more scans before you buy.

LABELS: Look for anything that can give you some care advice. Most times we buy vintage as occasion wear so the need for heavy-duty washing isn't there but if it is a day-to-day piece, try to suss if it's a dry-clean or hand-wash.

SEAMS: Give the seams a little tug. Some older garments are made with threads that can now be disintegrating and will fall apart during wear.

CARE: Look out for dry-cleaning tags on things like suits, outerwear or dresses. This for me is always a JOY. It means the garment was well cared for but also lets me know how I need to care for it if there's no label. I love to find lots of tags on an inside pocket and even better if the dry-cleaner's name is still there; it's one of the first things I search when I get home to piece together the life of the item.

CHECK FOR DAMAGE: It's rare to get a reasonably priced vintage garment without a little damage so assess fully. Look for discolouration, staining, fading, tears, moth holes and loose fastenings. In newer items they could have been discarded due to damage so don't skip this!

INSIDE: Turn the garment inside out fully. There can be stains, damage or wear and tear and it will be too late if you only discover it once you have it home. This especially goes for the crotch area of bottoms, there can be a host of issues here and it's best to know in-store if something is worn or torn beyond repair.

ISSUES: Don't forget that preowned garments usually have some minor issues. This doesn't need to be a turn-off and the price of a small repair, such as a zip replacement, can still mean a massive overall saving.

SUPERIOR QUALITY: Clothing quality was superior before and high-quality vintage clothing will reflect this. A coat that would cost hundreds can be picked up for a fraction of the price second-hand; you just have to know what you are looking for. I look for as many costly details as possible to figure out quality. No exposed edges, immaculate finishes, great use of fabric, details to enhance wear and comfort and so on.

WHEN YOU GET HOME

MOTHS: Your garment may well have lived in a moth-infested environment; it's just how it is. You can find out how to treat moths on page 213. It can be near impossible in-store to know if a garment has moth larvae so I would always suggest a wash, steam or a few days in the freezer before popping your purchase in your wardrobe.

FASTENINGS: Assess all fastenings before wear. I love gold button meauxments and have learned first-hand the heartache of losing one that can never be replaced. I will reinforce special buttons now before I wear them.

HEMS AND SEAMS: Suss these out by turning the garment inside out and inspecting from top to bottom. You want to make sure any gaps in seams are sewn up, anything you could catch a heel on is resolved and pocket holes are sorted. No more lost lipsticks.

WASHING: This isn't always a must, but you may have noticed a strong odour. Pop to page 161 to see how to tackle this.

STEAMING: One of the best things you can do for a preloved item coming into your home is to give it an all-over steam. It will freshen up the fibres and remove bacteria and mild odours, etc.

THE FAST-FASHION IMPACT

This area of the market has sadly been taken over by fast fashion in a bid to catch the now-emerging considered shopper. You will start to see well-known online brands tout new ranges with words that suggest they are reworked garments, preloved garments or true vintage. This is rarely the case and it is usually a design team using techniques to make new, mass-produced clothing appear like it was made years ago. Always dig a little deeper when a brand synonymous with fast fashion is covering something for the preloved market.

Right, you've assessed, and you've selected. Before we get to trying on, let's take a meauxment in the online world.

4 Virtually Speaking

SO LET'S START with the upside. The rise of online shopping has been a gift when it comes to finding clothes that are right for us. It has opened a whole new world in terms of accessibility and options. Let's also not forget speed and ease, instead of traipsing around shops on a Saturday you can shop from the comfort of your own home. Delicious.

In a few clicks, we can access brands, sizing and price points that may not be readily available to us where we live. There are massive advantages to being able to sell online for brands as it means they widen their customer base without the hefty spend a store would bring.

The major solid that online shopping has brought to the world is that the customer and the brand are no longer reliant on just their local stores to give them what they need.

But online shopping does have its negatives. It's been one of the leaders in the spread of fast fashion and low-quality clothing as it cuts out one main part of the shopping experience: physical time with the garment before deciding to buy it.

Its ease means there is a tendency to over-buy and under-wear. The journey of being at the physical store means there are more stages to us being able to assess if it's really something we want to carry home. When we shop online, we lack the real-life experience with the garment that can give us a reality check.

Then there are the price points. Have you ever seen something in-store that had a higher price point but the more you looked at it you could see why? Perhaps it was the fabric or the finish and you could see the reflection of the quality in the price. The opposite happens with online shopping; we have much less connection with the garment and so the price expectation lowers. Instead of the store atmosphere getting our blood pumping, we have low prices drawing us in.

Another issue is lack of transparency. It is not uncommon for the faster-producing fashion brands to try to mask poor quality or bad fits by presenting garments in a certain way online and not giving vital information that could turn us off. Online shopping has become more of a game of roulette and the trust just isn't there like it used to be. To take back control and be more mindful as well as aware, there are steps we can take to be savvy online shoppers.

A lot of the information you need is there somewhere online, it's all about knowing its relevance and where to find it. Online shopping doesn't have to be all about fast fashion; there are incredible brands out there that we cannot reach in person and the virtual stores allow us to peruse their stock with ease.

A PICTURE PAINTS A THOUSAND WORDS

Now that you are an expert in the physical examination of garments, you can use this knowledge to assess images on an online store. You may think it's impossible to spot bad quality from an image but you would be surprised. If a brand is trying to get a trend out quickly, little consideration will be taken when it comes to the prep of the garment for photographs. Also, there are a lot of bad-quality red flags that just cannot be covered up.

LOOK THROUGH ALL PICTURES: Even if you think she is good to go from image one, try to pick up if something is being kept from view. For example, if I see arms crossed or the same pose being used in the first few images that cover the same part of the garment, I skip to the image that shows it. Multiple pictures are there to give you a view of every part of the item, but people usually only look at a couple and can miss a red flag. I will also search the description and brand in a Google search to see if someone else is selling it and look at their images. Seeing it in a different pose can highlight the good and the bad. The same goes for review pictures which many online stores have if you scroll right down.

ZOOM IN: Most stores will have a zoom option. Use it. Loose threads, puckering, wonky hems, poor use of fabric and so on can all be spotted easily. It should also allow you to see seaming and hems clearly. These will help you to understand if the garment is put together well and can be worn a lot.

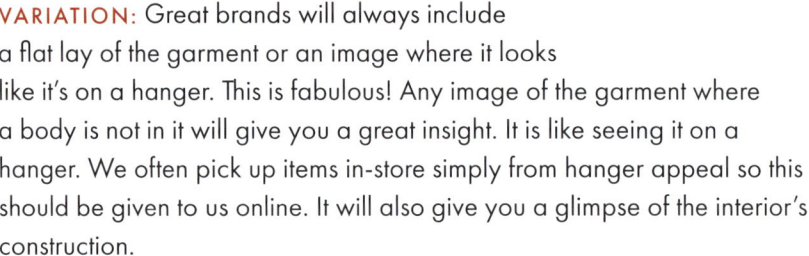

VARIATION: Great brands will always include a flat lay of the garment or an image where it looks like it's on a hanger. This is fabulous! Any image of the garment where a body is not in it will give you a great insight. It is like seeing it on a hanger. We often pick up items in-store simply from hanger appeal so this should be given to us online. It will also give you a glimpse of the interior's construction.

POSES: A massive, massive red flag is not providing an image of the garment on a body in a neutral pose. When a garment only has a twisted/motion/fashion pose and no neutral pose at all, it makes it almost impossible to make a wise purchase. Posing is how a brand will hide a bad fit or a poor-quality indicator. If the body poses are all contorted in some way, look for the above flat lay. Sometimes gold seal samples will not be ready for photoshoot time and so the brand will have to shoot a bad fit and then provide a flat image of the good one.

DEVIL IN THE DETAIL: For good-quality brands, detailed shots are always there. This is usually of the neckline or waistline so you can get an understanding of the workmanship and finish. Any image where the interior of the garment is shown – stunning. Don't expect to part with a lot of cash for a garment that doesn't haven't their details in clear images.

INFORMATION

Buying online is no different to buying in a store in terms of the information you need to make your choices.

FABRIC
If you like a garment, the first thing to check is the fabric composition. Remember, having a lot of different fibres isn't a good thing. You want to see large percentages, not lots of little ones. Get to know what a brand means by their fabric, too. If they use a premium cotton or a recycled poly, it will be shouted about. If I am buying a t-shirt or a sweat online I will Google the brand's cotton statement. If they use extremely good, long-staple cotton they will have a blurb about it somewhere and it gives me peace of mind that I am not wasting my time.

FASTENINGS AND FUNCTION
There should always be a note on how you get in and out of the garment. This will help you see if the garment has been constructed well. Don't always assume it's not an elastic waist or that the pocket zips actually work. Look for these in the description. Bonus points for a detailed description and one that is easy to understand.

CARE LABEL
This is a must. When I see 'online only', one of the first things I look at is

the care label. Many brands won't put 'dry-clean' clothes on the shop floor now. Sometimes online-only is done because the garment has zero hanger appeal, it was bought in a very small quantity or will be an absolute ball-ache on the floor in relation to their hangers and fit out.

Knowing the care instructions will help you gauge if it's something you want in your wardrobe. You may not want something that you need to wear a lot but cannot wash at home, for example.

LENGTH

There should always be some kind of length noted. The inside seam, front leg or nape to hem, for example, should be available to you so you can take it into consideration. Stating the model's sizing and height for me just doesn't cut it. If you know the exact measurement of the length you'll be able to suss it out properly in relation to your own body. Great brands do this.

SOURCE

It is now getting more and more popular to be transparent about where and in which factory the item was made. This allows people to know the chain properly and make a more conscious purchase. This level of transparency is a great step in the right direction for fashion as it ensures brands publicly commit and stand by their supply chain. It may not be on the garment's page but brands will usually have it somewhere on their site.

SIZING AND SILHOUETTES

All brands will have a size guide and good brands will note if the item differs in any way from it. Get familiar with the size chart and look more at the measurements than the dress size. You want something that works for your body.

Aside from size guides, the sign of a good brand is a fit guide. If you are not using a lot of fast-fashion styles and are committed to your brand silhouette you'll be able to clearly show the customer what shapes your t-shirts, jeans and so on come in. Have a browse through the fit guides to see which silhouettes suit you and you can search for these only. This also takes out a load of searching, I will look at the fit guide and be able to only search for the fit I want when looking for something like a white tee.

SUSTAINABILITY

You don't just have to check the retailer's site to get a grasp on their ethics and sustainable measures. There are many sites now dedicated to helping you see who treats their supply chain terribly in the name of fashion and who is making strides in reducing their impact on the planet.

BEFORE YOU CHECK OUT

CHECK THE RETURN POLICY: Don't rely on it being a perfect match or having a long return period. It can help to pop the deadline in your calendar so you don't miss the window.

BE AWARE OF DELIVERY TIME: Look at the fine print of the delivery just in case it is a time-sensitive purchase. Buying for a holiday and being away for the returns period could leave you with unwanted clothing and waste cash you could have spent on margs under a sunset.

PRELOVED: Another plus is seeing if it is being sold preloved. As mentioned in the Buying Vintage section, this isn't always readily available on a search engine so I will usually search for a fashion app that sells a lot of the brand or similar price point. Savvy sellers know to pluck the description from the website to attract more eyes and it can help you to buy the same garment for much less.

SIMILAR ITEMS: As well as your preloved search, pop the description into the shopping section of Google or any social channels you use. This has often led me to a similar look with far better quality, detailing and price. Sometimes the item is a trend many brands are covering, and you can get the lewk for much better value elsewhere. I never purchase online without doing both of these searches.

I hope this helps your next round of online shopping and leads you to some gems that will last a long time. The main takeaway is that low-quality clothes will have low-effort listings. When you see very little information and images, it will be minimal for a reason. My main advice is that if you are struggling to get a feel for the garment and its durability or suitability, it could be a sign that it is not built to last.

Next up, we are about to get real again and take a step into the changing cubicle.

5 The Changing Room

YOU'VE SUSSED the garment within an inch of its life and now it's time for a road test. It is tempting to slink out of the store sans try-on – especially when the queue is out the door and you have tights on – but a try-on before committing is essential so don't skip it. It doesn't even have to be in the store itself. It can easily be done at home or, if you buy online, once you have it. Just remember to do it within the returns period and never do it on the day you want to wear it. Trust me, bebe.

The 'changing room' is the final boss in video games, the reunion of a *Housewives* season, she is the last thing to do to round off a successful purchase. There will only be a very small note here on how the garments look and that will be more of a quality note than a body reference so please know you are safe from the word pear or apple being mentioned … . This is more about how the garment will feel, wear and last. I've read some wild changing room tips in the past; wear a full face of make-up, only ever shop in heels, bring an honest friend … gag. Instead, let's just focus on making sure the garment is right for you.

PREPARE

Before you begin trying things on, gather what you need to properly assess the items. A stylist will never have someone try on one garment and then get them to imagine the rest, now would they?

THE LEWK: Garments that you intend to wear with the item you are considering buying are vital to have to hand so you can see if the length, shape and style are what you are after. You'll never get a feel for a skirt if you're assessing it in just your bra but want to wear it with tees. It's not a must to tote around bits from home, just grab them off the racks, if needed. You don't have to even consider buying them but it's great to have an idea of whether it goes with the silhouette of what you usually wear. For example, when I am jeans shopping (I hate jeans shopping with an actual passion, I'd rather shop for my own coffin), I always grab a white tee so I can see what they will actually look like when added to my wardrobe as that's what they'll mostly be worn with.

ORDER OF SERVICE: Hang the items together in outfits. I know this seems mad, but it will help add an order that leaves your mind and eye less busy and you can focus. Changing rooms are stressful places; any order will help.

WELL-HEELED: Don't underestimate the right shoes being part of the game. The silhouette of a shoe can also make or break a lewk and a trouser can sit differently on various types so you want to make sure you get it right.

WEAR

Once you have put on the garment, do your usual front and back sconce to see if you like it. We are all different and will be after different things aesthetically, so I'll leave you to it from that point of view. Then consider the following:

COMFORT: How does the garment feel on your skin and from a comfort point of view? Good quality won't feel bad to wear and you'll know it's well-made as you pull it on. Take in how the interior feels as well as the exterior: for example, whether the pockets are bunching up or the lining is catching.

POSITIONS: Most people will try something on, put one foot in front of the other and a hand on their hip, like a QVC model. Tell me, lover, how often do you stand the way you pose in a changing room mirror during an average day? Move your arms in the positions you are likely to when wearing it. Bend down if you'll be doing it, open fake doors, turn imaginary steering wheels, do the splits if you're Kyle Richards. For example, I will hang off a faux Tube pole when trying on winter coats as I need to make sure my usual body position isn't going to be stressing the garment out so much that it will wear out buttons and shoulders quickly. I don't want to have to wear something that doesn't feel nice when I am in my most common body positions during its wear. Jumpers, jackets, dresses and so on all need this test to let you know if it's for you. Simple but most common movements will also point out any negatives quality-wise. If a seam isn't up to scratch or the facing moves, it will become obvious.

WALK: You don't have to stride up and down the communal areas of the store, a few steps forward and back will do. Some garments that are really trend-led and shipped quickly won't have had enough fitting done to assess the wearability. Walking could feel restricted or make different parts of the garment react to each other negatively or there could be a bad fit that makes it bunch in places.

SIT: Most dressing rooms will have a wee stool (if you're at home, any seat will do). This will allow you to pop yourself into a seated position and test the comfort as well as durability and suitability. If you are going to be commuting in a seated position in your winter coat, for example, you'll want to see how comfortable this is and if the buttons will annoy you or be under a lot of pressure. If you are buying a dress for an occasion, sit and see if it wrinkles in a way that is not going to be okay for you once you stand. You could wear the garment mainly seated and need to see if the waistband is comfortable or if the crotch is irritating. Sitting down in a garment tests it out as you'll easily spot something that is a no-no for you.

POCKETS: Check that the pockets are good to go for what you need them for. Pop your hand in, pop everyday items in and see how it feels. If the items are valuable, assess how safe the pockets are, how they close and so on.

ACCESSORIES: If you wear a bag, get it on. Some garments will have buttons, seams or embellishments on shoulders or across the chest and it's wise to see if they will be affected. See how it feels when you wear a bag and if will cause damage or wear to the garment.

FASTENINGS: You've probably already done a bit of this on the shop floor but do it on the body. The main question here is: can you be bothered? If the fasteners are difficult or uncomfortable, you won't want to wear the garment as much. If they feel flimsy or hard to use, they could be low quality and only last a few wears.

AFTER

TEMPERATURE: As you hang the garment back up, consider if it felt breathable or made you overheat, and if the use of this garment suits this.

DAMAGE: Assess the garment for any damage when it's off you. If threads or seam finishing have deteriorated in any way during a try-on, then the garment is most likely not fit for purpose.

CAN IT BE EDITED?

If you really like a garment and have done all the assessment tests but there's just something stopping you from reaching for your clutch, it's worth thinking about whether the elements you are concerned about can be altered – either by you or a professional.

HEMS

Hems are one of the easiest things to edit, provided there is enough allowance to allow you to do so. Be sure to check:

SEAM FINISH: Take into consideration if there is stitching visible on the outside. If there is, will it affect how the hem looks when being let down or taken up? If it's a synthetic, it may be hard to remove needle holes, for example.

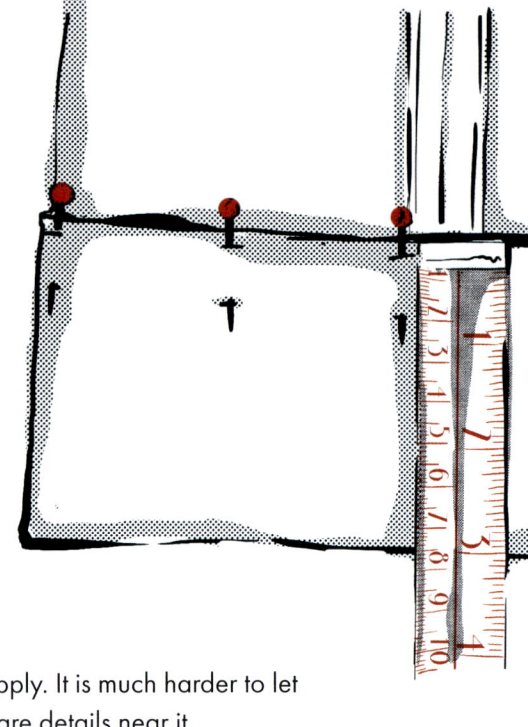

DETAILS: If the hem has a detail like a cuff, frills or banding, you'll need to think about how this will be done. Usually a good tailor will take off the detail, shorten the fabric and then reapply. It is much harder to let down a garment's hem if there are details near it.

PRINTS: Does the print finish in a way that would be negatively impacted if you reduce or lengthen it? Would you need to shorten from the other end to keep the flow, and would this be tricky?

FIT

Fit can be a little trickier but there is a way to get it right. Common fit issues are jacket shoulders needing to be brought in a little, torso, chest or hips being taken in or out, a more tailored look overall or the shape of a trouser leg being edited to suit your style. Some of these alterations – shoulders, for example – demand a professional or at least someone with experience.

EDIT DOWN: It is always said to shop for your biggest measurement and then edit in from there. This gives the tailor more to work with and you can work in from seams, which is much easier than letting out and risking visible needle marks. If you find there are areas of a garment that are tight, but the rest is fine, be sure to go for natural fabrics if possible as they are more likely to be able to remove needle holes.

DETAILS TO EDIT: Look for seams close to the area you want to edit as these are what will be adjusted. Darts, zips and seaming will all help to bring a garment in or out.

SEAM FINISHING: Clock the seam finishing. Well-made clothing will have good seams that are easy to open and adjust. Fast-fashion seaming often does not leave a lot of seam allowance and it can be badly damaged once opened.

TAILORS

If you need a professional tailor, you can find them in local directories or online but the best way is by recommendation. Ask the best-dressed person you know who they go to. I don't mean someone who wears a lot of expensive clothing, I mean someone who looks after their clothes. Style has nothing to do with the amount you shop, so someone you know who looks for quality and

wears their clothes often is bound to know of a good tailor. Even if they have not used one in your area, birds of a feather flock together and they'll get you a good rec from a pal.

Most tailor regulars will have two, if not a few, whom they go to for different things. This is mainly down to cost and ease. For example, their local dry-cleaner may be who they will ask to sew back on buttons or a fallen hem. They may go to a speedy and cheaper tailor to fix a broken zip. One thing they will not do is take more complex edits to anyone who specialises in basic repairs and alterations. Tailors who specialise in intense edits and bespoke jobs will do a far superior job but the price will reflect this. This is why you won't book them in for a hem. If you need to do a bit of online research, look for reviews that are weighty and mention the repair type or include images. The same goes for if you want to do a simple repair.

If you are shopping and know you want to tailor an item before you wear it, ask the store you are buying it from. Many will have an alterations service in-house or have a company they recommend. This is also usually discounted.

WHEN TO GO

Try, if you can, to give yourself some time for your trip to the tailor. It will give both you and the tailor the necessary space. Rushing in with an urgent request could rob you of some valuable time to talk it through and hear what the expert would advise you to do. It is much easier to ring a tailor and ask when their quieter times are to come in or if you need an appointment. The more direction and input you wish to have, the more time you will need so make sure you allow for it.

WHAT TO BRING
You may be asked to try on the garment so be prepared!

Always bring the footwear you are going to wear (use your common sense here, if it's a halter neck crop top, they may not be needed unless it's a thigh boot) and anything that will be impacting its lewk. The impact footwear makes on most garments is substantial, so having them there will make sure your alteration is as you need it.

If you have something in mind that you don't feel you can describe accurately or you don't know the correct lingo, bring an image. A few pictures from Pinterest will be helpful for anyone to see before they start to pin.

WHAT TO ASK
Be prepared for a conversation. If you drop off with a one-liner such as, 'Mere, please take that hem up by 3cm', that is what you'll get. The finish, seaming, stitching, thread used and so on will all be assumed. You also will not get an expert's opinion on whether the measurement is the right one.

It's better to be more detailed like, 'I would love these taken up to sit well with this shoe. Would you recommend finishing the hem in the same way it is now and with the same colour thread?'

The great thing about getting something tailored is you can change the look of the garment a little and make it more you. I would always ask if what I have requested is the best option or if I can alter the look a little. Their feedback is invaluable, and they will always lean you towards classic alterations rather than trends so the garment will live longer.

If it's a repair and you cannot imagine the outcome, ask to see something similar so you know what to expect and you can see if it's definitely what you want. If the finish is exactly what you're after it's helpful for the tailor to know so they can crack on.

If it is an alteration, ditto. You may be asking for a different finish to the existing one and it's good to see a real-life version. You may want to edit the colour of the thread or opt for another finish.

Pricing is always a must as sometimes it can be more expensive than the whole garment itself so you need to consider if it might be preferable to find a better version of the garment in question.

If it's a fastening edit, ask what kind of fastening they use. Zips especially. Make sure it's a good brand and that the style and tape of the zip are what you want.

Don't talk in measurements. It's better to allow them to pin it on you and you can decide by eye. Some garments need to be longer at the front, for example, and if you ask for a certain amount off it will affect its overall look. When it's pinned, the tailor won't expect you to stand still and say you love it. Move around a little, as you would in the changing room. They will always be happier to get the pinning perfect so the sewing is only done once.

I will always enquire if the job can be a no/minimal cut one. I know my taste and body will no doubt change and I like to have the option to edit it again in the future.

Ask for a price and job description slip before you head off. I tend to keep these so I can keep a log of what was done to a garment and whether I need to bring cash on pick up and to avoid any awkward convos if one of us forgets what we agreed. Remember pricing can vary from any price list you may have seen so don't assume. Different fabrics and finishes can add to a repair or alteration and mean the tailor has to work for longer on your piece.

AT PICK UP
Don't be tempted to run out the door once you have picked up the garment.

Try on the piece to see if it's as you needed. It's best to be in-house to raise any edits.

Ask if the washing method will need to change. Some repairs or alterations can add things to a garment that can change how it will react to the original washing instructions.

SEW IT YOURSELF

You may be wondering if some repairs and alterations are worth doing yourself. When it's a small edit, I think so. While there is nothing like having something professionally done by a good tailor, it's not always possible. Learning how to repair and edit clothing yourself will also mean you are more likely to get it done and wear the garment more. This is especially vital for things like hems. A dropped hem left for too long can cause more damage than you think. We will go through some of the basic alterations in the Repair and a Spare section to keep you covered.

Now it's time to bring those pieces into our lives and find out the best ways to look after your garments.

CONVERSATIONS AROUND CLOTHING are usually focused on the time prior to purchase, and we hear so little about what to do to increase the lifetime of the garments we already own. We are convinced that the only time we can make a difference in the overconsumption of clothing and its effects on the planet is at the browsing stage.

However, you can shop all the sustainable garms you like, choose the right fabrics, only opt for eco lines, go preloved, vintage, repurposed and other simply stunning moves ... but if you are not looking after your clothes, storing them correctly, washing them properly and ensuring you can wear them for a long time, your kindness to the planet ends on the shop floor. *clicks fingers*

ONCE SHE'S MOVED IN

Previous chapters have taught us to be more selective in what we bring home to live with us but, after purchase, what happens once these pieces have settled in and become part of our lives? Garments losing their integrity is one of the main reasons we tend to let them go. Premature fading, stretching, staining and so on are avoidable with a little know-how. Maintaining a long-lasting wardrobe is key to being a sustainable queen and reducing consumption. Even better, it isn't too difficult, costly or time-consuming to become a stunner at it. How gorgeous!

If we have spent so much time and effort selecting and sourcing garments suited to us, it would be simply bonkers to let our considered thought process and attention to detail stop there. After all, how you do anything is how you do everything. If we want a wardrobe that lasts, we need to be considerate about the wear, tear and care of each piece and this section is going to cover just that.

This will all also apply to garments already in your wardrobe. That reliable jumper you pull out year after year? The one-in-a-million vintage mini that looks divine with those metallic platforms, the one that you could just never seem to find another quite like? Those are all just as valuable as the Miu Miu-esque sparkling A-line you have just unpacked. In fact, they are MORE sustainable than something new and should be treated with the same, if not extra, consideration. Looking after what you already have will reduce your need for more.

YOUR TIME TO SHINE

After a garment has met you, your time to shine, sustainably speaking, really starts to kick in. Buying less is one of the key parts of sustainable fashion as its impact hits every part of the cycle.

BUYING LESS MEANS

REDUCTION IN PRODUCTION
When there is less demand, there is less production.

Shopping trends are always analysed in detail by brands. They are constantly responding to the shopper and their production follows suit.

If there is a slowdown in purchasing, there is a slowdown in producing.

QUALITY RISES
When we buy less, we are buying well.

As with volume, brands are all looking at exactly what the week's 'best sellers' are.

When something of better quality becomes popular, brands don't take long to learn that it's the quality that did it. And so, the details, fabrics and workmanship start to be considered in new designs and development.

LESS TO LANDFILL
When we buy less, our shop floors have slower-moving trends.

This means we, the shoppers, are discarding less as our wardrobes are lasting longer.

This impacts the number of lines, trials, styles sampling, fault coverage and overstocks a factory has to produce, and so we are reducing their landfill contribution too.

A LONG-LASTING LOVE AFFAIR

To truly shop less, you need to wear more, wash less and repair more. If you can master the art of garment care, your need for newness will drastically reduce. So how exactly is it done?

Every long-lasting love affair has a common thread: nurture. We already know not to expect strong, long-lasting relationships with people, pets, places and possessions if we don't apply the necessary care and nurture to them. If you don't water a plant, you don't expect it to grow. Equally, if you overwater a plant, you don't expect it to flourish. Today's actions, in relation to most things, are tomorrow's results and this could not be truer for your clothing.

For a wardrobe that can live with you long term, it is key to know how to look after, prevent the preventable and mend the unexpected. Let's get cracking on one of my favourite aspects of living with your wardrobe: we will cover laundry, storage, accidents and even parting ways. *clicks fingers*

6 La-La-Laundry

WE HEAR IT more and more: to be more sustainable with your fashions and keep them longer, you must wash your clothes less frequently. Frustratingly, after this line, we don't usually hear how exactly washing less is mastered and what it achieves when we do it. This usually leads people to ignore such solid advice and stick to their usual routines for fear of the unknown.

However, it's unavoidable. The easiest but most effective way to keep our gorgeous, well-selected clothing lasting longer (and in turn reduce our consumption) is to wash them less.

Washing less is all about consideration, it's not about shoving everything onto an eco setting once every two weeks, shutting the door and click-clacking back to your day.

When I talk about washing in a more considered way, I'm talking about the art of washing with the life of the garment in mind. The importance of knowing how and when to launder is a necessity when we want our clothing to last. There are two very important cogs in serving a lewk over and over again.

A WASHOUT

As a white goods enthusiast, my love affair with the washing machine has been a long and adoring one. She brings so much to any home that I don't like to speak badly of her ... well not in front of her anyway. *whispers* Vurry little is mentioned of how much she is responsible for the negative impact of clothing on our planet and your pocket. I know! A cleaning appliance having a hand in how we as humans are destroying the world rarely comes up in conversation but it's one we need to have. Take a seat, we should face some truths at the start of our laundry goddess journey to help us wash better.

The main ways washing your clothing impacts the world negatively are threefold:

ENERGY AND WATER
MICROPLASTIC SHEDDING
STRESS ON GARMENTS

ENERGY AND WATER

A no-brainer. I don't have to break this down for you in detail but bear in mind that unnecessary washing is

wasteful on many levels. Products and cycles cost not only your wallet but also take from the environment in some way. It can have different impacts in different locations, but I am sure you're already up to speed for yours.

MICROPLASTICS

You'll know the damage MPs are doing from the fabric chapter. You'd be forgiven for thinking, 'Well, I'm not a clothing producer or hopping bottles into the sea on a regular basis, so my microplastic contribution is non-existent.' Well, I'm afraid you are probably contributing more than you realise.

Every time we wash a garment made from synthetic fibres; we are sending microplastics out into our ecosystem. It's just a fact and one we need to get to grips with asap as laundry is one of the main contributors of primary microplastics. It is said that just one cycle of laundry can contribute up to 12 million microplastics … more than a yikes, babes. We will tackle considerate washing further on in the chapter to help reduce and possibly eliminate our contribution directly to water systems in the future.

STRESS

Laundry is, of course, a necessary part of life, but these days, as with most things, we tend to overdo it. We are washing like crazy right now and one true sign of it is the condition of our clothes and how short their lifespan has become as a result. The stress laundry puts on a garment is down to the physical strain during a cycle as well as the chemicals, water and temperature it has to endure during each wash. *Mon Dieu!*

The main way a machine cleans your clothing is by making it rub against other clothing. This rubbing, agitation, friction, whatever way you dice it, loosens fibres and wears out the garment wash after wash. Add heat, enzymes and lashings of water and your garment will have had to endure a lot while in the drum.

Washing in general – but mainly over-washing and incorrectly washing – breaks garments down to a state where we no longer want to wear them. This causes more landfill and, of course, more shopping, which inevitably leads to more production. The worst part is that this is all preventable. Making clothes last starts with knowing how to wash them properly and knowing if you need to wash them at all.

Let's get into the ins and outs of the perfect load and keeping our whites white, brights bright, stop the snags, oust the odours, suss the stains … (I could go on all day).

THE ART OF A WONDERFUL WASH

As well as being stressful on fibres, washing is also tough going on dyes, prints, fittings, seams, hems and shape. Each time we wash we are reducing something in the integrity of the garment, be it obvious to the naked eye or not. There is a hidden cost in every wash and it is the garment that is paying the price. This must be kept in mind when we launder.

WASH TESTS

Washing endurance plays such a pivotal role in deciding the quality and price of a garment that it is even taken into consideration during the development stage. Prior to production, most garments go through what is called a 'wash test'. This is where the supplier or factory washes samples of the garment a certain number of times in a domestic machine.

After each wash, notes are taken to detail the changes that occur. This could be anything from fading colour to loss of shape or weight. Many lower-priced brands will have a strict four-wash rule, where the garment must be able to show no major changes in appearance for a minimum of four washes done in accordance with the care label; higher-priced brands will have six and so on. (There are, however, instances where a premium product shows signs of wear after two washes but that is for another day!) These wash tests allow both the brand buyer and the producer to make tweaks to either the garment or the care label in advance of production to help keep it within the brand's standards. This means shoppers can be guided on how to make the garment stay 'as new' for longer.

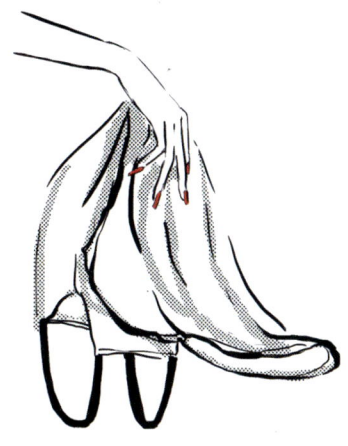

Some brands, or cheaper lines within brands, will have no wash consideration at all and just have general advice on the label. This is where fast fashion is doomed from the jump. If we cannot expect a dress to be the relatively same after a wash or rely on the care label to match up to

the washing requirements of the garment itself, we are washing our money down the drain.

So, what can we do, when washing is a necessity but we also want our clothing to last? Strap in for the ride of your clothing's life.

A GREAT LOAD

Who doesn't love a good load? Getting your load right is pretty straightforward when you know how.

STEP 1: UNDRESS AND ASSESS

Allowing your clothing to skip unnecessary washes is an instant way to prolong its brilliance. Ask anyone known for their stunning style how often they launder their key pieces and they will tell you not that often. Instead, they wash only when it's truly needed and also reduce the need for washing by wearing the right things under their more loved or expensive pieces to save them from frequent washing.

WELL WORN

A no-brainer at the other end of the scale. Garments like underwear, socks and anything else that sits close to the body or gets put through its paces when you wear it, need to be washed after each wear to reduce odours, remove sweat, body oils or staining. These can get tossed into the hamper post-wear, no bother.

GENTLY WORN

Since you will wear most garments with something underneath, the main offenders, like armpits and other sweat stations, should not be directly impacting the garment. This means many garments do not need to be washed each time you wear them. They will simply need a freshen up Inspect the garment for any staining. The longer you leave a stain, the more it gets to know the fibres and won't want to leave. You can easily spot-clean most garments without having to run through a full wash. More later.

Turn the garment inside out and leave it to hang in a room with good airflow for a day or two. For example, once undressed, I hang the garments on the outside of my wardrobe door until the next day. This will freshen up the fabric that has been against your skin and allow it to breathe, releasing odours so it is grand to pop in the wardrobe afterwards, ready to wear again.

ODOURS

If odour is the only reason you are washing, try these options instead:

STEAM! Steaming is the best way to remove odour on fabric with very little harm and suits most garments. It can loosen trapped odours and bacteria quickly and also give a lovely freshen-up post-wear. Steaming is one of the best ways to avoid washing garments and still keep them feeling fresh.

OUTDOOR GALORE: If you can, hang it outside. If it's in sunlight, it's a bonus. The sun is one of the best eliminators of odours and an hour or so outside will always freshen up a garment. Hang inside out to avoid sun bleaching and to allow odours to be released.

NATURAL GIRL: Bicarbonate of soda is a simple item that can be a wonderful way to rid odours all over a garment. Simply place the garment in a pillowcase and sprinkle in about two tablespoons. You can then shake the pillowcase and leave it overnight. The following morning shake off the bicarb from the fabric and the odours will leave with it.

THE FUTURE: Many leading appliance brands now have devices that can eliminate odours from clothing using no water whatsoever. These are a great investment for a long-lasting wardrobe. From handheld devices to integrated systems, these are the washing machines of the future!

WASH WITH CAUTION

There are some garments that you should be super-mindful of washing in general, no matter their soil level, as their integrity is so affected by the agitation, water and temperature of a wash.

KNITWEAR: Knits naturally lose a lot of fibres during a cycle, purely down to the composition of the yarn. That wonderful stretch and warmth you get from a knit are down to how loose the fibres are in there, and these gals get washed away very easily. Knits are also prone to shrinkage, bobbling and dye loss.

For true knits to last a long time, barely wash them. This doesn't mean cutting about in dirty jumpers. Instead, get into the habit of wearing a cotton piece under your knitwear to keep them fresh. Go as light or heavy as you please but keep a barrier between the skin and knit to lower the chances of it needing to be washed and for optimum comfort. The cotton piece will take on any deodorant, sweat or body oil stains and leave the interior of the knitted piece only needing an airing at most after wear.

If you do need to wash, some experts say more than once a year is too often, especially for a pure wool jumper. Don't use a machine and go for a hand-wash with a mild, wool-friendly detergent or just cool water, squeezing the fibres gently. Wring out gently and then remove excess water by rolling in a towel, then leave to dry flat.

Wool knits contain lanolin (from sheep, it gives it waterproof qualities), which can smell almost sour after washing. This, along with the massive shrinkage potential, leaves many people with spot cleaning and airing their woollens as their only options.

If your knits are natural like cotton, she'll be able to withstand a machine wash but go easy. If they are synthetic, I would recommend hand-washing to keep their integrity for as long as possible.

HAND-WASH OR DRY-CLEAN ITEMS: Hand-wash or dry-clean only advice on the label can be due to a variety of things. Some garments can't take the stress, others can't take water, some finishings won't cut it in a wash and so on. The warning is mainly there to imply that there will be immediate and visible damage to the garment if you machine wash. Listen to this advice. (More on dry-cleaning on page 209 if that's made you panic.)

PROTEIN NATURALS: Silks and other protein queens will break down in washes like no others. Follow the care guide to a tee! I tend to only steam mine gently.

DENIM: Denim is a sturdy girl that can go for a long time between washes but that doesn't mean she can get through frequent machine washes unharmed. She is affected by heat mostly, but the agitation of the wash is not great for keeping denim looking good for a long time. This especially goes for stretch denim, which is the worst off after frequent washing. You'll most likely notice baggy knees and crotch and a warped fit due to the elastane breaking down.

Most denim experts will advise up to 10 wears, or once there is a stale smell, before she needs to see the sight of a drum. Some will say wait even longer and only air in sunshine, inside out. There are denim enthusiasts out there who swear that washing at all will degrade the denim quality so much it is never worth it and keep their denim collections unwashed.

The bottom line is that denim has the potential to last for a long time so be considerate before throwing her in the drum. All she may need is a light steam to freshen or an afternoon hanging in a window.

GENERAL

When it comes to other garments, my motto is, if in doubt leave it out. If you cannot see obvious staining or there aren't any body odours that a good airing or steaming won't eliminate, she doesn't need to undergo the duress of a washing cycle. This also goes for anything that is super-bright in colour, heavily tailored or has embellishments that you get a feeling could lose their lustre in the chaos of a cycle. Let her live.

STEP 2: LINE UP THE LOAD

Now you know what you are washing, you'll need to separate your loads no matter what. Many people will recommend having multiple piles like lights, whites, delicates, darks, brights, blacks and so on but for most homes there will never be enough of each category to fill a load for weeks. If this is the case for you, you can separate more simply.

DARK AND LIGHT

Matching the tones of the wash will do one main thing and that is stop dyes from ruining lighter clothing. When we wash darks and lights together, especially those made from natural fibres which both lose and take on dyes quicker, we risk the lights absorbing dye and becoming dull or badly discoloured. Colour matching is also great as it means we can treat a load accordingly. Darks and brights react to certain detergent ingredients and temperatures much differently than whites and so separation does more than prevent colour runs. Trust me, it is worth holding back clothing to wait for the right tone of load.

So now you will usually have two main piles: darks and lights, which can then break up further as per below.

CARE LABEL

Once you have washed something a few times it will be a no-brainer but getting to know the care labels on all garments and matching them to similar garments in order to fill up a load can take time to get your head around. I promise you it is worth it. Don't worry if a few items are rogue temps. If you find that you have a lot of 60°C and only a few 40°C items of the same colour, throw it all in at the lower temp. If you have some heavily soiled garments in there, simply pretreat (more on this later) to make up for the lower temp.

To brush up on our knowledge, here are what the most commonly used laundry symbols mean to help you make your move.

WASHING

MACHINE WASHABLE

All washes are A-OK.

MAX TEMP

Exceeding this temp will cause damage.

DO NOT WASH AT ALL

Don't do it, girl. Not even a hand-wash.

PAWS UP

Hand-wash only here. Usually a gal that can't hack too much agitation so be kind.

GO EASY, BABY

This means less speed and lower temp like a synthetic cycle.

EVEN EASIER

Gentle wash. This is for delicates or wools.

DRY-CLEAN

Machine washing or water may cause damage so dry-clean only.

DON'T DRY-CLEAN
No to dry-clean but if there are just letters in the circle they are a note for dry-cleaner.

DRYING

TUMBLE AWAY

She's grand to tumble dry on any heat.

TEMP NOTE

One dot is low heat, three means high is grand.

NO!

Don't tumble in any way.

DRIP DRY

Best on a clothes horse usually as less stretching.

DRY FLAT

Dry on a flat surface. Usually knits.

HANG DRY

Is fine to hang from a line or hanger and won't reshape.

DE-WRINKLE

COOL IRON

Max 110°C.

WARM IRON

Max 150°C.

HOT IRON

Max 200°C.

DO NOT IRON

NO STEAM

COMPOSITION
Synthetics and naturals are different in many ways and one massive difference is their endurance levels when it comes to washing. Naturals, like some cotton for example, can hack warmer, more hectic cycles, whereas synthetic just cannot deal with a lot of agitation or heat. If you have enough to separate again into naturals and synthetics, go for it. If not, don't worry, just cater to the weakest garments in the load.

SOIL
Underwear, socks, bed linen, tea towels and so on all need more water, hotter temps and at times a stronger detergent to rid them of bacteria, body oils and protein stains. This is fine as usually these are made from fibres that can hack this kind of a cycle.

So, keep these together and the most effective is a weekly hot wash, so you can be more eco and money conscious for the cycle. It also means other garments that are synthetic or have a lot of dye can be washed more peacefully together separately and not have to undergo such a stressful wash in order to make up a load.

STEP 3: PREPARING THE LOAD
Even though laundry ads and tips will never tell you this, there are ways your garments need to be prepped for each wash. These steps will keep them from faring badly and also affecting others.

INSIDE OUT
Turning garments inside out has a twofold effect. The inside is what will have touched your body so you're getting straight to the juicy stuff. The other reason is that you are protecting the exterior of the garment. This will help hold in dyes, fittings and pleats. Denim jeans, in particular, are

absolutely stunning if washed inside out as they are mainly cotton and need your help holding on to their beautiful indigo tone. This will also slow down the pilling process as the outside of the garment is not rubbing against other harsher fabrics. Different fabric compositions can harm other compositions in a wash, so it is better that the garment is basically washing itself.

OPEN ALL BUTTONS

This will make sure there is less stress on threads, buttonholes and other parts of the garment as she moves around.

CLOSE ALL ZIPS

You don't want the teeth of the zips sinking into fabrics of other garments, scratching hardware or snagging threads. It is also important to keep zips closed right up to the top for the zip itself as it can help the zip avoid damage. An open zip can wreak havoc for your machine too as it can get stuck in the holes of the drum. If a garment has a hook and eye at the top of the zip make sure you close this too.

SEAL ALL VELCRO

This will destroy so many fabrics so you want to make sure it is fully closed and turned inside out for extra protection.

EMPTY ALL POCKETS

Aside from the absolute chaos of a pocket tissue let loose in a wash, you want to avoid anything getting stuck in the machine's filter or losing valuables like jewellery altogether.

UNFOLD

Turn down hems and t-shirt sleeves which will catch everything from detergent to lint.

STAY AWAY

Remove collar stays as these can do more harm. Washes can cause these to bend and it will lead to your collar warping. Stays that got stuck in the filter of the washing machine were a regular repair call-out for me so that's another reason to remove them!

COPING WITH ODOURS

As you start to prep your bits you may notice some garments holding on to body odour or have some sweat or body oil stains but have a cool wash on the label. This will usually be down to it being a synthetic garment that cannot release sweat or bacteria properly and so builds a strong smell. These will need a little help in place of hot temps.

SPRITZ THE PITS

A 50:50 mix of white vinegar and water spritzed onto the inside pits of the garment before washes can help to rid the fabric of pesky odours. Don't forget areas like collars on shirting as these can have a lot of body oil build-up which could do with a good spritz too to break down the protein stains that cause discolouring. Gym gear can always do with a spritz! I tend to do this around 30 minutes to an hour before washing.

STAINS

There is a section on stains coming up, however, if you feel something is just heavily worn and more stained by body oils and sweat, pretreat with a soak in water and a dash of white vinegar or a small drop of detergent for at least an hour before the wash.

VINEGAR RINSE

If the load, in general, needs a good freshen-up but it's going to be a cooler wash, throw a cup of white vinegar in the fabric softener compartment. She'll take care of it.

> ### QUEEN V
>
> When it comes to vinegar for clothing, what you want is distilled white vinegar. Forget the balsamic, cider and other gals – distilled white is where it's at! It's gentler than cleaning vinegar, which is great for tough household cleaning, but distilled still packs a punch in terms of acidic realness. When you go for distilled white it's kinder to fibres and your machine but will still soften, brighten and cleanse.

STEAMING

Try a light steam as this can often release odours prewashing. It is my go-to for garments that I want to last a long time and preserve, especially occasion wear.

STEP 4: LOADING

A full load is usually one where there is enough space that you can put your hand on top of the clothing. If you can't fit that gorgeous wee hand of yours in, she's too packed.

A full load is the best load for most cycles. This is not only for environmental reasons energy-wise,

it also means you'll have fewer microplastics released in the wash due to less agitation between garments. Less agitation also means less friction, so the clothes will rub as much as they need to, but not overdo it. Emptier loads also mean the clothes are so saturated that even more fibres and microplastics are released. And of course, dyes will be more affected.

Before you apply this to every wash, have a browse of your manual and see what her weight advice is for each cycle type. If you are buying a new machine, this is also worth checking out in advance as the kilogram-load-per-cycle note is based on optimum performance. If you frequently wash a specific composition (e.g. cotton) and your machine needs you to reduce the load, it may not be a perfect match as emptier drums mean more fibre loss as well as not being able to wash as many garments at once.

REDUCING MICROPLASTICS RELEASE

What's a gal to do when she needs to wash her synthetics but doesn't want to wear them down or release a ton of microplastics each time?

Enter eco-washing bags. Using eco-washing bags can reduce the release of microplastics from synthetic fibres and help prevent degradation of synthetic garments.

Like mesh washing bags, these will stop the garments from mixing with the rest of the load, keeping agitation to a minimum and reducing stress on the garms. Plus they trap any microplastics that are released and prevent them going down the drain. Hurrah!

As most machines don't have microplastic filters (yet), these are a genius way to consciously wash synthetics with the bonus of garment protection.

After the wash, you'll need to dispose of the fibres that are inside the bag by putting them in the regular bin so they go to landfill and not down a drain into the ecosystem.

PONDER YOUR PRODUCTS

DETERGENT

Choosing a detergent is rarely done in relation to our clothing and usually done by selecting the brand we feel is most reputable in our price range. The best bang for your buck, let's say. However, for a product that is a higher-ticket grocery item and something we buy consistently, we tend to know very little about the product itself and how it works, never mind how to truly shop for real value. No matter how low the price of your detergent is, if she's not right for your clothing, she's costing you more than you think.

The wrong products can lead to fast-fading, sour-smelling clothing, natural fibres not being able to thrive, whites dulling and many more things that are too easy to avoid with the right intel under your vintage Moschino belt.

Luckily, we have all we need on the packaging to help us make the right decisions within our budget. The ingredient list as well as other taglines on the packaging can

help us to choose more wisely what is best for our washes and what will help us keep the integrity of our clothing wash after wash.

The easiest way to think about how laundry detergent works is to split it into two parts: the perceived and the actual results.

THE PERCEPTION OF CLEAN

Our *perception* of clean clothing is a MASSIVE selling point for detergents. Babies on soft towels, tablecloths hanging from clothes lines in rolling fields, tropical flowers, the list goes on. These are all marketing visuals to sell you the concept of cleanliness and smelling 'fresh' and new. This goes beyond the marketing and packaging and follows right through to the ingredients.

DYES

When it comes to detergent colours, blues, greens and whites are often used in cleaning products as they are affiliated with fresh outdoors and sterile environments. Pinks, purples, oranges and yellows tend to hint that we will be getting natural colour added in as the affiliation is usually with exotic plants and flowers.

Far from rainforest raindrops or alpine air being infused into your detergent, the colour is down to the dyes added to the product. These dyes have absolutely nothing to do with the cleaning power or the fragrance in the product and are simply there to trigger you into picking her up and associating her with cleanliness or freshness.

FRAGRANCE

We have been convinced for decades that to truly be clean it must smell clean. Funny isn't it? For something to actually be called clean, it would be cleansed of all dirt and soiling and then rinsed thoroughly, leaving its own natural scent. It would hold no synthetic smell at all afterwards.

'Clean' has become a scent in itself and one which crops up all over the place, not just on laundry. Fresh car smells, fresh hair smells, fresh home smells, clean kitchen smells, clean toilet smells ... you get me. However, 'fresh laundry' is now in a league of her own with candles, air fresheners and even perfume emulating this manufactured scent.

BRIGHTENERS

These don't work by cleaning your clothes any more thoroughly to make them whiter. The reason they make whites sooo bright is that they play with the UV light waves to make them bluer. This means we see less yellow and more blue in the fabric, it is not that the fabric has had more dirt lifted. You will see these on the packaging as 'optical brighteners'. While they will make plain whites appear whiter, they just won't cut it for other colours as these can end up looking older and more faded due to brighteners.

As you can see, the perception of 'clean' can end up costing us more money and creates a cycle of frequent and unnecessary washing to achieve something that has nothing to do with the garments actually being dirt free.

THE ACT OF CLEANING

A lesser talked and thought about element of detergent is how it actually cleans. Here are the star players in most detergents.

ENZYMES

The main enzymes present in detergents are proteases and lipases. Proteases go after protein stains (think anything that comes from that divine body of yours or anything else that's living, such as blood, grass, sweat, milk) and our lipases have their eye on lipid stains (think oils and fats so you have butter, grease, cosmetics, lotions).

These enzymes are present to help break down very stubborn stains on fabric. They do a stunning job even in cooler temperatures, which makes them a marvel for modern times. Cooler washes are the hot girl on the block when it comes to long-lasting clothes and lower bills, so enzymes allow these to be more effective.

SURFACTANTS

Also known as surface active agents, these are major in the stain removal process as they help lift the stain from the fabric by removing surface tension. Enzymes will work on breaking down the heavier stuff, while surfactants will work their magic on lifting any unwanted stains from the fabric due to the way it makes the surface react. When you read a detergent's label you'll probably note two types of surfactants: anionic (charged) and non-ionic (no charge). The reason there are two types is to balance the surfactants and reduce the risk of skin irritation but also because non-ionic can work away even in hard water.

BUILDERS

These gals are present to soften the water. Even in the softest of water areas, you will have minerals in the water that will change how effective your detergent is at cleaning. These work by changing the pH of the water to improve its cleaning potential.

Lastly, you will have things like stabilisers, fragrances, dyes, chemicals that stop the dirt from going back onto the fabric and so on.

So now you know what is hype and what is going to work at cleaning your clothes properly.

HOW TO SELECT THE APPROPRIATE DETERGENT

BIO
Bios' main boast is that they contain enzymes.

BEST FOR: clothing with a lot of protein or fat staining or well-worn clothing.

NOT SO STUNNING FOR: natural fibres of the protein variety. Their enzymes can break down the fibres as they attack proteins so save your silks by avoiding.

COOL WASH CLAIM
Modern magic that helps us use lower temperatures.

This is a great sign on the label as it means the wash doesn't need to be hot to make the detergent work well.

BEST FOR: avoiding fibre loss as long, hot washes will wear the clothing down more.

Microplastic shedding is reduced in cooler washes.

Dyes won't fade in cool temps.

Your washes will not cost as much.

ENZYMES AND SURFACTANTS
Cheaper brands will have less of these and so less cleaning power.

If you see a sale on detergents, clock the ingredients and look for these to be further up the list and with a higher percentage. This way you can keep this for more well-worn and soiled clothing and use a cheaper less enzyme- and surfactant-rich detergent for lighter worn or daily bits.

NON BIO
These don't contain enzymes and many experts say they are better for sensitive skin.

BEST FOR: baby/child clothing; anything worn by someone with respiratory allergies or sensitive skin.

NOT SO STUNNING FOR: These will be weaker than other detergents so may need warmer washes

OPTICAL BRIGHTENERS
These will give the appearance of whiter whites.

BEST FOR: whites.

NOT SO STUNNING FOR: anything that stays on after the wash is not going to be good long-term for the clothes.

Washing darks or dyed garments with this detergent will fade them much faster.

WHICH FORM TO CHOOSE

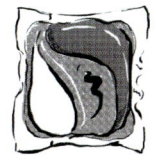

LIQUIDS

BEST FOR:

More likely to find one that works with cooler temps as they don't have to break down first.

Less hard going on the machine (if cool temp compatible).

More powerful per wash.

Can easily be used to pretreat stains before the wash.

NOT SO STUNNING FOR:

It can be harder to find choices with eco-friendly packaging.

Usually more expensive.

PODS

BEST FOR:

Quick and easy to use.

No risk of under or overdosing a load.

Can come in cardboard so less wasteful packaging.

Pods can pack quite the punch and be more effective at stain removal as well as being designed to work in all temps.

NOT SO STUNNING FOR:

It can be harder to find choices with eco-friendly packaging.

Usually more expensive.

POWDERS

BEST FOR:

buying more cheaply and buying in bulk.

NOT SO STUNNING FOR:

Harder to break down in cool temps or quick washes which leads to blocked pipes, residue left in garments and build-up in machine parts.

Less effective on oily and protein stains.

ECO-DETERGENTS

So you've decided to switch to an eco-detergent? Divine! Eco-detergents, as well as being better for your skin and the planet, are far better for your clothing. As with anything eco, you'll need your wits about you as it can mean various things.

Top-tier eco-detergents will be made from ingredients that are not harmful to the environment, the people who make them or the wearer, their dyes will be natural and so will their fragrances. Packaging will be sustainable in some way, and you will be guaranteed to have a cruelty-free label. *C'est bon.*

However, as with all 'green' products on the market these days, it can take a meauxment to spot the real deal on a shelf of imposters. Greenwashing in laundry is big business and it is not uncommon for detergent brands to have an eco version of their detergent with only a few small tweaks. Instead of a well-rounded environmentally friendly detergent, you may sometimes find that an eco-detergent that shouts from the rooftops that it is a green gal only ticks a few green boxes. This can mean it has all the same ingredients as a regular detergent once you clock the back and its eco credentials only stretch to recyclable packaging or a natural fragrance.

Here's what you should be looking for in eco-detergents.

SURFACTANTS

It can be next to impossible to find a surfactant-free detergent that cleans well but not all surfactants are created equal; you need to read the label and choose wisely. If you just see 'surfactants', it's a red flag. True eco-detergent brands will have their surfactants listed so you can suss them out. Many contain palm oil and come from petrochemicals so when you want a true eco-detergent, check out the brand's stance on their use of palm oils. If they give a fuck it will be on their label or website and easy for you to find.

BRIGHTENERS

The impact of brighteners on ecosystems is still grey so great eco brands will avoid them completely.

PACKAGING AND PRODUCTION

For genuine brands, these are as well considered as the ingredients.

You'll probably have heard that you simply must have multiple detergents in your home to match multiple fabrics. That is all well and good if you will use them before they go off. Instead, think of the actual wardrobe you have and what you wash most often; this will help you choose the right detergents for you.

QUEEN V

A lesser-spoken-of laundry queen is vinegar, distilled white vinegar to be exact. The advantages of adding vinegar to your laundry routine are as follows:

BRIGHTENING

Vinegar is stunning at removing stains and brightening clothes. It also doesn't affect dyes so can be used on all colours.

ODOURS

The acidic realness of vinegar can help to remove odours from clothing without covering them up with something else. Yes, she dries odourless so you don't have to worry about wearing Eau de Chips afterwards.

SOFTENING

Vinegar has a stunning fabric-softening quality. This is because she can release fibres of build-up that makes clothes feel harsh. Her acidity loosens minerals found in water, product and detergent build-up and other fibre-harming residues.

You don't need to use vinegar in every single wash but, every few washes, it's great in a half-cup measurement in the fabric softener compartment. This is because fabric softener is released before the rinse stage and not washed away by detergent, meaning the vinegar has some space to get to work.

FABRIC SOFTENER

Now for something you need to ditch from your routine. This can start a war when I say it *deep breath* ... the fabric softener needs

to go. It isn't good for your clothing, the wearer or the environment. Modern detergents have all you need to wash your load thoroughly and effectively, then see themselves out with the waste water.

GETTING TO KNOW HER
They say it's better the devil you know so let's get to know FS a little better to understand why we don't need her.

Who is she? FS came about when the handfeel of cotton was tragique due to the dyes and drying back in the 1900s. It was found that applying an oily coating (one that would not break down in water but would stay on the fibres) would create the softer handfeel that producers were after. Another bonus was her static-reducing qualities. As new fabrics were being developed, static became an issue. (All you need to know here is that all fabrics have a charge, the charges can be different in each, and opposites attract. This creates a static cling that we all hate.) This added coating helped to keep this at bay. Plus it replicated the effects of a stunning outdoor dry for the months we would dry inside.

More take-up came from pressure for the 'woman of the home' to be a better person through better results in her cleaning and home care. *screams internally* I mean, not much has changed here. We are still being told that how clean our homes are equates to how successful and likeable we are as people. Adding another product to our cleaning routines was always going to happen.

While fabric softener had a purpose, it is now used in ways it truly was never designed for (don't start me on it being used as a room spritz puh-lease), with many people not realising its intended use. This can be detrimental to a long-lasting wardrobe as it is a product that can cause a host of issues over time.

BREAKING UP WITH FS

Fabric softeners work by coating the fibres. In theory, some of the chemicals in this coating make the fibres react by standing up and separating (this is what drying on a windy day will do as well), making them feel softer to the touch. This all seems pretty harmless, *non?*

Well … it is until we go into the other elements. Fabric softener enters the drum at the rinse stage of the cycle and the reason it is so famed for its odour is that it doesn't wash off. The reason it doesn't wash off is down to its oily ingredients, which are water resistant. These oils often come from animal fats, which most consumers don't realise. It is this fatty layer that can wreak the most havoc as it's not going anywhere any time soon.

PRODUCT BUILD-UP

If something is designed to not wash away in a cycle, it will build up over time and clog fibres. This can lead to damaging clothing quickly. If fibres are loaded and sticky, they will trap more dirt and minerals from water. This can eventually lead to harsh-feeling fabric and us discarding things like shirts and towels and other cotton items that were once naturally soft due to their crispy handfeel.

ODOUR

Many people will complain of a wet dog smell from their clothing over time and it can often be down to fabric softener. With fibres overloaded, lack of correct airflow can lead to odour build-up and even a damp smell from freshly washed clothing. If you overuse fabric softener you also risk building up the layers so much that it prevents detergents from being able to interact with clothing and washing them properly.

PERFORMANCE

If a garment has performance qualities that you rely on, like moisture wicking, breathability and even fire resistance, these can all be reduced by the coating that fabric softener leaves behind. Some clothing labels will even state not to use FS on the garment, like sportswear, children's sleepwear and even towels. Yes, towels, the thing you see in most fabric softener adverts. When we use fabric softener on a natural fibre like cotton, it will affect its absorption potential as the fibres have instead soaked up all the product and there is no room for water when you are drying after a shower. Fire-resistant coatings will be hampered by the coating it creates over it, which is a no-brainer, and sportswear with overloaded fibres won't be able to perform as it did either.

STEP 5: DOSING

Don't be fooled into thinking that the more product you use the cleaner your clothes will be. On the contrary, they will be less clean than if you follow the correct dosage guidelines. This is down to one thing: water. Increasing the dose and not the amount of water used is going to result in the product not getting the chance to be fully washed out of fibres, which is never good. Product build-up leads to clothes smelling, fibres loosening, stains setting and a host of other unfavourable actions, so be sure to stick to what is on the packet.

Where to put your dose is another issue that can affect your clothing and how they wash.

PODS

Pop these in the drum before the clothing to allow water to get to them first when it starts filling up the drum. Pop it to the back to avoid it ending up on the rim of the door. Giving the pod more time with water will help it to dissolve fully and for the water to be fully loaded with her when it starts to wash.

DRAWER DIVAS

Incorrectly loading the compartments in your machine's drawer is bad for your clothes, bad for your machine and pretty awful on your wallet due to the waste it creates. 'I don't know which section is for detergent so I just pour it into all of them.' Je téléphone à la police, babe.

Loading products to their correct drawer section is VITAL in ensuring that they are used well during the wash and that your clothing is cared for properly during each cycle.

The incoming water flows through a series of spray holes only into the compartment holding the product required for the upcoming cycle stage; it does not wash all the product into the drum at once. This is why you'll hear that gurgle at the start of the wash and then again towards the end when she's about to get rinsing. This ensures that only the relevant product is entering the drum at the exact time she is needed so she can enhance and not hinder the washing process.

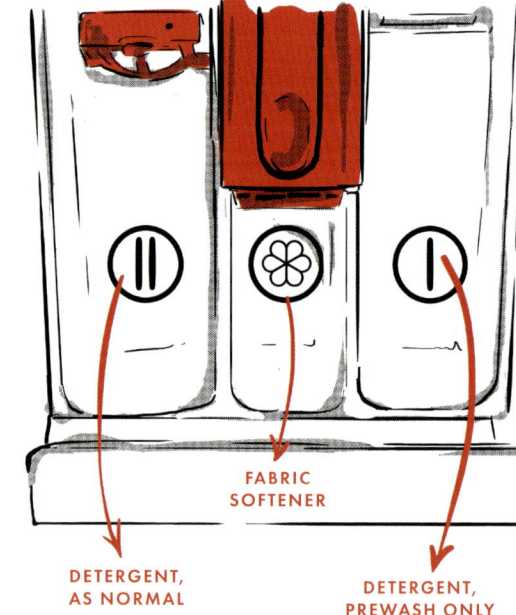

FABRIC SOFTENER

DETERGENT, AS NORMAL

DETERGENT, PREWASH ONLY

If you pour detergent into the fabric softener section in error and leave the detergent section empty, not only do you risk your clothes washing only in water and coming back to you unclean, there can be other issues. The fabric softener compartment is usually flushed before the last rinse and so you essentially won't have enough water meeting the detergent to wash it from the fabric. This will lead to a build-up of detergent in the machine as it can't break down properly and a build-up on the clothing too, which will affect how it looks, feels and functions.

Your manual will break it down for you rather quickly but a rule of thumb is to follow the symbols that are usually allocated to each compartment.

CYCLE

CYCLE SELECTION

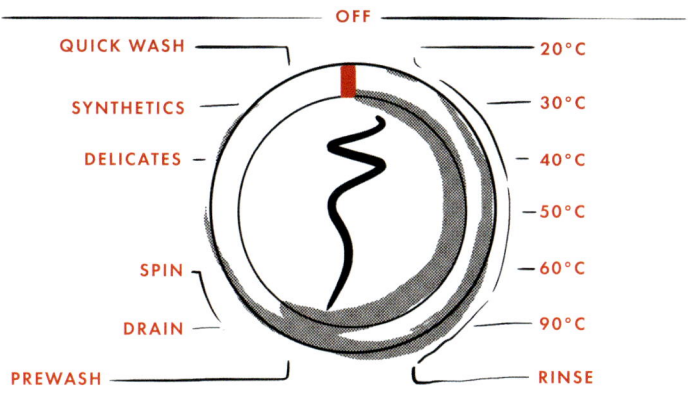

If we think about how a washing machine works, we can see why it puts garments under pressure. There are two drums in a washing machine, the inner drum, which rotates, and the outer drum which holds water that pours through the inner's sieve-like holes at intervals. This water is pure at some stages (rinsing, for example) and loaded with detergent at others (washing).

Once water has entered the drum, you'll get some soft spins and then the clothes will start to agitate as the speed begins to pick up.

Here's the elevated tea ... this agitation is not the same in every wash. Machine manufacturers know that some fabrics and staining need a more thorough clean, like cottons as they are so absorbent and worn close to the body. Whilst other fabrics, such as synthetics, need a slower pace and a more gentle meet and greet in the drum. For this reason, the cycle you choose could really affect the life, handfeel, effectiveness, fit and overall fabulousness of your garment.

To be able to use our washing machines to enhance the lifetime of our wardrobe we must consider four things before we wash:

SPEED: How fast the wash is can tell you how much the clothing will be agitating each other. Only durable fabrics can hack a high-speed wash.

TEMPERATURE: Higher temps are great for ridding fibres of bacteria and some stains but horrific in terms of fading, shrinkage and deterioration.

WATER: Studies have found that it is the excessive water that encourages microplastics to be released and we should be considering this if we want to reduce the amount we shed each wash.

FILL: How full the drum is will impact how aggressive the agitation is. If you think of the thrashing a load will get in a half-full drum between each other and the water, it is not hard to see why.

You may be thinking these are tricky to figure out but have no fear! The manual will guide you through all of this. Take a meauxment to look up the consumption chart and cycles and it will let you know the speed, water, temps and energy. Depending on the brand, it may have some stunning advice about which garments are best for which cycle but unfortunately it is not guaranteed.

Here is a guide to help you match your load to your cycle.

SYNTHETICS

GREAT FOR:
Synthetic fibres
Brights and darks

BAD FOR:
Not much but if you have heavily soiled items, choose your detergent wisely.

BEST FOR:
Fragile queens, those synthetics, which is why they need a little tenderness in washes. Synthetics are also the gals that release microplastics during washes so choosing a synthetic cycle will keep it to a minimum.

Most fast fashion will be made from synthetics and most fast fashion is dumped because of incorrect washing.

Low and slow is the name of the synthetic cycle game so you'll have less agitation and a softer speed. This will help your synthetics stay as they should for far longer.

ECO WASH

GREAT FOR:
Lower temps and less water mean great for gently worn. Pretreat stains here.

BAD FOR:
Will suit most loads once you have product to chomp through heavy soiling.

BEST FOR:
This gal uses less water (perfect for reducing microplastic release) and lower temps – welcome to less energy use and keeping dyes divine!

MIXES

If you have a garment that is a mix of fibres, cater to the weaker element. Say it's a poly-cotton pair of knickers, opt for the softer cycle but choose a bio detergent to take care of the protein stains. Also, you always have the option to pretreat with a vinegar spritz.

COTTONS

GREAT FOR:
Durable cottons
Bed linen
Underwear and socks

BAD FOR:
anything else really.

BEST FOR:
This is a hectic wash, make no mistake. Cotton washes are high on speed, which makes them high on agitation.

They are mainly designed for bedding, towels and underwear, which are soiled by the body and so need a stunning scrub.

Temps are usually high and the wash time will be longer. The drum will change direction more often in a cotton wash so you want to make sure what is in there can hack it.

Don't let your synthetics near this divil. I would also keep brights and darks out of these two as, you guessed it, the dyes don't need this chaos. Keep this cycle for white sheets and undergarms.

DELICATES

GREAT FOR:
delicate fabrics that have a 'fine to wash' care label.

BAD FOR:
synthetics due to the amount of water used and microplastics released.

BEST FOR:
Knits, laces, silks and so on are what are meant to go on a delicate wash ... but the first port of call is whether these should truly be washed in a machine at all. It will be rare to have a whole load to pack into a delicate wash so I say, hand-wash as needed instead of waiting for one to pile up. If they are so delicate they need their own cycle, they probably could do without the whole affair and would prefer a meauxment with your soft hands and the bath instead.

Secondly, this cycle is a disaster for the life of clothing and ecosystems as it sheds microplastics more than any other cycle. This is down to the large volume of water (usually around twice as much as a normal cycle) it uses to complete its cycle.

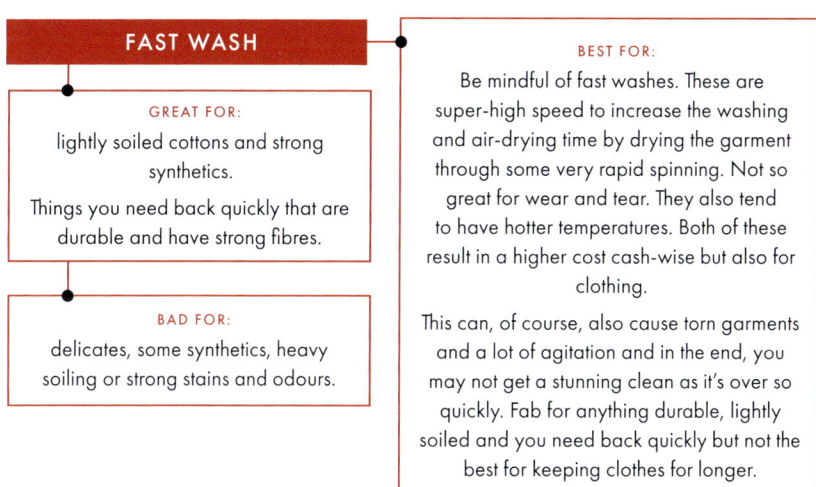

TEMPERATURE

The heat of your wash is mainly to be matched with soiling but composition should also be considered to keep your clothes from being greatly affected by a wash. Turning your temperature down will increase the life of your clothing massively. There are also other benefits:

IT'S CHEAPER

You can save around three-quarters each wash by switching to 20°C. You're also reducing your impact on the environment.

HEAT FADES DYES AND PRINTS

If you want to keep those brights vivid and darks deep you need also to keep cool.

Low temps are the new gal on the block for so many reasons and 40°C is the new 90°C. Here are the best temps for your load; some may surprise you.

In summary, the composition of the fabric and the dyes should be where you match your temperature. The soiling will then come into play. If you have brights or darks that need a thorough clean, you can always spot clean or give them a vinegar spritz before the wash.

FAST FASHION

This is a special note for fast-fashion garments. Buying fast fashion isn't just for the one-time wear girlies; slow lovers have them too (unavoidable in many cases these days) and it can be a mare trying to get their laundering right as even one wash can change them forever.

Fear not! There are some extra measures you can do which will help these garments last. Washing in general is going to deteriorate a low-quality garment in some way so consider these issues.

- Does she need a machine wash? When she needs to be cleaned fully, a soft hand-washing with a nice gentle detergent will release fewer fibres and keep dyes for longer. Use spot washing when it's a small mark and airing and spritzing if it's odours.
- If she needs to go in the drum, low and slow speeds with minimal water and spins here please and make sure that it is a full load to reduce the chaos.
- Wash in a synthetics bag to keep agitation to a minimum.
- Temperature should be as low as you can go.
- Keep your detergents gentle.
- Air-dry to avoid any further damage.

SHE'S GOT ISSUES

Consideration in laundry doesn't stop at what goes into the machine, you also need to think about the machine itself and her maintenance. Here are the most common issues that impact your clothes getting washed as you intend.

DETERGENT DRAWER NOT EMPTYING

If you notice that certain compartments in your detergent drawer have product in them after a wash, this is really common so do not fret. It means that the spray holes above the relevant drawer section are clogged (usually down to a calcium build-up from hard water). This can affect loads as product is not getting to them. Simply take a dental brush or similar and use it to clear the blocked holes. She'll be back to normal for the next wash.

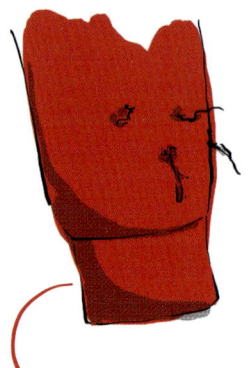

PULLED THREADS AND FABRIC DAMAGE

If garments are coming back torn, it could be a damaged drum. When something like a cord or zip gets stuck in holes in the drum, they can cause damage by being pulled back out through the force of the spin stage. Short of replacing the drum, a quick fix is to get a small hammer and gently tap the sharp edge so it is concave instead of convex.

SMELLY DRUM

It happens. Washing machines often build up odour as they aren't given a chance to dry out and this can affect each load. To solve this, let your machine air after each wash. Pop your drawer and the machine door and leave it open as long as you can.

DIRTY MARKS ON CLOTHES AFTER WASHING

If you are getting dirty marks on clothing after washes this is usually a clogged filter. Your manual will show you how to open this, release the blockage and prevent the issue from happening again.

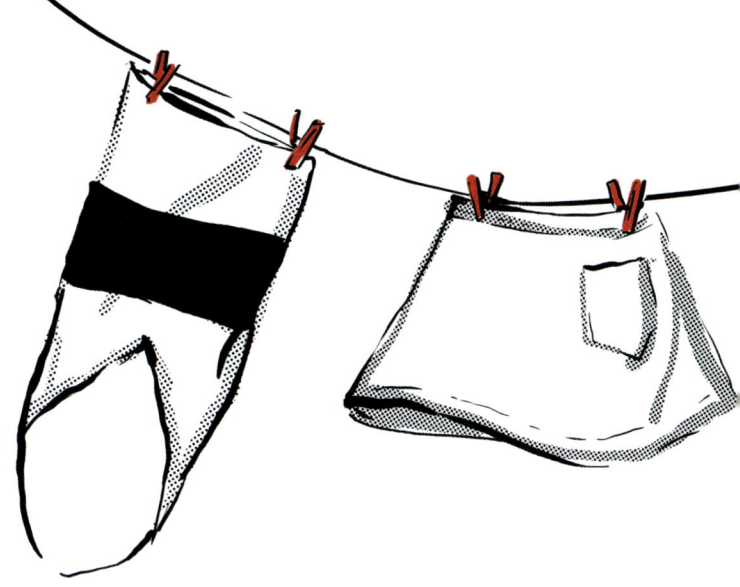

DRYING

You may be wondering if tumble drying your clothing is better or worse for them. All I ask you to think about is the lint filter after a tumble. Yes, it is a little bit like brushing your hair in that some of that was going to be coming out anyway but most garments that you want to keep the integrity of are best air-dried.

The most premium air-dry is an outdoor affair. Sun and wind give the best fibre dry around, hands down. You may notice clothing that has been outside to dry comes back the softest, then next is tumble dryer softness and last is indoor air-drying. You may also notice that it is only natural fibres that seem to be most affected. This is because they are the gals that will basically dry to a new structure after being soaked in a wash.

This is all down to the evaporation stage and how fibres bond during it. The reason an outdoor dry leaves them so soft, is down to movement. 'Tis a grand day for drying' will imply a dry day with a wonderful breeze. The same goes for tumble drying, the constant movement and airflow mean the result of drying isn't as rigid as not as many bonds form between fibres.

On the other hand, when clothing goes from wet to dry with zero movement, like on a clothes horse, more tight bonds form and it causes a rougher handfeel. Don't worry, there's a way around it.

PREPARE TO DRY

No matter which way you dry, but especially if you are using a clothes horse, shake garments before you leave them to dry. Within reason, please, nothing too delicate or sopping to the point that a shake deforms it.

Shaking out your clothing before drying does a few great things: it helps the garment dry more wrinkle-free, prevents large creases that can make the garment take longer to dry and, of course, opens the fibres up to give a softer handfeel and reduce the stiffness after washing. A good aul shake is a stunning start to any air-dry and I would even recommend another tszuj when you're rotating for good measure.

INDOOR DRYING

You may not have outdoor space to hang your loads and, regardless, we can't do it all year anyway, so here is the best way to air-dry indoors.

DON'T BE EXTRA: Don't be tempted by an extra spin. Doing an additional spin cycle after a wash to rid the load of extra moisture will only suit strong cottons and other durable fabrics. Anything else will not enjoy more speedy rotations after it has been washed too much, so additional spin cycles are best left to something like bedding, socks and towels. If you find you want to dry the clothing a little more before air-drying, a much gentler way to do this is to roll it into a folded towel, which will absorb the excess but not harm the garment.

THE RIGHT HANG: What you use to hang your clothes on is extremely important. Free-standing clothes horses are a popular choice as they can be moved around when needed, popped in front of a summer window or on a balcony. Wall-mounted dryers are great for space saving but be mindful of the airflow in their location, and heating dryers are the holy grail for many. These types of dryers have minimal contact with the clothing and allow a lot of air around the garment to speed up drying.

Don't be tempted to put clothes directly onto a radiator, as this can increase mould in the home and also prevent the room from heating up properly as you are blocking its heat with your garments.

VENTILATION IS KEY!: When you dry indoors, you're adding excess moisture to the air and this can add to dampness, mould and so on. Ensure your clothes horse is in a well-ventilated spot and you are airing the room afterwards. It's always a great idea to air-dry in rooms with extractor fans (give the fan a light vacuum

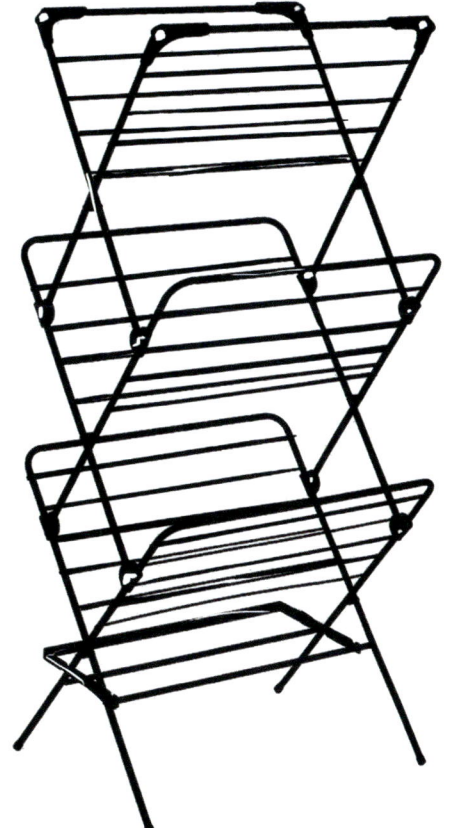

quarterly). A small dehumidifier placed near the clothes horse can be super-beneficial if your property suffers from excess moisture.

AIR MOVEMENT: Great air movement is also a way to speed up air-drying indoors so consider a small fan. Solar-powered desk fans are an ideal way to get clothing dried faster when it's too cold to have a window open the whole time.

GIVE HER SPACE: This may sound like a no-brainer but don't overload your clothes horse or use it incorrectly. Space out clothing to ensure good airflow and if you are using just one for an entire load, put lighter garments on hangers. Most clothes horses will have plastic covers on the top corner with holes in them for hangers, some will simply have holes in the metal frame. Hanging something heavy when wet can stretch it so stick to lightweight garments.

EXTRA SPACE: A smaller airer that can clip onto the clothes horse for socks and underwear will free up space massively and you can unclip and carry it to your bedroom once they are dry for ease of putting away.

I hope this chapter has made you see how vital a considered washing routine is for your clothing. It can help or hinder when it comes to a long-lasting wardrobe! If ever in doubt just remember to keep her low and slow and that not everything needs a full wash cycle after wear.

7 She's Living

SO YOU'VE LAUNDERED like a goddess, what's next? How you put away your clothes will surprisingly make a difference to the longevity of your wardrobe. Incorrect storage can change how the garment fits and can cause odours and damage as well as impact how often it is worn.

To get the most out of our clothing it is important to know what they need to stay their best. These easy meauxments on storage will help you continue the consideration post-wash.

PRE-STORAGE

It should go without saying yet it happens so often: only put away clothes after a wash that are completely dry. Damp clothing can lead to a host of issues that will damage the garment.

If you are storing it for a long period, ensure that the garment is dirt and odour free as well as dry. Popping a worn garment back on a hanger is fine if she has been aired and is free of any stains or odours. If you let odours or stains sit on the fibres during a long unworn period, it can make it harder to remove them later.

Have a storage system. Hanging and folding garments in groups according to wear will help more than you can believe in terms of reducing consumption and up your wear per garment. When we go to grab a t-shirt for the gym and are faced with 15 each time, we will be less likely to impulse buy another in the future.

Being confronted with the amount of each type of item we have for an occasion is at times alarming, although fantastic in the long run for a stunning wardrobe. Another advantage to a wardrobe system is that it shows us our obvious gaps. You could be super-abundant in terms of trousers for work but have very few formal tops. Next time you shop, this will be immediately on your checklist, saving you from another pointless purchase and ensuring you are getting more wear out of what you have already bought.

HANG OR FOLD

Whether you hang or fold can depend on what storage you have to hand but it is good to keep in mind some basic principles.

WOVENS AND NON-WOVENS: Wovens and non-wovens behave differently on the hanger. Non-wovens have a stretch to them and, unless they are lightweight, are best folded. Something like a knit cardi will be miserable on a hanger. Wovens, on the other hand, have zero stretch – think a work shirt – and can suit a hanger better as she won't droop. This is usually the kind of fabric used in something that relies heavily on its silhouette being pristine so hanging can ensure fewer wrinkles.

DELICATES: Linen, lace, silk and anything else that you find creases heavily, should be hung. Letting them free flow from a hanger will ensure they are perfect when put on and have less maintz in the long term.

PRESSED: If something requires pressing before wear, such as a trouser or a shirt, even if you are not doing it before storage, always hang. It will give the garment a meauxment to take shape and be easier to iron later.

TAILORING AND SUITING: A no-brainer. No tailoring should be folded as it distorts the shape. Think jackets, suit trousers, structured dresses. This also goes for anything with details like frills, pleats or folds as they can lose their natural flow when folded frequently.

JEANS: Jeans can realistically be hung or folded, depending on your set-up. Either way, just make sure they are flattened out and fastened to help them store well. If they are super-stretchy, be sure to fold them gently to avoid warping over time.

TEES: Tees are fine folded and will be fine hung. If you have some lightweight t-shirts that crease easily, in summer you may want to hang them to avoid ironing.

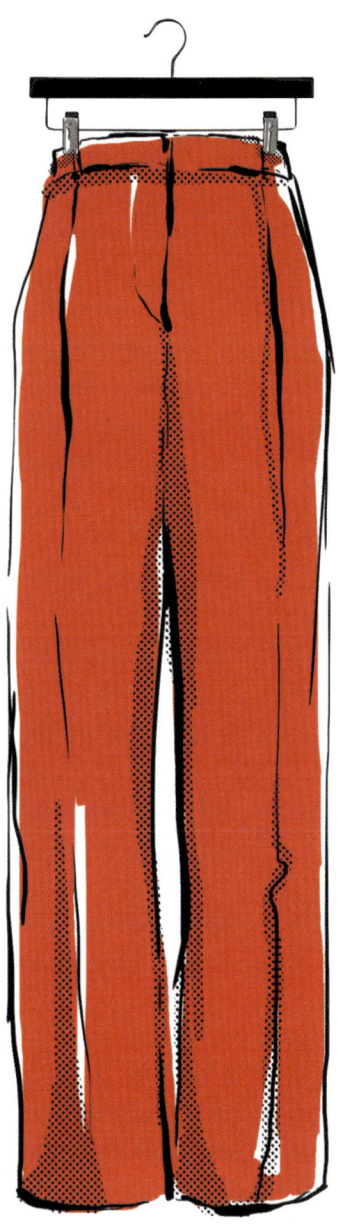

> ## A WEE NOTE ON KNITS
>
> Knits are a more pricey item that has the potential to last year after year after year if we wash and store them well. A lot of knitwear is discarded due to losing shape when this is easily avoided. All you have to do is never hang and only fold.
>
> Knits have great elasticity but literally grow on the hanger from their own weight stretching them. You can be as elaborate in your folding as you wish – everyone's wardrobe storage is different – but try to work with the garment's shape and fold loosely. Little parcels make big creases. Loose folding will also allow airflow which knits just LOVE.

WELL HUNG

Hanging properly can ensure that the garment keeps its shape and doesn't warp or stretch while stored. It will also prevent it from forming impossible-to-remove creases or sitting oddly after storage.

If you iron, keep a stack of hangers nearby and hang the clothes immediately after you press to get the most out of your hard work. Drying, as we know, does a lot in terms of setting the garment's shape, so some lightweight items, like a work shirt, can make easy work of ironing if hung mid-dry (fully fastened and on the right hanger).

HANGING LOOPS

Originally, hanging loops were designed to take some weight off the garment while it was hanging to avoid stretching and pressure on certain parts of the garment, like shoulders or necklines. Their placement would be very well considered and not affect how the garment appeared in-store or during wear. As well as discreet, they are usually of good quality and long-lasting in well-made clothing and a tell-tale sign that something was designed and constructed with consideration and will last well.

However, you have probably noticed that hanging loops are far more frequently used now and tend to break easily. With stores stocking so many styles each season, having multiple hanger types to make the garment look better on the floor is only sucking from the margin so cheap loops are used to enhance the garments' 'hanger appeal'.

For this reason, it can make sense to snip cheap, impractical loops from cheaper clothing.

HANGERS

There are many different types of hangers. One recent trend is to have all your hangers in one colour to give the wardrobe a more streamlined look. This can be good for the grid but bad for the garms.

Different types of garments will need appropriate hangers to preserve their shape and prevent dents, creases and marks. You don't need to go out and buy a whole new set but do consider these down the line when storing something that you want to preserve the shape of.

When buying new hangers, your first consideration should be the types of hangers you need and how many of each. Next is size: the most common size you'll see is around 43cm. This can be too small and cause denting or too big and cause stretching; it depends on both you and the garment. Make sure you consider which size works best.

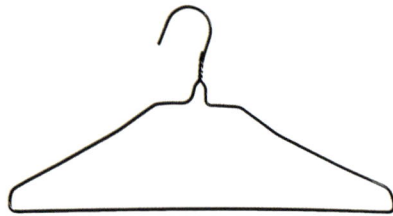

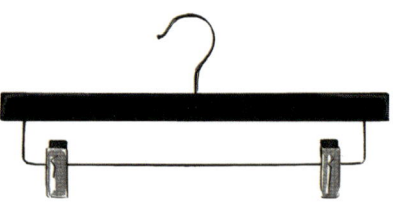

WIRE HANGERS

These are not great for garments due to how thin they are. They can end up creating a crease along the shoulders and a little bulge at the upper arm or shoulder. Phase these out where you can or only use them for something like a sleeveless jersey, garments you wear under sweaters or other tops where creasing is not a biggie and the garment is lightweight.

CLIP HANGERS

Not all trousers are best folded or hung over a hanger bar. Clip hangers are ideal for keeping the garment similar to how it will be when worn. Just be mindful of the clip on fabric. Leather or delicate fabrics will need something like a piece of card (I use business cards given with the bill at restaurants) folded over the waistband to create a buffer.

SUIT/COAT HANGERS

These can come in a variety of compositions but are great for your good jackets or anything with a shoulder pad as they keep great shape. Suit hangers will have a bar to hold the matching trouser/ skirt and coat hangers will have none, just the contoured shoulders.

WOODEN HANGERS

Durable and sturdy, these are a great long-lasting option. They take up more space than others so save for shirting, light tailoring, blouses and formal sweats. One of the most eco options is bamboo – it's stunning.

 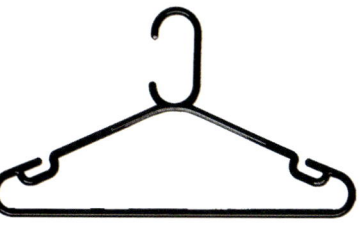

FABRIC HANGERS
Hangers with any sort of padding will be gentler on the garment and less likely to dent or damage clothes. These are great for delicates or protein queens.

PLASTIC HANGERS
These aren't so stunning long-term as they can snap and bend but are best suited to lightweight garments.

CONSCIOUS HANGING

When you hang, literally dress the hanger. It sounds a little odd but it will pay you back, I promise. Also, the more contact we have with our clothing outside of wearing it, the better. It not only keeps us up to date with how the garment is doing but also makes how much we own much more tangible.

Pop the garment onto the hanger, straighten it and ensure it is hanging evenly to avoid uneven weight or pulling on shoulders. This should be done both front and back. For example, on a dress shirt, you will want to make sure the yoke along the back shoulders is running flat and straight to ensure the shoulders are in the right position.

FASTENINGS
One common mistake when hanging or folding clothing is not doing up fastenings. This can cause the

garment to take on a shape, fold or position you don't want it to when wearing.

You'll be able to see if someone does up their shirt buttons or not at a glance. It will look a little something like this:

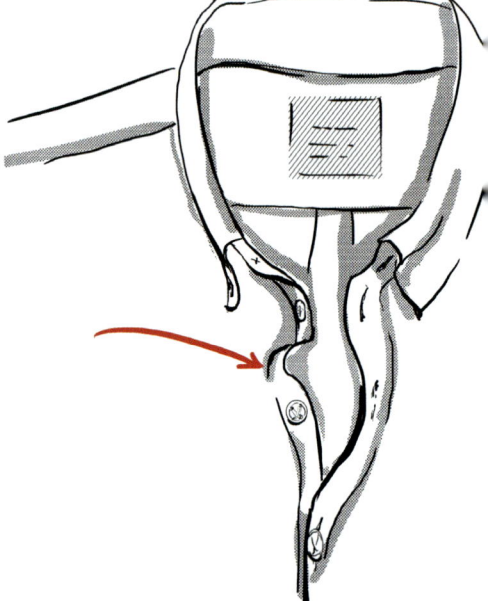

Not a major issue but something easily avoided. When you do up all the fastenings, it also means the garment sits on the hanger properly and has an even weight distribution, so seams and fastenings are not under any added stress.

When hanging, it is not super-important to button a shirt from bottom to top, just the top three to four buttons will do and every second on the way down, if needed. However, when folding, go the whole way to avoid warping the button stand.

Just like in the wash, zips and Velcro are better with their snagging elements hidden and fastened fully.

OFF-SEASON

There are items we will not wear all year, and these are best out of the way to allow you to focus on what you need now. Taking time to set up a clothing rotation system will be something you won't regret. Not only will it free up space and make dressing a simpler affair, but it will also help you to wear your clothing more and reduce the feeling of 'I have fuck all'.

When you go to rotate again, you will get the feeling of newness before a new season begins. Pulling out gems from last year and setting them up for the coming season can be a joyful task in itself. We can also easily see gaps in our wardrobe which help us to buy only what we need.

LOCATION, LOCATION, LOCATION

Rotating according to season doesn't have to mean packing it up into an attic. Most of us will only be able to store our clothes in one room. Besides, things we pack too far out of reach tend to stay there longer than intended.

The easiest place to start is to put all that is not currently in season to the less accessible parts of your wardrobe, rather than out of sight completely. Some garments need to stay hanging – they just don't need to be in your way. Keep what you will be wearing now to the front and centre.

Cool, dry locations are best for clothing, which is why you won't get much trouble in a bedroom as it tends to be a cooler room in the home. You may be able to pop things to the back of shelves and drawers and the sides of rails. If you need to make use of under-bed or overhead storage, be mindful of the following points.

FLOOR STORAGE

The bottoms of wardrobes and cupboards are where many of us will store baskets, bags and boxes of clothes and accessories. However, this can be an area that gets mouldy or damp without you realising it. It could be

anything from excess moisture in the air to a leak from an ensuite, but the effects of damp in your wardrobe are usually not realised until it has done some damage.

If you are storing on the floor or bottom of a unit, use props to keep the boxes elevated and allow airflow underneath. You know those glass ramekins we all inexplicably have dozens of? These are great for creating little legs for boxes stored at the bottoms of cupboards. They won't get damaged and will have enough airflow under boxes, leaving your garms unharmed.

If you want to make sure that your clothes are well protected, be considerate about how they are stored. There are many ways to ensure that your garment comes to no harm when out of the way.

STORAGE BAGS

Once your items are not of the moth-enticing variety, they are best stored in natural fibre storage bags. These allow them to breathe, don't encourage damp and don't cause that stale odour unworn clothing tends to get. If space is tight, you can also find stackable cotton or linen clothing boxes that allow good airflow.

HANGING BAGS

A lot of occasion wear is stored in garment bags. These can be divine ... or deadly.

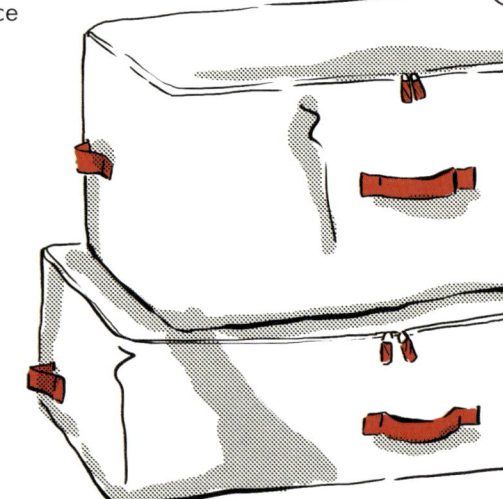

Storage bags are, in theory, supposed to protect what is inside and keep the garment looking great for longer. When you unwrap it, it should look just as good as when you stored it away.

Whether this happens is down to what they are made of. For example, dry-cleaner plastic bags are an absolute no-go for long-term storage; the packing is only a temporary measure. As well as the wire hangers you get from a dry-cleaner, the plastic covers are also bad for your clothing.

It's two-fold: dry-cleaning uses chemicals and your clothing cannot breathe inside the plastic afterwards. Free those fibres up. Plastic also traps moisture and promotes the growth of mildew, mould and, of course, moths – another important reason to take off the plastic cover before you store. If you wish to use a garment bag, make sure it is a fibre that's allowing the garment to breathe.

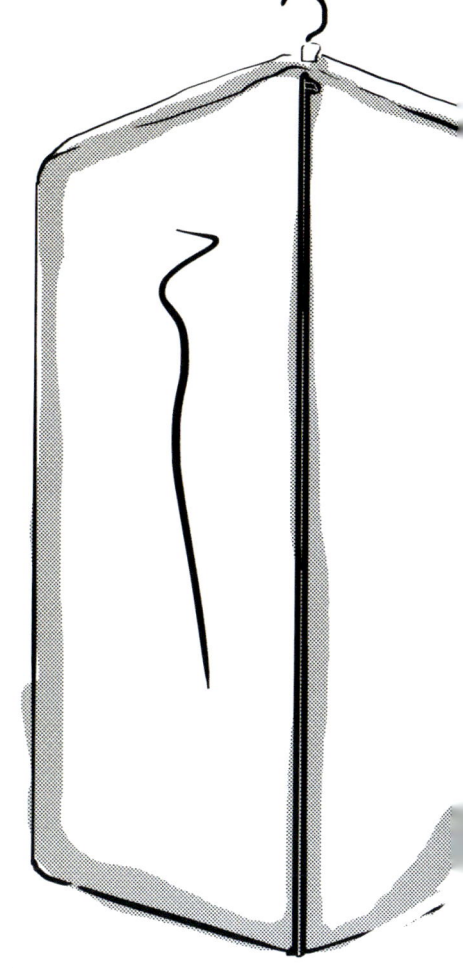

VACUUM BAGS

Don't be tempted to use vacuum bags for your out-of-season clothing. Natural fibres HATE to have all the air sucked out of them and need to be able to breathe to keep their integrity. When you suck the air out of

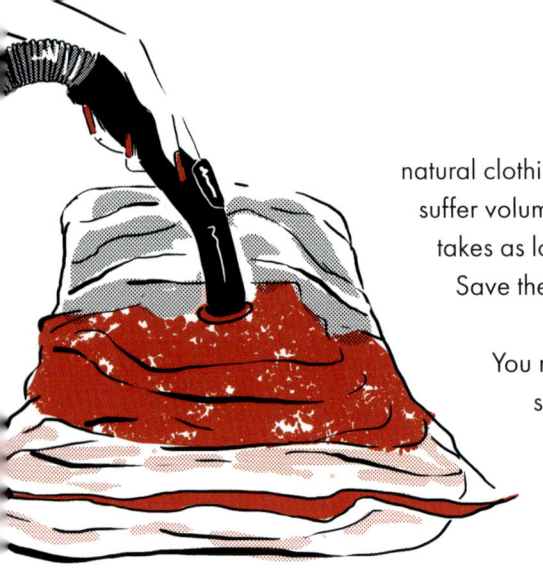

natural clothing, knits and filled outerwear will all suffer volume loss. It is said that this volume loss takes as long as the stored time to recover fully. Save these for folded or hung storage.

You may be sliding that hand over to synthetics as we speak but there is a caveat here too; odour transfer is real. You can end up with plastic-smelling clothing if you leave them in the bag too long.

One last thing here if you do use vacuum bags, don't use a vacuum! Opt for the ones that you can roll the air out of as it won't stress the garments out as much.

OCCASION WEAR

A little note on occasion wear! Items you don't wear often shouldn't remain untouched until you do. When you are rotating your wardrobe, even if they are not involved, pull out your occasion wear. Suits and dresses should all be allowed to air at least twice a year. All you need to do is leave them out for a day or two. Let those fibres breathe! This will also give you a meauxment to inspect them and see if they are doing okay.

DRY-CLEANING

Dry-cleaning is something we tend to not know enough about so dry-clean-only clothing can remain hanging up in need of a clean or in a laundry basket for months. Let's get to know her a little more to understand how to best live with our dry-clean-only gals.

Why do some clothes say dry-clean only and others are grand in a wash? Well, dry-cleaning isn't truly a dry clean, it just means the garment is cleaned with chemicals instead of water, for various reasons.

- The fabric or the dye will show an immediate reduction in quality when a lot of water is applied. This can be anything from fading to shrinking to warping.
- There is embellishment or detailing on the garment that will get damaged during the agitation of a wash.
- The garment has fusing. This is mainly in tailored garments, where it is added to certain areas to add shape. The same goes for shoulder pads that cannot be removed. A machine wash will distort these completely.

Don't assume dry-cleaning is there purely due to the item being delicate and think it is safe to hand-wash. I will often ask my dry-cleaner why it's dry-clean only and if it's safe to hand-wash before I do.

As dry-cleaning is pretty much a chore, and an expensive one at that, it's good to be aware of the golden rules.

NO PLASTIC: Never, ever, ever, ever store your dry-cleaning in the plastic garment bag it gets returned to you in. Ever. As we have already said, these are for the dry-cleaner as a temporary measure only. As chemicals are used in the process, you immediately want to strip the garment of the bag and let her breathe. Always air a dry-cleaned garment once it is in the door; I tend to hang it on the outside of my wardrobe for a day. Then if it is a garment that you want to preserve, use a breathable garment bag.

NO WIRE HANGERS: Don't leave the garment on a dry-cleaner hanger; again, this is a temporary measure. These hangers are so thin they can damage fibres and leave creases in some fabrics. If you must, bring your own hangers and slip the garments on in-store.

ALWAYS INSPECT THE GARMENT IN-STORE: Once you're out the door, there is not much that can be done if there is an issue. Errors can happen. Even the most skilled of dry-cleaners can come up against a garment that is just not fit for dry-clean and the brand has not done enough due diligence to label it in a way that helps reduce any damage. Your dry-cleaner will chat through the options for resolving the damage and they are the best person to do so.

HOW MANY DRY-CLEANS?: Ask your dry-cleaner how many times the garment can get away with cleaning. It's my first question when handing in a garment for its maiden dry-clean. Just like other clothing, every wash will reduce the garment's integrity and it's good to know how fast that will happen.

STEAM: You don't always have to go straight to the dry-cleaner. Steam is a

wonderful way to deodorise, remove bacteria and freshen up garments. Don't put dry-clean only in the laundry basket, even if it's for a few days. The odours and bacteria, as well as wrinkling and fibre damage, won't be worth it.

CLOTHES MOTHS

We cannot talk about living with our clothing without bringing up these gals. Clothes moths. They will strike fear into any cashmere lover and can be pretty stressful to discover for anyone. This is mainly down to us not having a huge amount of knowledge about why they are there and how they operate.

Let's start with some myth-busting. You know the moths you chase around? These are not the ones chomping through your Miu Miu. Those gals don't have mouths so no biting is happening. Fascinating, right? Once a moth transforms from larva into an adult moth, their sole purpose is to mate and lay eggs on fibres that can provide food. Then the cycle begins all over again.

The culprits here are the larvae. Different types of moth larvae need different types of food to grow into adult moths. For clothes moths, it's the protein keratin. Remember back in Fabulous Fabrics we spoke about natural fibres that are derived from animals? Well, these gals all contain keratin and this is what adult moths seek out and drop their eggs on, to feed from. Yes, they are also the most expensive fibres to use in clothing so it is always a balls when you discover you have moths, as you know it's your premiums they are after. Silks, cashmere and wool are all a fine dining experience for clothes moths.

Fibres aside, moths need darkness to thrive. They are not out in the open doing their bits and egg dropping, so you will usually find them in creases and pockets and the depths of wardrobes and drawers. Moth larvae are like teeny tiny threads that can barely be seen unless you know what you are looking for so are often missed.

HOW TO KNOW

Moth season traditionally ran from early spring to late summer but with modern living and climate change, they are becoming a problem all year round. They need heat to thrive and instead of cold winters shutting down the cycle, heating our homes has kept them going. Yikes. You will know if you have moths these days around springtime. This will be due to sightings of adult moths in rooms with clothes storage. Unfortunately, their eggs may already have hatched from being dropped in the previous season and so the damage could be done. If you see a low-flying moth, this is usually one that is laden with eggs so you may be able to catch it in time as we are at the start of a new season.

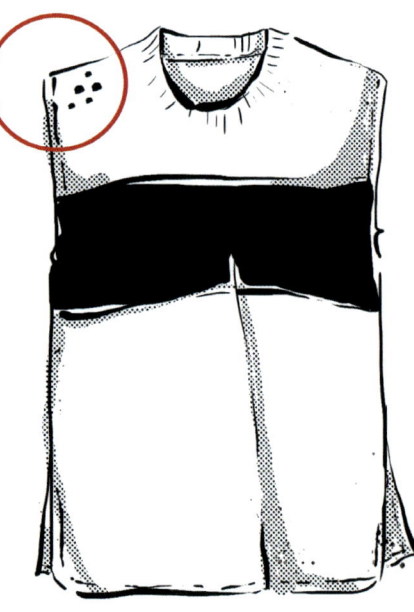

WHAT TO DO

When you see moths, pull out your wardrobe and start to inspect. Although they only go for keratin, which is in animal-based fibres, don't forget you are a producer too. So, clothing that you may have sweated a lot in or that contain your bits can also be a target. Examine garments, especially in areas that have folds and creases, such as pockets. If you see a hole, you know they got her. If you don't, it still doesn't mean she is safe. Divide your garments into keratin queens and others, then you need to treat them. As moth larvae are impossible to see easily, here are the best ways to get rid of them.

HEAT: 55°C to be exact, so a 60°C wash will help to kill them. Add a cup or two of white vinegar to the load as vinegar is divine for tackling moth larvae. However, this may not suit your garment so do be sure to check. Wool, for example, usually cannot be washed at this temperature.

STEAM: The best thing to do when you see a moth is to steam all garments that could be a target. Check your steamer goes up to this heat and the garment can take it and pay attention to the areas moth larvae can be nestled.

COLD: These gals are super-sensitive to extreme temps. The larvae are so delicate a meauxment in the freezer can solve the issue. If you have a few affected or suspected garments, pop them in a plastic bag and into the freezer for a few days.

Yes, you can use harmful sprays but these tend to drive the adult moths out into the open rather than killing larvae so all you are doing is killing off what you see and still letting next season's bebes fester.

PREVENTION

Once all your clothing is out and the girls in danger are being taken care of, it is very important to vacuum and wipe down your storage with a mix of white vinegar and water. This will help kill any lurking larvae. Don't forget to empty your vacuum afterwards.

BREAK THE CYCLE

Pheromone traps are very useful for breaking the cycles in your home. You can hang them in the darkest part of your wardrobe and they will call to the males. These are usually glue traps and so will prevent mating and, in turn, larvae decrease.

Be careful with these, having them out in the open near windows can cause moths to flock to your home. Make sure they are hidden in storage to draw out what is already living with you.

REPELLENTS

Don't bother with toxic repellents; you are more important than your clothes and you have to live with them too. You can use things like cedar hangers, peppermint and other non-toxic solutions but the best way to prevent is to upset the environment as often as you can.

This is another reason seasonal rotation is great as it disturbs. If you have items you are absolutely freaked over protecting and are in the midst of a moth invasion, treat them with heat or cold and then pop them in a sealed box that allows them to be kept free from harm.

As you can see, how we store our clothing can help us massively in maintaining a long-lasting wardrobe.

Not only is it better for the integrity our garments, it also has an impact on our consumption levels and how we wear our clothing in general. From hanger to hamper and back again, if you treat your clothing with a little care, she will pay you back threefold.

Up next we have a little meauxment for one of my favourite topics ... stains!

8 YIKES

No matter how careful we are with wearing, washing and storing our clothes, there can be some little mishaps along the way that can make a garment unwearable or less likely to be worn. In this section, we are going to learn how to deal with common stains, odours and other issues that crop up in the lifetime of our clothing.

STAINS

Stains stop us from wearing clothing that is otherwise in great condition. That one drop of guac on your fave white tee doesn't render it only wearable under a jumper for the rest of its living days. There are quick and easy ways to rid fibres of stains, all it takes *swishes hair* is a little know-how.

Stains happen all the time. It could be the obvious like dropping food or a drink on a garment or perhaps sitting on something. It could also be from dye transfer in a wash or simply wearing deodorant.

Stains are broken into four main categories:

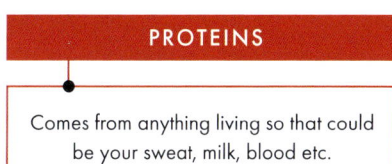

PROTEINS

Comes from anything living so that could be your sweat, milk, blood etc.

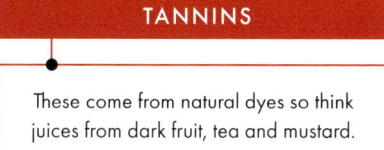

TANNINS

These come from natural dyes so think juices from dark fruit, tea and mustard.

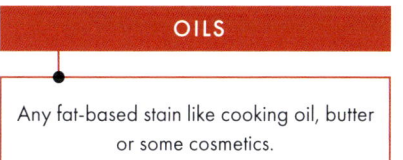

OILS

Any fat-based stain like cooking oil, butter or some cosmetics.

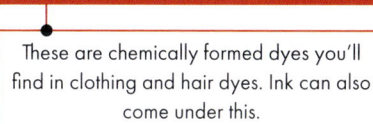

DYES

These are chemically formed dyes you'll find in clothing and hair dyes. Ink can also come under this.

Luckily, thanks to modern technology, we don't have to go out in search of toxic stain removers, lotion and potions. Most laundry detergents, as you will see, have enough enzymes and surfactants and so much rinsing will be done that stain removal is a cinch.

However, before we depend on detergent alone, it is essential to know what the stain is before popping it in the wash, as many will need certain temps, specific drying or maybe a pretreatment to help it on its way. The wrong treatment can make some stains worse. Let's look at the ya-yas and nah-nahs for the different types of stains.

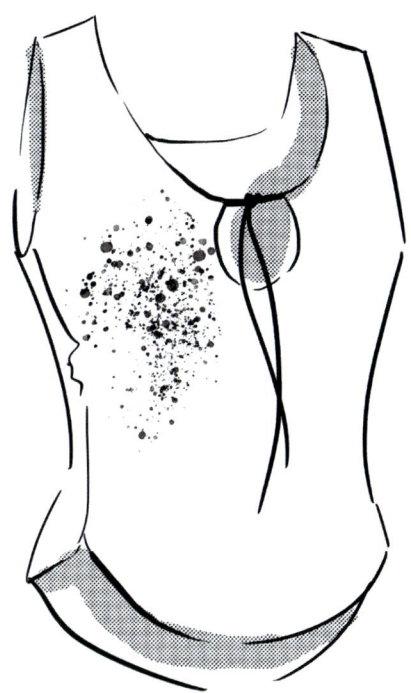

PROTEINS

When it's a neat protein stain and not mixed with anything, a bio-detergent's enzymes will happily chomp through it.

CAVEAT:
Heat is your enemy here. If the stain is strong in colour, it can set the stain into the fibres. Make sure the wash is set to a cool temp and air-dry with zero heat until you are sure the stain has gone.

CAVEAT:
Wash these as soon as you can and don't leave to sit for days. If you can, keep the stain wet where possible to prevent it from setting.

OILS

Pretreatment is best on these stains to ensure they come out after washing in a regular detergent. A dab of washing-up liquid rubbed in before washing will do nicely

The most common tannin stains will be a hot drink like tea or coffee. These can be pretreated with a spritz of white vinegar water before a cool wash.

CAVEAT:
Flush the stain with cool water before washing to remove as much of the tannin as possible, then use a detergent with oxidising properties. No heat, please!

TANNINS

CAVEAT:
Heat is a nightmare here. In production, heat is used to set dyes into fabric and it will do the same with your stain. Avoid!

DYES

Tricky gals these dyes. As many natural fibres will drink up the dye, it is important to flush out as much as possible with cool water before washing.

Regardless of how you go on to treat it, when you notice a stain, the correct action can help save the item of clothing.

FRESH STAINS

It is simply stunning to work on a stain as soon as it has happened. It gives it less time to get to know the fibres and decide to settle in.

CHECK: Always check the care label before any stain removal to ensure it can hack what's about to happen.

STOP THE STAIN: The first step is to prevent the stain from getting worse. Depending on what has caused the stain, either blot or scrape off excess to stop it in its tracks.

FLUSH: Flushing the stain off the fabric with cool water can work wonders. Just be mindful to do it from the opposite side of the fabric to the stained side. The aim is to flush the stain off and not through.

KEEP IT DAMP: Keeping the stain damp will often stop the stain setting on most natural fibres. We now know about the bonds that happen during drying and this can lead to stains locking in.

COOL IT: As heat can be a mortal enemy of stain removal, wash and air-dry with zero heat until you know the stain is only a memory.

SET-IN STAINS

There will be times when we have the stain removal process bang on but the stain remains after a wash. There may also be daily stains that you cannot avoid happening and will end up with after every wear.

ARMPIT STAINS

As someone who loves a white tee but also lives in a constant state of fight or flight (kidding ... ish), I have encountered many a pit stain and odour. Combine this with my penchant for fake tan and we have one hell of a stain party. After years of relegating tees to under-jumper wear only, I started to tackle it head-on to find a proper solution and can now let it rain, rain, rain with less fear of the aftermath.

KNOW SWEAT

You will hear all the time that sweat is odourless and colourless. This is true for the most part but understanding our sweat a little more will help us prevent sweating – a natural part of the body's care for us – hindering our wardrobe's performance.

Sweating is a stunning way for the body to regulate its temperature and cool itself down. It's a part of life but can also be a part of why we dump clothing prematurely. Sweat can cause strong odours that seem to never wash away and also discolour areas heavily. You may have noticed that even though you sweat all over, it is mainly your pits that are the issue. There are a few reasons, but the first port of call is the kind of sweat that is produced there.

Our bodies have two main types of sweat glands in our skin: eccrine and apocrine. The latter is the one that is in the armpit, and other areas where there are lots of hair follicles. This sweat is naturally oilier and lipid-loaded so it has more protein and ammonia.

It is thought that the bacteria in hair follicles are the reason that sweat will smell. The sweat essentially goes through these to be released and so picks up bacteria on the way. This odour can, of course, also be altered by things like diet and other bits it meets when it's on the skin, like perfumes or more bacteria.

WORK WITH IT

The reason it is so heavily advised to wear natural fibres against areas with apocrine glands is to help it lift off our skin. Natural fibres will wick the lipid-rich sweat from our skin and then, because it's breathable, it will help it evaporate.

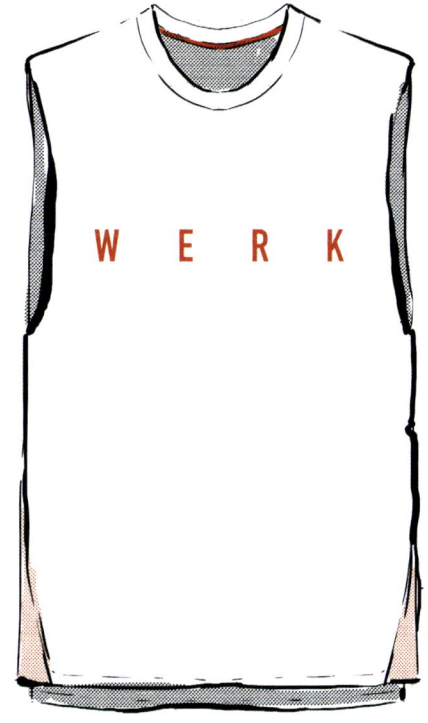

You may notice that synthetic garments are the worst offenders of strong-smelling pits and this is down to how breathable it is. Once it has absorbed the sweat, it cannot let it go in the same way a natural fibre can – and hey presto – bacteria grows.

BO BE GONE

If you have some synthetics that are still smelling wash after wash, I have your back! This will most likely be gym gear as it is a question I am always asked. Don't ditch the kit! There is a solution and it's pretty easy.

Most gym kits need to be synthetic as it's a performance fabric, which helps with your workout. Instead of hindering, like a cotton that will absorb sweat and get heavy, synthetics are designed to not get in the way. So many gym garments are thrown away each year due to their odour which, as you can imagine due to their inability to break down, is pretty bad for the environment. So, how to solve?

First up, you are dealing with synthetics so we need to use something that will help release these protein-based stains from her fibres and break down build-up.

Second of all, I fear you may be using fabric softener or a detergent that contains some. This is designed to stay put in the fabric and so will be adding another element that traps odour-causing bacteria and will make the whole thing worse. *Mon Dieu!*

STAGE LEFT

Who can enter the ring and come out on top? Why it's Queen V, of course. Who else? Vinegar is fantastic at eliminating odours and also stripping clothes of fabric softener. She'll also give your machine a wee once over while she's at it.

FOR LINGERING ODOURS: These need a trip to the spa. All you need here is white vinegar, water and a sink, bath or basin. Add a cup of vinegar to warm water and then leave your clothing to soak for 30 minutes. This will loosen and freshen the garments, which can then be washed as normal in a machine. You should notice after the cycle that the clothing is now smelling fresh. If one or two bits are still smelling, have another go, as some fibres are a bit more stubborn.

KEEPING ON TOP OF ODOURS: For maintaining clothing that tends to smell after wear, spritz them before each load. For this, I use a mix of distilled white vinegar and water (50:50) and spray the fabric on the most odour-producing areas, like the pits. If you have a particularly bad top you love, spray it 30 minutes before a wash.

Something great for gym kits in general is to add half a cup or a full cup of vinegar – depending on how bad they get – to the fabric softener drawer when washing. This will help to free up those fibres and keep you fresher for longer.

DEODORANT

Even if you have banished odour, you may notice that underarms are holding sweat stains after washing. This is mainly down to the presence of antiperspirants and deodorants.

Antiperspirants contain aluminium to reduce sweating. To put it simply, aluminium melts down to block the sweat ducts and limits the amount of sweat coming out. Hence the name, antiperspirant.

When aluminium meets the protein in our sweat, the compound created causes the sweat to take on a colour. This is why we get

yellow stains on the armpits of clothing when we use an aluminium-based antiperspirant. There are also other ingredients in many sweat-managing products that will be there to help it stay on your skin. This will also help it stay on the fibres.

SOLVING THE PROBLEM

One thing you can do to reduce the yellow stain potential is to use a product with no aluminium. But there are other ways to reduce the impact of sweating on your clothing.

CHOOSE NATURALS: Choose the products and fibres that sit against your armpits wisely – natural gals are the best.

BREATHE: Allow your garments to breathe after wear. This especially goes for anything super-sweat-laden being thrown in the laundry hamper. Even hanging it over the edge is better as it allows for odour and bacteria release. Allowing it to fester in a pile of clothes will make it worse.

SPRITZ: Washing clothing prone to sweat stains immediately after wear is the first step in successful removal. However, it's not always possible so adding a vinegar spritz to your washing routine is wise! All you need to do is to spritz the pits with a 50:50 vinegar–water spray before you pop it into a wash. Give it a good soaking directly to the pit area. Remember, you want to spray the interior of the garment. Don't forget to wash it inside out.

GO BIO: Use a bio detergent to help lift the worst culprits.

SWEAT SHIELDS: There will always be items that you want to wash less but know you will sweat in due to their composition. This could be anything from synthetic vintage to highly embellished pieces. These will greatly benefit from sweat shields. All you need to do is either tack or safety pin the shield into the pit of the garment, allow it to absorb any moisture or product during wear and then wash only that after.

LONG-TERM SWEAT STAINS

If it's an old pit stain or strong sweat odour that has built up over time, you'll need to remove the build-up of the product as well as the sweat itself. This is done using either vinegar or bicarbonate of soda, but not both as they could cancel each other out.

BICARBONATE OF SODA: Mix with water to make a face mask consistency. Apply to the stained pits for a few hours. Scrape a portion off to check progress and leave for longer if needed. Pop in a wash as normal with a bio detergent.

VINEGAR: Soak in a mix of 70:30 vinegar and water for an hour. Check progress and leave for longer if needed. She can be washed as normal with bio detergent.

If the whole garment is smelling, leave it to soak in a 50:50 mix of vinegar and water for a few hours, then wash on a cold wash as normal.

OTHER COMMON STAINS

You'll almost certainly have come across some of these common problems and have the solutions in your kitchen cupboards – you just don't know it yet.

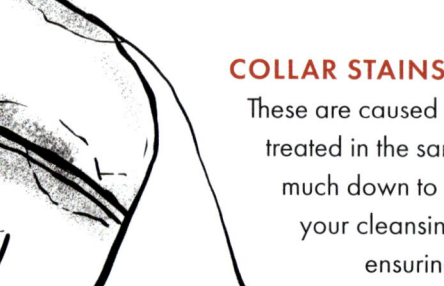

COLLAR STAINS

These are caused by body oils and sweat and can be treated in the same way as pit stains. Prevention is pretty much down to ensuring your neck is not forgotten in your cleansing ritual, pretreating before washes and ensuring cosmetic and hair products are not affecting pores and fibres.

GREASY FOOD STAINS

There is so much advice out there for this and so many products we are told to add to our cupboard. However, something that never fails to work for me is a product we already have in the home: washing-up liquid. Simply dab a bit on your finger, massage into the stain and wash in the machine as normal. This also goes for grease stains that have been there wash after wash. Try it!

BLOOD STAINS

Blood can be tricky. Not only is it a protein stain so it can linger, but the same thing that makes blood clot is what will make her bond with fibres. She loves it!

Fresh blood stains will usually be fine with a bio-detergent. I would recommend acting fast once you notice a blood stain. First, flush with cold water from behind to wash as much out as possible. If you're not washing that instant, keep the stain wet until it enters the drum to stop it from bonding during the drying period.

Blood stains that have dried will have set into the fibres and are another issue. These will need to be pretreated. All that is usually needed is for the stain to be soaked in neat vinegar for at least 30 minutes. Once this is done, it should be loose enough to be removed by a bio detergent. No vinegar? Some neat detergent for 30 minutes prewash will also work well.

RUNNING DYES

Mega yikes. It can seem like the garment is a goner when it comes out of a wash laden with dye from another piece or there has been some dye transfer during wear.

DYE TRANSFER DURING A WASH

If you are pulling the wet load and notice that the dye has run, you are still in luck as it is the best time to save affected garments. Have a rummage, remove the culprit and pop the rest on to wash again. Make sure the temp is low for this cycle as heat will not be your friend here. Usually, this will be enough to free the fibres of the dye.

DYE TRANSFER AFTER DRYING

When we apply heat to a dye, it sets. If the fabric has been machine-dried it can mean it is more difficult to shift. You have two options.

Provided the garment is suitable, you can soak it in water with a cup of vinegar added (do more if it's pretty bad). An hour or two will usually do and then you can wash as normal. This can also be good for garments that have not been affected all over but the transfer has been caused by the item rubbing against a dye.

If you're having a true mare, you may need a specific product designed to tackle colour runs. Read reviews, read labels, read warnings.

As you can see, stains are a lot easier to solve than we think but don't be afraid to ask for expert help if you need it. Even if a garment is not dry-clean only and you are struggling to lift a stain, you are best to take it to a dry-cleaner who may be able to remove it with the right chemicals.

9 ADIEU

IN THIS TIME of overconsumption, to alleviate our bursting wardrobes, it's rarely promoted to just shop less. Instead, new ways to manage our stuff tend to trend and we keep on buying *Andrea True voice* – More, More, More.

We have gone through online clothing storage crazes in recent years. You know the ones whose roots began with experts teaching us about living neatly with less? Yes, those ones that eventually got taken over by consumption-driven tutorials on how to cram as much as we can into 30 plastic bins and 20 drawer dividers.

Thankfully, lighter living is creeping in, but following the era of over-shopping and under-wearing, so is throwing out clothes.

The general attitude seems to be that donating is the eco thing to do, and guilt-free – be it a clothes bin at the side of the road, a bag to a charity shop, home pick-up or whatever. Donation has very positive connotations in the current fashion world and is often used to counterbalance overbuying. In truth, we don't ever actually throw anything 'away'. It goes somewhere.

I'D LIKE TO LEAVE IT ON, PLEASE

Overconsumption of fast fashion wears a mask – we know this. It appears glamorous and even aspirational. But clear-out culture is becoming a strand of fast fashion as people struggle to live with all they buy and her mask is starting to slip.

When it comes to clothing, we all have a tab. How long the tab is, is not only up to how we consume but also how we cast off. It can be easy to think no more of it once you have bagged up clothing and it has left your home. However, how and where they are sent heavily impacts their chances of being repurposed, repurchased or recycled and reduces any damage they could potentially cause.

BYE, BEBE

We cannot treat all clothing the same as we send them back out the door. Their condition and composition will be the main things that impact their ideal destination but to get there, they need your help. Whatever you are getting ready to ship out will usually come under three main umbrellas:

RESALEABLE: Good condition and able to be resold by you or someone you donate to.

RECYCLABLE: Unsellable or damaged and in compositions that will be accepted by clothing recycling companies.

REPURPOSED: None of the above, but can be repurposed.

SELLING

Reselling to a new buyer will instantly lengthen the life of the garment, if done right. If you choose to send your garments for resale, with the profit either going to you or a charity, making sure it is a good match for the audience is a must.

To increase the chances of your garments bonding with a new owner and going on to live a long life, let's get into resale.

SELLING IT YOURSELF

There are so many options for selling items online from the major apps to local groups. It might feel a little overwhelming but here are the best places to start.

TIMING

Firstly, timing is key. You will get more traffic for a bikini sold in warmer months than in December. It is also worth reading up on current trends to relate the item to in the description.

Sometimes people are simply shopping for a certain look, for example, the 90s, and your piece could easily get missed. Knowing what is popular for preloved trends is a really smart way to get your ad up the algorithm and get it in front of the right audience.

EXECUTION

After timing, how you execute your advert will be the next aid in making sure it is not only sold but sold at a good price and to a mindful buyer. Quite often, when preloved is sold at a knockdown price, it is snapped up in a fast-fashion mindset and those who are looking for a long-term garment can think there is a fault and move on.

When an ad is detailed and the price is a true reflection of the piece, it will be less likely to be bought by an impulse shopper and more likely by someone more considerate about what they buy. Conscious shoppers tend to be drawn to adverts with better photographs and more information and won't have as much of an issue paying the right price as they are not seeing it as a one-time wear.

HIGH END

If it's a high-ticket item that you feel could sell quite easily for a good price, selling it through a reputable company is the first port of call. If you are not selling through a consignment company, always look up multiple previous online sales of your item as you will most likely have to choose the price point. Not only will this help you with price, but you'll also start

to familiarise yourself with what comes across best in terms of description, details in pictures and condition notes.

The more info the better with anything high-end, to help people see it is genuine. Many online sellers are seasoned professionals and know exactly what makes a good sale so their ads will be pristine. Don't forget, it is always better to have obvious photos of wear and tear as it avoids hassle later. No one is expecting perfection from a used item but they will expect details of exactly which parts have wear and tear.

APPROPRIATE PLATFORM

When it comes to the platform you sell on, look into the percentage they take and what exactly is involved in the sale. Some companies require you to have a minimum amount of 'stock' before you can start selling and a specific style of photograph as well as shipping and packing guidelines. The cut that they take can also massively vary, with some having hidden extras. Look for info on admin fees, if the percentage changes based on price and the time it takes to receive your payment.

Some of these may be a deal breaker for you and they are worth knowing before you begin the process.

You should also look into who is best at what. Some preloved high-end stores and platforms are very good at bags, for example. Others are known for their denim or outerwear and this can help you to secure a good buyer.

HIGH STREET

As we know, there has been a massive uptake in preloved high-street clothing in recent years, with a lot of even well-worn high-street items being snapped up. Again, you'll need to suss out platforms and their cut as well as what guidelines suit you best. Be mindful to check:

THE AVERAGE PRICES FOR CATEGORIES: Fast fashion exists in the preloved market too and the price expectations and quality will be the same. Some high-street resale platforms are known for selling at really low prices and are geared towards the one-time wear market. This is where fast fashion often goes for its second and final wear. If you feel your garments are matched to a higher price and quality level, find the platform that matches. It will save you time and effort in the long run.

SHIPPING METHODS: Are they on your dime and time? Think about what each purchase entails for you as the sender.

TSZUJING UP YOUR ADVERT

INSPIRATION: Look at guidelines on designer selling platforms. These have more money and expertise poured into them and their guidelines are often full of gems that help your item look its best and attract more serious buyers.

MEASUREMENTS: Lay the garment flat and measure. (There is a measuring guide on page 59–60 for this.) Use your phone to overlay text and arrows and it will give potential buyers plenty of useful info.

UNIFORMITY: Take all photos in the same way to create the feeling of a 'store'. This builds trust in the shopper as it looks more authentic and considered than a mishmash of backgrounds and photo styles.

SERVE ANGLES: Take a lot of photographs. Just because it's a low price doesn't mean it needs less work to sell it. Including the front, back, details, brand labels and so on are all an easy way to make a quicker sale.

CARE INFO: Care label details and fabric composition are a must to ensure that the piece is not skipped over for lack of info. More and more people want to know if they are buying polyester and other synthetic fibres.

HONESTY: Be open about the life of the garment. Describing items truthfully as 'gently worn', 'well worn', 'occasionally worn' and so on all help you to build more trust. Be open about any faults to ensure your reviews are good and help you to keep selling in the future. It is also the sound thing to do and will come back to you, I am sure.

STYLING: Mention trends and what the item can be styled with or the occasion it could suit. Describing something as a 'Y2K party dress' rather than 'pink shimmer mini dress' could get you more traction.

BE PATIENT: You can spend an entire afternoon photographing and uploading with no movement on your stock, but it can take time to sell.

DONATING

Donating unwanted clothing seems to many like a no-brainer. You can over-shop and then a charity profits from selling off to a new wearer. However, most donors have very little idea of where their clothing is going or how to donate properly, which is leading to a massive issue.

DONOR BEWARE
The necessary research into where we are dropping off our clothing is not

happening as much as it should. It is rare that one bag of mixed-quality, mixed-condition and mixed-use garments will be 100 per cent usable by one destination. When we don't divide, prepare and donate properly it can result in, amongst many things:

- Charities not receiving the high-quality items they have in the past. This is reducing the level of quality stock, which leads to fewer shoppers.
- Charities being left to deal with your rubbish. Charities have to spend thousands each year on damaged or unsuitable donations that don't fall into their donation guidelines.
- Garments that were intended to be given to someone in need being sold off to be recycled for profit.
- Wearable, sellable and recyclable clothing being sent to landfill.

DONOR PREPARE
DIVIDE

The first place to start is to divide the clothing into categories and then you'll decide where to send each of those categories. Usually where we send depends on what we want it to do: whether that is to be given to someone in need at no charge, sold for profit either in-store or in another country, or used for recycling.

Sorting into categories will increase the chances of clothing being reused in the right way. It would be pretty rare for you to only ever be getting rid of great condition, unworn clothing so be honest in your categories. If you have items that have never been worn, even better if they have tags still in place, many places need them more than a clothes bin that ships them off to landfill. Or is it something only fit to be repurposed or recycled?

TIMING

As you can imagine, timing is really important when sending clothing to charities. Clothes that can be sold right away and don't have to be stored until they come into season will increase the chances of it ending up on the shop floor.

PREP

Preparing each category well is essential. It not only means that the place you send them to has less work to do, less will get wasted and more has the potential to be re-worn.

Always ensure your garments are clean and in a sellable condition. Bagging and labelling can also be really helpful. There will be a person receiving and sorting your donation and having it divided into categories like 'Men's winter coats' will help massively.

PROVIDE

If you want your clothing to go somewhere where it is benefitting someone in need, without any cost to them, this involves more research and time. I am sure you will agree it is worth it.

UNWORN AND GENTLY WORN

Online you can find information from local shelters, refuges and clothing drives that are looking for donations that will be given directly to someone who needs them. Winter coats and accessories, for example, are always worth sending to a local charity.

Smaller, local places will know their recipients' needs and wants very well, so they will usually be very clear on what they will and will not accept. If this is not on their website, a call should always be made before a drop-off. Be sure to check what categories of clothing they are looking for and if there are any specific requests. An example that you will often see is suiting or clothing suitable for interviews in a specific size. Also enquire about condition, as many women's refuges, for example, will only accept new (tags on) clothing.

GOOD CONDITION AND PRACTICAL

Sadly, there is often a demand for emergency clothing in countries where people have been forcibly displaced. Good-quality clothing can be a great way to support those in need.

The specific garment requests here will most often be for protective, practical clothing and accessories. If you would like to donate to a clothes drive for people in need abroad, be sure to do your research. Charities will have clear guidelines on what is in most need and if all is going to the cause rather than being sold for profit.

PROFIT

You may want to donate your clothing to a charity that can make a profit from selling them. Before you send it to a charity shop, check what they require. Most will have guidelines on what they accept or need. It is always worth giving them a call to check if they are currently taking donations and how they like them dropped off.

Charity shops should be donated to with a lot of consideration. If you wouldn't wear it in its current condition, why would a charity want it on their shop floor?

Charities will also send clothing to be recycled. This is a way for them to be able to make money from unsellable clothing donations that they end up with. Garments that cannot be sold or are surplus to requirements can be sold on to a company that profits from selling clothing abroad or recycling. Be sure to ask if they take these donations and package them separately.

PRIVATE COMPANIES
There are many private companies that will buy large quantities of unwanted garments from charities, brands and even you.

If a garment is still wearable but not of the standard for local demand, it can be sold off to another country, usually a developing country, where the used clothing trade can turn a big profit. This also goes for clothing of poor quality that is barely worn or in otherwise new condition.

An example of where this has caused a lot of harm is Africa where a lot of the world's used clothing was sent due to previous demand. This was down to the demand for the lower price of good-condition, well-made garments that could be sold there. This demand for imported sold-on clothing had a massive impact on local production of new clothing, which led to bans on imports. While these donations can create jobs and industry, poor-quality donations are now causing havoc and starting to build up in places that just don't want or need low-quality used clothing. We are essentially making our rubbish someone else's problem and someone is profiting.

CLOTHING BINS

Many people are opting to use clothing bins out of convenience and the misconception that they are an easier way for you to use your wanted clothing to help those in need.

Many of these bins are run by companies that make a profit from sending your unwanted clothing away and are not part of a charity. Sometimes, a small percentage of this profit will go to a charity but it will be heavily branded.

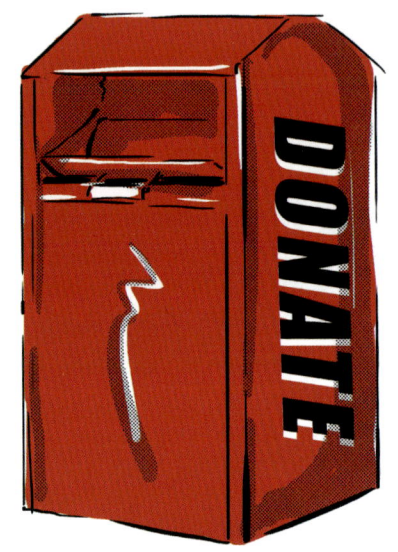

Not all clothing bins send clothes to be re-worn. Instead, they will sell off according to fibres for recycling.

These bins aren't unnecessary just because they are for profit. Their ease of use helps clothing avoid landfill and be used in some way.

THE GREAT UNSOLD

As our experience of used clothing is mainly through shopping for it, we don't tend to be exposed to the sheer volume of what is discarded. It appears on the outside that clothing

donation is a well-oiled machine taking care of anything we don't want, saving it from harmful landfills and moving clothing seamlessly from wardrobe to wardrobe.

Aside from buying less, which in turn leads us to buy better quality, we should be mindful of how we discard our unwanted clothing. It is still our responsibility.

If you have some clothing which you don't want to let go of but feel needs a little love, the next few chapters are for you. We will be covering how to give clothes a new lease of life through mending, dyeing, repurposing and revamping. Needles at the ready!

WELCOME to a gem of a section! Repair and a Spare is all about arming you with the information and skills you need to be able to carry out the most common repairs, edits and updates yourself.

A stitch in time saves nine, they say, and this section should help you do just that. The following chapters are all about being able to save a garment yourself and keep her going for longer.

With a rise in social media repair hacks, there has also been an increase in methods that just don't last and instead, clothing can only be worn a few more times. This section is all about applying the reliable and trusted ways of generations past to new, modern garments. We will look at the most common repairs – like rips, tears, fallen hems and broken zips – that happen to clothes made by some modern methods. We will also venture into button changes, hem edits and dyeing in our lessons in garment transformation. Divine!

All this cannot be done, of course, without learning some basics, so from building a sewing kit to stunning stitches, we will be taking a deep dive into the foundations of sewing. This will either help you get to grips as someone new to it or help you to polish your skills if you have done it before.

Repairing, sewing and creating clothing has been a passion of mine for as long as I can remember. Armed with skills first taught to me by my wonderful (and patient!) grandmother and then topped up during my degree, it has always been a relaxing and mindful process to get lost in. I hope this section will help you to find your escape in mending and making. It is a glorious skill set to have and one that can bring a lot of joy.

So let's start our journey to becoming our own seamstress.

10 Building a Sewing Kit

WE ARE NOW perfectly poised to discuss something all of us can benefit from having in the home, no matter what our style. The sewing kit. *closes eyes, palms to chest* This chapter will focus on helping you build one to last.

Just like a tool kit, a sewing kit is a stunning addition to anyone's home and one you will be so glad to have to hand at certain points in your life! You don't need to be a crafty queen to have a great sewing kit; think of it more as a repair box for your wardrobe. They are made up of such small elements that they don't need to take up much space and, as long as you look after them, they can last a lifetime.

I absolutely LOVE to see people's sewing kits; they are always such a gorgeous little meauxment in a home, a little collection that has been built up over time. Getting to see one that has been around for a while – or even through generations – is a sight to behold. Don't even get me started on how glorious they smell.

A NOTE ON PURCHASES

A sturdy, long-lasting and dependable sewing kit is pretty inexpensive (and a joy!) to build. Once you have the basics, you can add to it over time and most people will find that what goes in will most likely stay in there. This means it's a good idea to start with good tools from the beginning so they last well.

Whether you are starting from scratch, simply adding to what you have or are looking for advice on replacements, here is the tea. Where possible, go preowned when purchasing. This is for tools and equipment but not threads (more on that later on).

Not only will you save money – these girls were made in a time when sewing kits were used frequently and are quite frankly made of stronger stuff. To buy the modern equivalent in similar materials and of similar workmanship, you would have to spend a lot more.

Also, there's the aesthetic. I'm almost mopping my brow as I write this. As they hail from an era where sewing was super-common and people were not of the throw-away mentality, the tools used were considered and ornate, they were there to add to the meauxment and live forever. *swoons* Silver plating, pearl handles, etching, filigree ... I'll stop but you get the idea.

My advice is to avoid the mass-produced, plastic tools where you can and go on the hunt for some preowned beauts. Look in vintage stores, car boot sales and, of course, online. You'll be spoiled for choice and after you find the ones for you, you'll be sure to cherish and mind them. It's always the way when you lengthen the shopping journey: things tend to be more considered and personal.

A good kit will not only ensure that you only buy once, but it will also make the simplest of sewing and mending a chic and stunning affair.

Below are the things most people will end up using no matter what they sew and the key points around them to help you avoid wasting money.

NEEDLES

A needle is a needle, is a needle. Right? Wellllllll, while you can sew with any aul needle in theory, for the best results, you need to know what kind of needle suits the task at hand. Getting the needle right for the fabric thickness, weave type and thread will make the process a lot more seamless. Pun intended, of course.

Most stores stock 'assorted' needle packets which have a variety of the most commonly used needles. Inside, on a good brand, is a guide to what is in the pack. This guide is usually made up of numbers and names and it's a good idea to get to know what these mean in relation to what you are sewing.

It goes a little something like this:

EYE:
The width and length are important as the eye needs to be able to be threaded with ease and not split or fray the thread during sewing. Some tasks, such as beading, will require an eye that is the same thickness as the needle and so on.

LENGTH:
How long a needle is will impact timing and accuracy, so this is why short, fine, sharp needles are ideal for something like quilting.

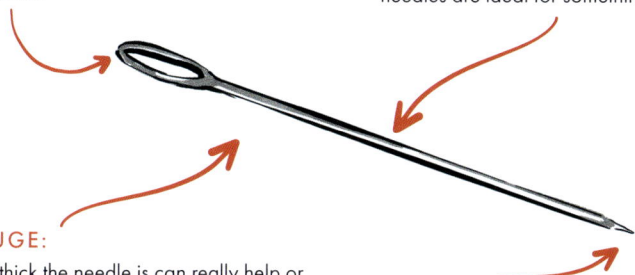

GAUGE:
How thick the needle is can really help or hinder the process. For example, the finer the needle the more accurate you have to be. On the other hand, a thicker needle will be able to withstand being pushed into denser fabrics.

POINT:
The sharpness of the tip. Some fabrics require a severe, sharp tip and some, like knits, fare better with a rounded tip.

In the best-case scenario, the wrong needle will just take you a little longer to use; the worst is that it will snap or cause damage to the fabric. Choosing the right needle will also mean that it won't have to overwork and so the needle will last longer as its tip doesn't wear down.

A short rule of thumb is that the finer your fabric, the thinner your needle should be. The thicker the thread, the wider the eye and the longer the task, the shorter the needle.

For a standard repair or taking up a hem, you'll mainly need to know what type of needle you require and how thick it should be. Here is a helping hand in figuring this out.

NEEDLE TYPE

Needles are made from wires. I know! The things you learn. They are pointed at one end then stamped and the eye cut at the other. The numbers on the packaging will refer to the gauge or thickness of this wire.

Unfortunately, there is not an official standard gauge reference for needles as most brands have their own size chart, but most packets will include the house rules as well as arranging the needles according to size. It will be pretty easy to match your thread/fabric to the needle once you have read the advice below.

SHARPS

Sharps are the middle of the road, all-rounders that can pretty much see you through most sewing tasks. They are, as you probably guessed, very sharp. Their length is usually medium.

BETWEENS

These are like sharps' sisters. They are also pointed queens and quite fine but are shorter in length. Shorter needles can speed up sewing time so quilters tend to like a between.

CALYX EYE/EASY THREAD

Can't thread easily? These gals have a slit at the top that allows you to pull the thread into the eye from above so you don't have to go in from the side. The caesarean of sewing needles.

BALLPOINT

You have probably already guessed it. She's like a sharp but with a less pointy end. When would you use these? Knits and stretch fabrics are ideal here as they don't need a sharp end for you to feed the needle through and they are less likely to damage the looser weave.

CHENILLE

These have a larger eye so can accommodate thicker threads or multiple threads as well as feeling better in a bigger hand.

BEADING

When beading, the whole needle needs to be able to glide through the bead for speed and accuracy. Beading needles are super-fine and have the same gauge the whole way up.

LEATHER

This needle has three areas of attack to help glide through such a tough material.

If you need to reattach a strap or belt buckle, make sure you go for the right needle to prevent snapped needles and sore hands.

DARNERS

Quite literally, for darning. You'll spot these by their longer eye, which can easily accommodate thick yarns used for heavier-duty repairs. They come in long and short lengths.

TAPESTRY

The reason a tapestry needle has such a large eye is to hold the thick thread. The rounded bottom is because it is not required to pierce through fabric, which is pretty useful as you are blind to it when pulling it through.

THREAD

In theory, you can use any thread for a quick stitch ... but if you want your mending to last and look good, I recommend having some options in your kit for different garments.

As I have mentioned, threads are something to consider a little deeper when you are buying pre-owned items for your kit. Many older threads were made of cotton, before the polyester years, and this cotton tends to have weakened over time. This doesn't mean that you should dump your vintage threads as they can be great for basting or a quick temporary stitch.

There are a few things you need to think about when purchasing thread.

COLOUR: Think of the garments you're most likely to sew rather than your whole wardrobe. For example, do your wide-leg, double-pleat work trouser hems frequently drop? Are you always adjusting the hems of skirts or fixing buttons on particular garments?

It is pointless and wasteful to match your thread to absolutely everything so go for the colours that match what you're likely to mend first.

COMPOSITION: Threads, like clothing, will always have their fibre composition on them and you need to match your fibre composition to the garment you are working on. In general, it is advised to use synthetics threads on synthetic garments as they will react to wear and tear in similar ways.

COTTON

Cotton is a great option when sewing natural fabrics as they share so many properties. There are many advantages to cotton and some instances where you may need an alternative:

PROS
- Has a gorgeous aesthetic and a lovely handfeel. Synthetics never quite look the same quality.
- Can withstand higher temps so great for garments that get ironed a lot.
- Cotton is often put through an industrial process called mercerisation that can give a wonderful sheen and enhances her ability to hold on to dyes.
- Organic cotton is the hot girl on the block right now as she does not undergo the same coating treatments and is more durable.

CONS

- The mercerising cotton undergoes means it has little give and can make it more likely to snap than a synthetic so don't use on areas that get a lot of stress.
- The dye can fade quicker than a synthetic so be careful with sewing brights you wash a lot.

As you can see, cotton is not suitable for heavier weights that will get a lot of movement and should be kept to looser lightweight garments.

POLYESTER

We already know plenty about this girl fibre-wise, but it is worth noting some finer points about poly thread:

PROS

- She will have the give that cotton does not, so is great on stretch and garments that endure stress.
- She is easy to pick up and colour match, as most brands will have a poly as their general thread.
- Her shiny nature means she slips through fabric more easily so she can be a lot smoother to use, especially if you don't sew often.
- Polyester is favoured by a lot of dressmakers as it can hold dye really well.
- There are now plenty of recycled poly options out there.

CONS

- Not a stunning fibre to be using.
- Won't have that same richness as cotton.

When you want the heavy-duty capabilities of poly but the look of cotton, you can go for the ever-popular thread that has a polyester wrapped in cotton. Use her for non-stretch garments like shirting or tailoring. She will always stay put, even after an intense wash, so she is great for keeping shape.

WEIGHT: Suit the thread to your fabric. Sewing a lightweight dress in a heavy thread designed for denim is not going to give as wonderful a finish as a finer thread. General thread is usually 50 in weight as that is the most versatile.

BRAND: There are many reliable thread brands out there and, just like lipstick, the well-known and respected (and a small bit pricier) ones are genuinely better. They are more durable, their coatings and compositions are of a higher quality and you'll get a much better result.

It is always worth spending a little more on good thread. Avoid unbranded multipacks. You're probably never going to use the majority of the shades and, if you do, there's rarely enough in these spools for more than a couple of buttons.

SNIPS

A small pair of scissors or snips are a must for a sewing kit. You will more than likely only use it for snipping threads so she will stay sharp for a long time. They are also dotey. A must.

When buying these, take into consideration that they don't need to look like traditional scissors. Thread snippers that sit into your hand are more comfortable to use and you can tie them onto your machine to use as you sew.

SHEARS

If you are going to be cutting fabric, a pair of good shears will be a godsend. These are designed to cut various weights of fabric in fewer snips so you can get a beautiful edge. They feel lovely in the hand and quite weighty, which means you can control them easier.

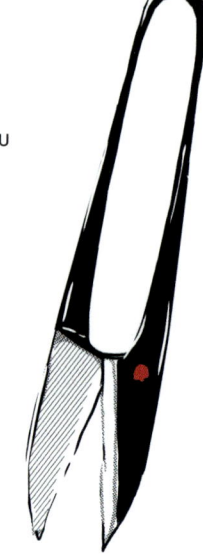

When buying your shears consider:

THE HAND YOU WRITE WITH: I learned to pattern cut as a right-hander and the dents in my fingers from late nights cutting heavy winter fabrics tell their own tale. Take my advice and get to the right grip early doors. The blades are also switched on left-handed shears, which means if you learn on a right, as I did, you need to relearn how to cut as that couple of millimetres makes a massive difference in the fit.

MATERIAL: Stainless steel is best as it is hard wearing and you can sharpen it. However, it can be heavy. For this reason, some like to opt for titanium but this can be much more expensive. A cheaper compromise is a plastic handle. Both of these lighter weights can be great for someone starting out as they are easier to use.

LENGTH: The longer the shears, the heavier the fabric they can work with. Heavier fabrics are usually used in wider and longer silhouettes, like coats and trousers, so the long blades don't tend to have the issues that come with more curved edges. If you work a lot in heavier fabrics, this is your gal. If you are more lightweight, you don't need to have a super-long and heavy pair and you will most likely need something shorter purely for the curves that come with lighter fabrics that sit closer to the body.

I have found the best, long-wearing and precise shears have been from Japanese brands so keep an eye out for these on the second-hand market.

Here is a lesson that will keep your scissors stunning for her lifetime: never *leans in* and I mean never, use your fabric scissors to cut paper. It will blunt the blades and you want to avoid having to sharpen them too much. The greatest shears you'll ever use are those that have never seen a sheet of paper. Not even a glance.

MEASURING TAPE

Trust me, you'll use these for a million things other than sewing over the years. I know this seems like a no-brainer purchase, but there is an art to making sure you only buy one good tape.

When it comes to buying a measuring tape, there are some things you need to be mindful of. There is a reason dressmakers will avoid the ones you get in a Christmas cracker.

SIZE: Get one that suits you. Measuring tapes come in different lengths and it is handy to have one that's right for you, so always check the maximum length. This isn't just for bust and hips, it also goes for height.

MATERIALS: Fabric tapes will fray over time and can warp and stretch, which will affect accurate measuring. This can also be the case with unbranded cheaper tapes. Fibreglass measuring tapes are your gal here! They won't stretch or fray and will last a lifetime. The great thing about them is that they are also soft, which makes them easy to work with and not harsh on the body. If your tape is hard and uncomfortable as you measure, she's probably not fibreglass. Coated polyester can also be a good, cheaper option but go for a brand with a great rep.

INCHES AND CENTIMETRES: I always go for both. Yes, I mainly work in centimetres but sometimes I will need to divide a measurement and it breaks down better in inches, or a size guide or pattern could be in inches.

DOUBLE-SIDED: If you have managed to find a two-sided tape with both cm and inches on each side, these are great. This means you can start at either end of the tape so it can be quicker to use during a long sesh. When you can only start at one end of one side, you'll have to constantly flip it back over.

THE TIP: Check the ends for how they start. The bottom measurement should be a perfect one and have a cap at the top to prevent this from changing. Cheaper tapes will have a flimsy top and your measurements will always start off wrong. Other tapes will have a gap before the start, and this can be annoying when space is tight as you have to curl the tape under itself.

PINS

A box of pins will never see you wrong. Even if you don't machine sew, they are great as a helping hand when hemming. They don't need to be

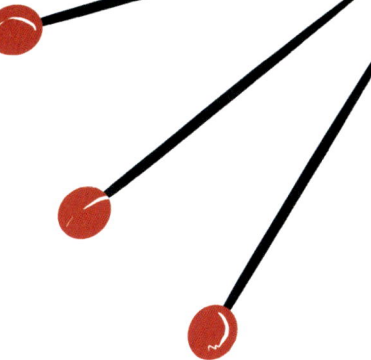

anything special – I find the standard full stainless steel gals great – but if you are going to be using heavy fabrics or quilting it can be handy to use pins with a ball or similar at the end as it is kinder to your fingertips when pushing through thickness and, most importantly, easy to find!

The boxes these come in when buying in bulk can be a bit flimsy and easy to accidentally open so I recommend buying in the standard cardboard (cheaper!) and rehousing the stash in something with a screw top that has more weight.

I have mine in a repurposed hair mask tub and face powder tub. They have been with me for years and have been so much easier to use, find and remove pins from. I also find that doling some pins out into the lid to work from makes it easier than digging in the full pile. You can also move the lid around with you and you're less likely to ever end up with the whole box on the floor.

PIN CUSHION

These are not a heavy must unless you are doing a sewing project. They simply allow you to keep your pins safe. It gives you easy access when you need them but also a perfect spot to pop pins you're removing. If you are going to make or purchase one, think about where it will sit. Some like a tabletop, others like a wrist.

If you are machine sewing frequently, I find making yourself a band for your machine a godsend. You can easily pop in the pins you've taken out as you sew without ending up losing any.

A MAGNET

See that pin box above? Sooner or later, you will drop it.

A magnet is super-handy for picking up a pile of fallen needles but also great to make sure you find any that dropped as you sewed. I also find them useful for finding needles lost in a big coat, etc. It can be a traditional magnet or there are many lovely vintage sewing magnets out there that double up as little pin boxes.

SEWING BOX

This can be anything you like. In fact, it can be something you love! A biscuit tin you saved? A cosmetics box you loved the font on? This kit is here to stay so make it something wonderful! Smaller boxes within make really handy dividers and will help you find things with ease.

If you plan to do a lot of sewing, you can invest in a professional sewing kit box but I have found my most used is a fishing tackle box with different-sized compartments, the largest ones to fit full thread spools and others to house everything from buttons to needles and fabric roses.

BUTTON JAR

Next time you are throwing out a small jar, consider using it for spare buttons. It can also be handy to divide a few jars into types of buttons. Boxes are, of course, fine but you may find you end up with lots of little boxes in your kit and it can be hard to use for something so small. A glass jar will always make it easier.

To get full use out of your button jars and not have them follow you aimlessly through life like a drawer of cables or a box of batteries – categorise. For example, have one for replacements for your knits and one for coats. You can also have a spares jar from garments you have cut buttons off.

When the buttons come in their own wee bag, it's a no-brainer: keep them inside and write the garment on it or a piece of paper inside. When something new has buttons attached to the inside label, snip these off and tape them to a piece of card or paper and write the garment description on it.

There are two reasons I don't love to leave buttons on the label and wear them. One, they can clatter as you walk, which is not only annoying, but it can chip or break them. Two, it's a sure-fire way to lose them. Washing and wear

can loosen the threads they are attached with and it's bye, bye, baby on your commute.

SHE'S ON THE GO

A travel sewing kit is one of those things you'll never know how you lived without once you have one. They can be super-handy for trips but also a dream for popping in your bag for an event, keeping in a drawer at work or your favourite date clutch.

If you look for a ready-made travel sewing kit, you may notice that some of the more antique styles will have grooming items as well as sewing tools. This is down to a wonderful item called an etui. Back in the day, women would carry an etui in their purse. *Étui* means 'holder', in French. I meannnnn.

This was a small ornate box or bag that would hold a sewing kit, tweezers, scissors and anything else you can't get on a flight with these days. These were always super-ornamental but extremely practical. Fabergé even created one called the Nécessaire Egg, which held all the bits a lady would need. Stunning!

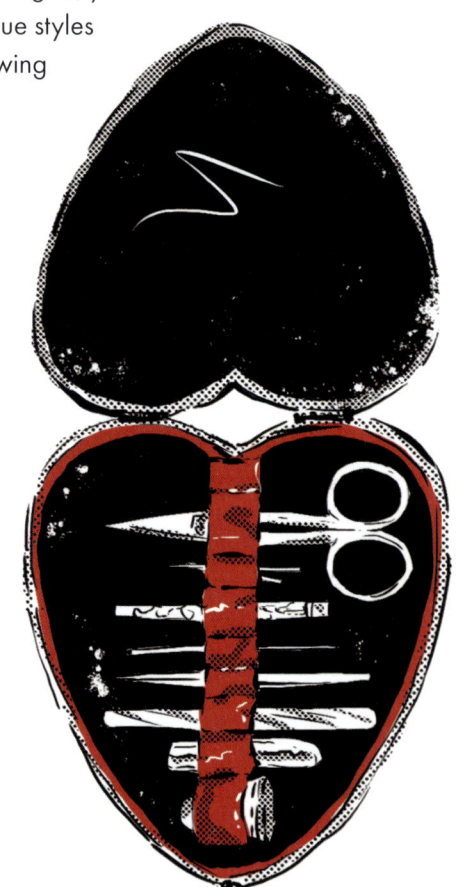

YOUR UNIQUE TRAVEL SEWING KIT

Our needs and wants are slightly different from those in the etui days, and will also differ from person to person, so making your own, to suit you, is easily done.

There are so many things you can use as your travel kit holder but one I find great is an old spice jar. The lids twist on so there's no risk of it popping off during travel and it's pretty slimline. It can prevent the needles from sticking through as you rummage for a pair of lace knickers on your first night out in Paris and it will also stand the test of time.

BUTTONS

Spare buttons. I would opt for one the size of a shirt button in the most common colour you'll wear and a larger button. Usually, the repair you do on the fly will be redone once you're home anyway so size is more important than colour. You essentially want something to do a coat or trouser and something for a shirt or top.

NEEDLES AND PINS

Just a few, perhaps secured in a small square of felt. Preloaded needles are also a godsend!

THREAD

Just as you would see in Christmas cracker sewing kits (the ones where the scissors fall apart at the first snip), it is wise to have pre-cut thread. Simply preload a strip of card with lengths of the colour thread you think you will realistically use. I load mine up with black, white and also light pink, which can be used on oranges, reds and pinks.

SNIPS

Usually, you'll only need to cut a thread on the go so scissors may not be needed as you can snap or use a lighter or nail clippers to cut the thread instead. Some airlines worldwide allow small scissors (blades under 10cm), but this is not always the case. For this reason, it can be handier to avoid carrying scissors when travelling on planes but if you are not, opt for a snips.

As you can see, you only need to add to your kit as you need it. She will grow so be sure to leave room for new additions.

A WALL-HANGING SEWING KIT

A bursting kit is usually a sure-fire way to lose a couple of buttons from a full set or your favourite needle. If you use your kit often and are pretty handy with a machine, why not rustle up a wall-hanging kit? This keeps your handiest bits on the wall and it can easily be taken down and rolled when you need it popped out of sight. I have found mine really handy over the years. They are best made out of non-stretch material like calico left over from another project.

Your sewing kit will grow as it needs to and there is no reason to have anything more than you will use. It's pretty common for crafts and hobbies to become areas of overconsumption with a feeling of needing to be kitted out and always fully stocked. You can throw that out the window for sewing as it is so personal. Enjoy building and looking after your own kit, she'll be a gem.

11 A Stitch in Time

MENDING CLOTHES is something that has fallen out of fashion in recent times. But I am here to tell you she is back with a BANG, baby. In a world of overproduction, I adore that this is entering our lives again. Clothes having stories and showing that they lived a life and hold memories is DIVINE.

There are many common repairs we can easily do ourselves but often avoid due to a lack of knowledge or a feeling that we cannot or should not. This is the same for SHE-iy, so many lovely, calming, mindful jobs that we could carry out and save ourselves money and time but, instead, we fear them.

In this chapter, we are going to run through some of the most common issues with modern clothing and learn how to repair them ourselves. Even if you never pick up a needle, it is great to get to grips with these as you'll know how to instruct and inspect a paid-for repair well. Also, you never know when you might want to try it! A heel could cut through hem stitching on your way out the door and you'll be glad you know how to sort it.

TIPS AND TRICKS

We know the art of SHE-iy is not just knowing how to complete the task at hand, but having some titbits of pro knowledge. Sewing is the same. There are so many little tips and tricks that can help the task run more smoothly and here are mine:

CUTTING THREAD
You may have not sewn before and will be wondering how much thread to cut. You want the thread to be at least a third longer than the length you are sewing, to avoid having to cut more. Simply hold the thread over the area and unravel enough to cover you for this.

DOUBLING UP
I will almost always work with doubled-up thread, it's something that I have found works well in most mending or making and it will last longer as well as be easier to work with. The only time I avoid is if the fabric is lightweight, or I need discreet stitches. For this, I just measure with doubled thread and highly recommend it!

A SNIP!
When you cut thread, always cut at a 45-degree angle so the thread ends in a really thin point. This makes it super easy to thread but also means the end left on the spool is less likely to get a splayed end which is hard to work with. No matter if you are hand or machine sewing, serve those angles!

ANCHORING

Consider how you will anchor the thread in the fabric so it never slips out. There are two main options: a knot or an anchoring stitch.

ROLL KNOT: This is pretty simple. Roll about the end of the thread between your thumb and forefinger to make a wee ball, then pull it sharply to the end of the thread and it will form into a knot. This works with single and double threads.

TIED KNOT: As you would with a balloon, knot the end. I tend to do two knots for extra security.

NEEDLE KNOT: This is where you wrap the end of the thread around the needle as if it's hair and the needle is a curling thong. Wrap around about six times, then pull it back down the length of the thread and it'll form a knot.

STITCHES: Sometimes you won't want a knot so the best way to anchor is to make a stitch in the fabric and go over it a few times to create an anchor stitch that goes nowhere. This is especially handy for the ends of side seams or top of splits as it will be more durable.

GOT TO BE REEL

Here is a tip not even most pros know! The reel of the most common thread brand we tend to have in our homes does far more than hold thread. She is great to utilise fully as it aids a more seamless sewing experience. Here is how:

1 The little bumps inside this groove are designed to hold the end of the thread to stop it from fraying and unravelling. Just slip the loose end in, and you'll hear a delicious sound as it slots behind the bumps.

2 The U shapes on the top of the spool are ideal for holding your needle when taking a wee break, instead of putting it on a surface and risking losing it.

If you are finished sewing for the day, never slide your needle into the thread to store it. This could snap yarns and weaken the thread.

Instead, push the needle fully into one U groove at the top. When you twist the top off the next time you sew, it will be held in there safely for you.

3 The top of the spool is also handy as a pin or needle collector while you sew.

A Stitch in Time

KEEPING SCISSORS SHARP

Scissors will go dull over time naturally and a great way to keep them sharp (aside from my no paper warning previously!) is to fold tin foil to about 3 or 4 ply and cut it several times.

PRESSING MATTER

When sewing most things, it is always important to give the garment a good iron before, during if needed, and after the process. Never skip the pressing as that will be what sets the repair apart from looking home done. Make sure you are using the steam setting (if the fabric allows) to not overheat the fabric but also to dampen the fibres and allow them to redry in the new position. Pressing will ensure the fabric is flat and in the correct place, making it easier to work with.

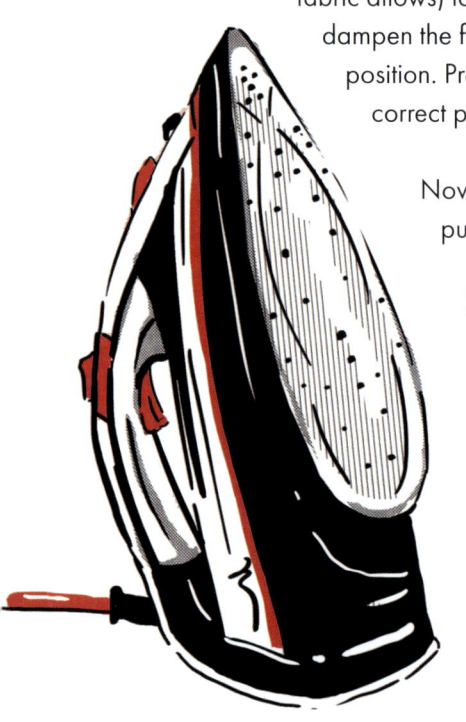

Now you have some pro tips to help you, let's put them to use.

SEWING

These basic stitches are all great to get to grips with as you will use them for creating, mending and general sewing.

THREADING A NEEDLE

This is how you thread a needle with ease and avoid repeat attempts that fray the ends of the thread and end up frustrated.

1. Make sure your thread is cut at a super angle for precision.

2. Hold the needle as far down as possible, with the eye facing to the side, not at you.

3. Put the end of the thread in your mouth and pull it through closed lips. It will flatten all the yarns. Spit queens.

4. Hold the thread up to 2.5cm from the top; too long and it will droop, too short and you won't see it.

5. Push the thread through the eye, tilting the needle back as you go to avoid the thread falling back out.

6. Pull her all the way through. Divine!

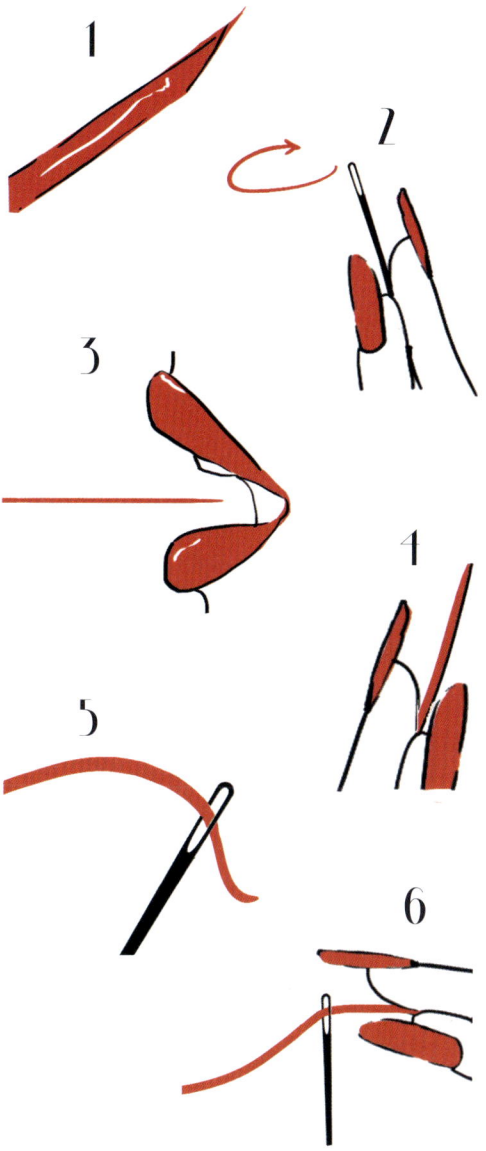

THREADERS

Gems that are often found in Christmas crackers ... but rarely used! These essentially work by acting as a larger eye for the thread, so many people will find them helpful. They can assist if you find threading difficult or want to speed up the process.

1. Slide threader's pointed wire through the needle's eye.

2. Keep pushing until the widest part bends to slip through the eye and you have the needle dangling but securely in place.

3. While the needle hangs out, thread the wire as you would a needle. Making sure you pull enough through that it won't slip out.

4. Pull the threader back through the eye and you'll have a threaded needle!

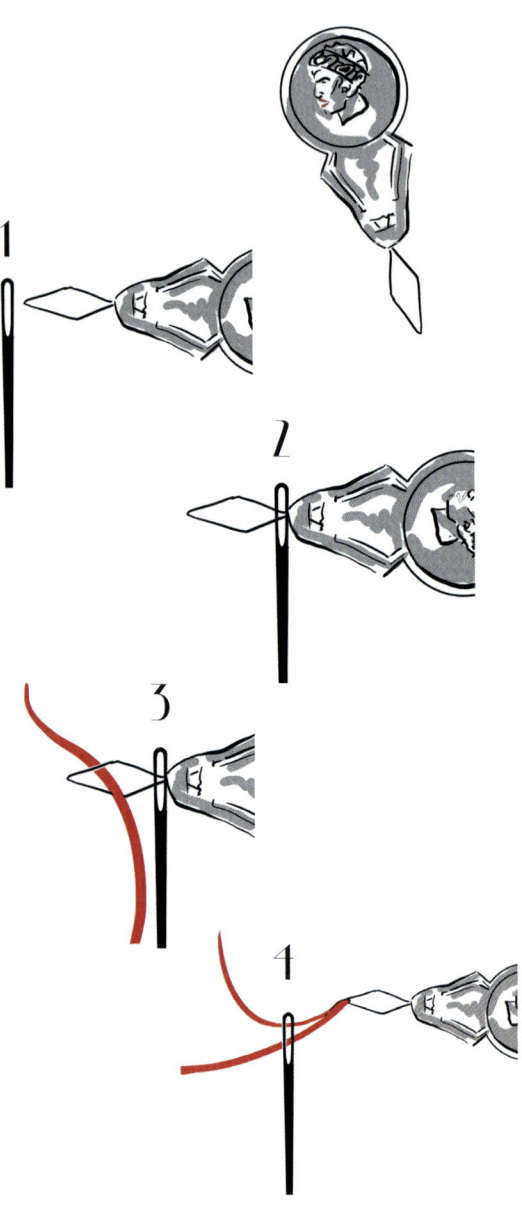

SHE'S A BASIC STITCH

This is what you will use to hand-sew fabric together in general. All you need to remember when doing this is the quality of the stitching. It needs to be straight, uniform and even to last well. If you are new to sewing, start here!

After you have learned it, you can use this for visible hems, side seams, creating a garment, adding on pockets, trims and so on. The best way to get it right is to practice by doing a sample first.

For this, we will draw a straight guide onto the fabric to follow but once you've mastered the art, you'll be able to do it without a guide. We will look into applying it to bust seams and coat pockets a little further on.

YOU'LL NEED:

- Threaded needle (make it a double length of thread for ease and tie the two ends in a knot – like a balloon)
- Two pieces of scrap fabric
- Snips or scissors
- Tailor's chalk and ruler
- Pins

1. You will almost always be sewing a stitch line inside the garment so be sure you have the right sides of your sample together and are working on the wrong side.

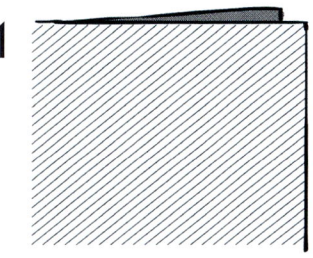

2   Start by drawing a straight line about 1.5cm from the edge of one piece of fabric. This will help you get into the groove of sewing a lovely straight line.

3   Pin fabrics together far enough apart to not disturb your sewing but close enough to keep the fabric edges in line.

4   About 0.5cm from the top, push your needle through from the other side.

5   Pull through until you feel the knot has hit the fabric, making sure you keep your thread taut so as not to allow it to tangle.

6   This is where you'll decide on the stitch length. Usually, in a repair, this will be following the other stitches in similar parts of the garment. For this, crack into a 3mm long stitch. It's a good all-rounder. So, pop your needle back through to the other side 3mm down and once you pull the thread through you have your first stitch! Divine!!

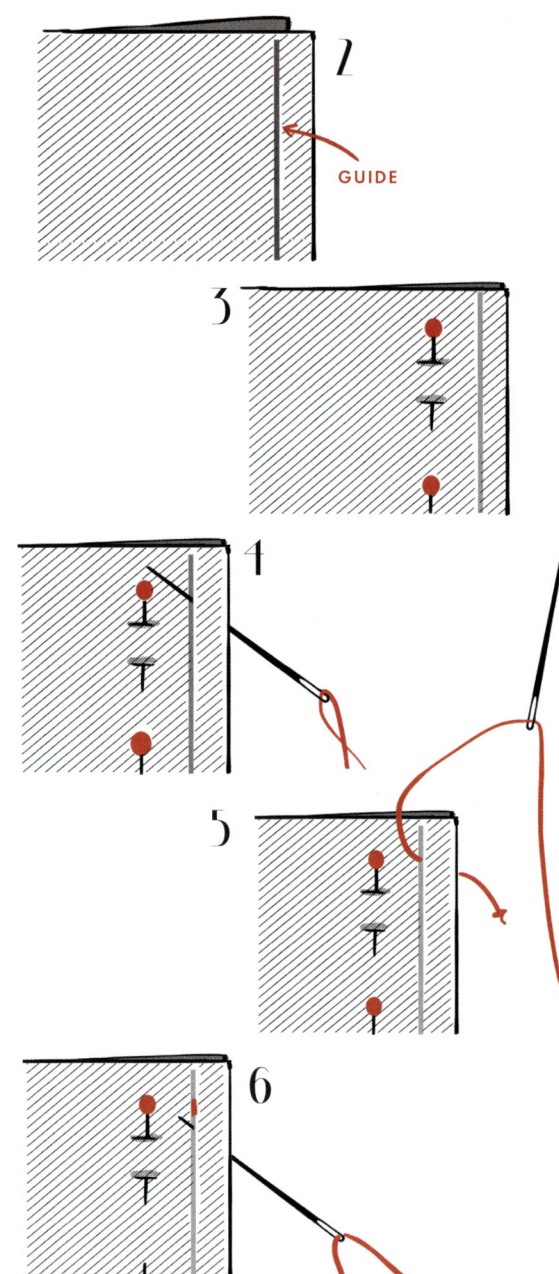

7. Leave a very little gap and repeat until you have your stitch line complete. As you sew don't forget to remember tension. That is how loose or tight your stitches are. You don't want it so loose that there will be gaps in the seams or so tight that the fabric bunches. It can help to stop every few stitches and pull your fabric flat to allow the slack in the thread to give where she needs to.

---

8. Securing your stitch line is super easy with double thread as you can snip, leaving around 6cm. Then knot twice right up to the fabric and snip the excess.

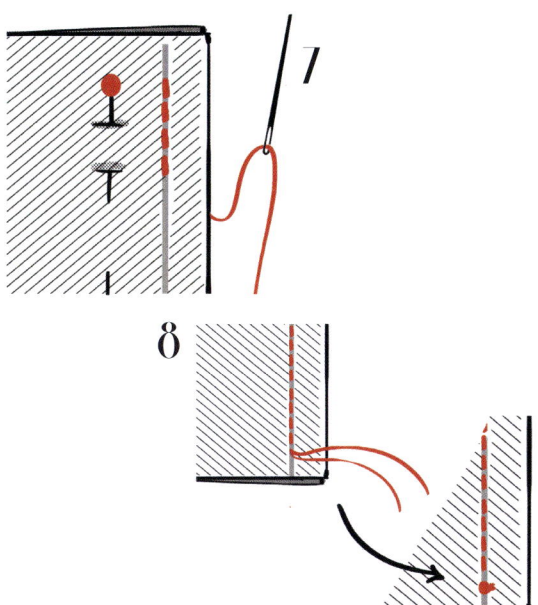

BASTING STITCH

She is a temporary stitch used to hold things in place as you sew, also commonly called a tacking stitch. She's a stitch that will be pulled out once you have sewn the fabric securely. She is done with thicker thread and in larger stitches but the principles are just the same as running stitch (a basic/straight stitch where the gaps between the stitches are the same length as the stitch.)

A basting stitch is often used to hold tricky girls like zips in place, secure lightweight or slippery fabrics together or pleats in place while you sew them. It's also great to use a basting stitch when matching up a print or stripes as it holds more precisely than pins would.

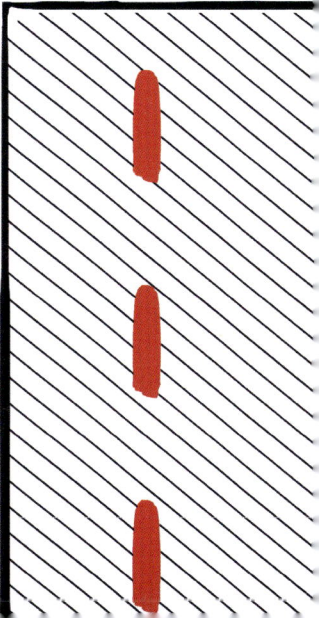

The main benefit to basting before you do the official stitching is that it frees up your hands from having to hold things in place and you are able to focus on beautiful stitchwork. Many tricky areas of garments relish the use of a basting stitch as there is so much movement during the sewing that pins can get in the way and affect precision. Thicker fabrics can also bend pins and be hard to keep in position so these love a basting before sewing.

If you are a beginner, it can be a stunning way to practise the task at hand before you go in properly. I also love it for sussing out a skirt hem length as the fabric can move more freely than with lots of pins.

Basting can seem like extra work but it can save you so much time as you can get the desired results in one go. Also, the drama of pulling out a basting stitch after you are done is lovely. These are the main things to remember with basting.

- Use massive stitches so they are easier to remove later.
- Choose a contrasting thread, as thick as the fabric will allow you, so you remember to remove it when you have finished and also to help you avoid sewing through the basting during your task.
- Baste as far away from where you are working as makes sense so it doesn't get sewn over. This is usually 5mm from where the real stitch line is going.

INVISIBLE STITCHES

These are also called slip stitches or blind stitches. They are most commonly used on hems or cuffs where you don't want any stitching seen, just a lovely clean finish on the exterior of the garment. Its application can also be good for seams you cannot get to the other side of easily like lined coat pockets. We will cover the how-to of these stitches in the next section – repairs!

REPAIRS

Now you have enough knowledge to get you through some common repairs for the modern wardrobe!

BURST SEAMS

Busted a dress while death dropping? Caused a trouser to split during splits? Maybe you've caught your trench on a bench? The basic stitch we just covered is fab for these little accidents. It's also a great one to know in general, as seam splits are very common in modern clothing that has had rushed production.

BURST SEAM

The main thing you need to remember in the case of a split seam is that you may not be in a position to resew the full stitch line. In this case, you will need to anchor onto the original stitch line, which is pretty easy. She'll go like this:

1. Turn the garment inside out and get to the place where there is a gap in the seam's stitching. Give it a good press and steam to get the fabric and threads acting their best.

2. Now you want to unpick the stitching, without snapping the thread. Do this until you have around 5 to 6cm of thread on either side of the gap. I usually use a needlepoint to coax them out of place.

3. You should have enough thread to knot your new thread onto and create an anchor for it.

4. It is wise to then start and end your new stitch line two stitches into the old stitch line and back stitch.

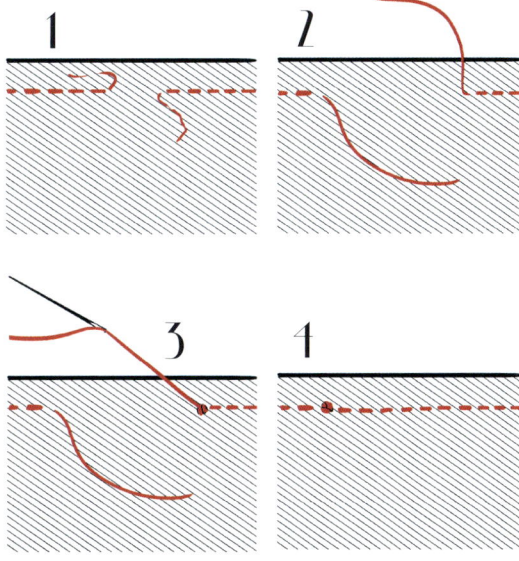

HEMS

There is nothing worse than a dropped hem where there are lewks to serve. Not only does it look sloppy, but it can also lead to a trip hazard as well as further damage to the garment. It is never something you should let go on for too long.

When it comes to a hem, you are better off undoing the whole hem and starting afresh. Many modern hems are not sewn nearly as well as your divine hands will do and only fixing a small area may not hold up for long. So whip out that seam ripper and gently undo the damaged stitch line.

Once finished, press with the steam setting on. A lovely hem will be easier to work with. You will need:

- Threaded needle (a single thread is better in finer fabrics and double in heavier)
- Snips or scissors
- Pins (remember to not pin too close to where you are stitching as it will affect the way you sew)

Turn the garment inside out and get to one side seam. This is the best place to kick off. Not only can you anchor your thread here, but you can also anchor the hem itself to it with a few extra stitches for more security with no effect on the exterior of the garment.

INVISIBLE STITCH

A wee note here is to remember that there will be very little done to the main part of the garment – the part that is seen – and most stitch work will be done to the hem allowance. This is why they are called invisible stitches.

1. Anchor the thread to the seam allowance, soon to be hidden by the hem, using a double stitch as this is the most secure.

2. Now that you are in, you want to slip your needle into that lovely crisp fold of the hem allowance only. About 1cm worth.

3. If the hem isn't double you can stitch across like this:

4. Now it's time to attach the hem to the garment. The key here is to only pick up one thread of the main fabric of the garment. This creates very little visual impact on the outside.

5. You'll repeat these steps until you get to the next side seam. Here you can do some lovely back stitches onto the seam allowance to make the hem sturdier. Then on again to where you started and cast off with a delicious backstitch and you're done sewing.

6. The last step is a press with steam and they will all live happily ever after.

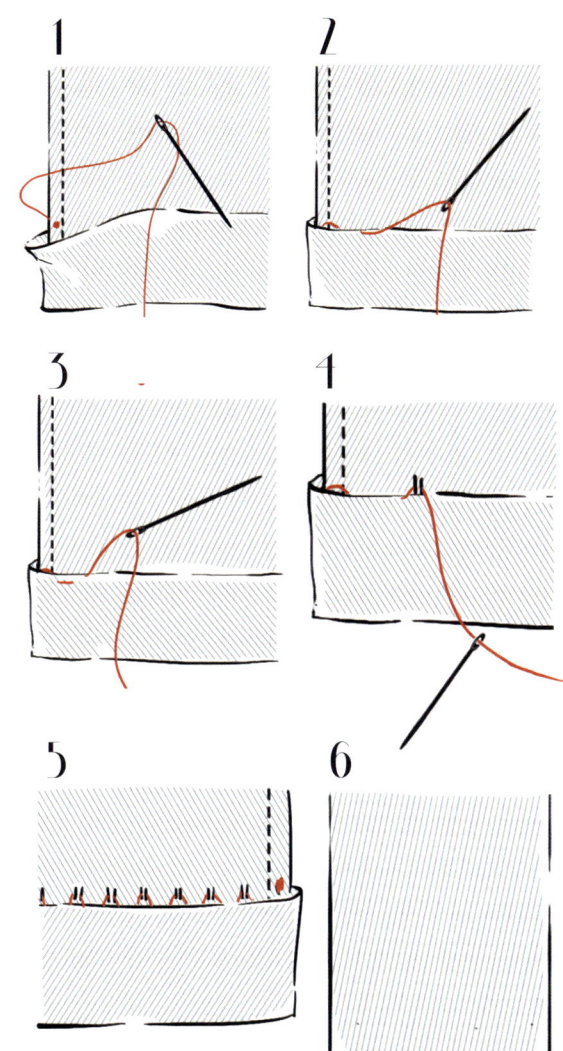

HERRINGBONE STITCH

If you have a heavier fabric such as wool or something that gets a lot of movement (I find this with really full trousers and skirts), you should do a herringbone version. This is more secure for them.

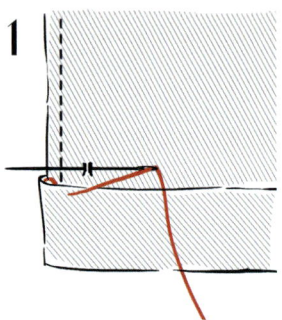 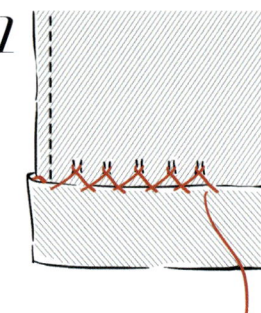

As you can see, you are crossing over each time and it gives a flexible security.

TORN POCKET BAGS (SLIP STITCH)

Rips in pocket bags can make the love for a winter coat severely dwindle. In October, you're wrapping her gloriously around you, however, come February, your keys are jiggling around the hem and you're cursing the day ye met. The longer you leave this, the harder it is to fix easily so act as soon as you can.

Here is how to solve! You'll need:

- Threaded needle (a double thread is better here for durability)
- Snips or scissors

1. We are going to be anchoring your thread to thread that is already there (just like the tutorial on page 277). So, this means you will need to guide some of the old stitches out to give you something to tie onto at each end.

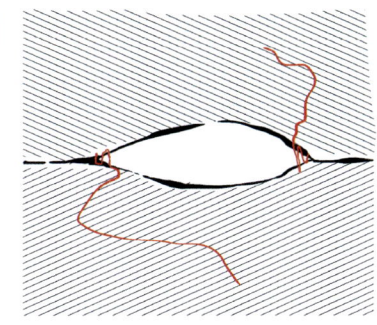

2. Anchored? Lovely. Now it's time for a slip stitch. This has the basic principles of the blind hem. However, you'll be taking a little from both sides. Every 6 or so stitches, pull the thread gently so the hole at the part you have sewn closes tightly.

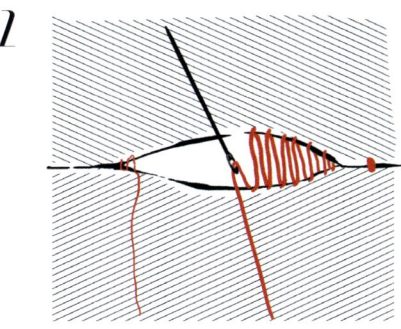

3. The last step is to double stitch and then snip the thread short enough so that when you pull the needle through and back to you the thread falls off inside. Bye, girl!

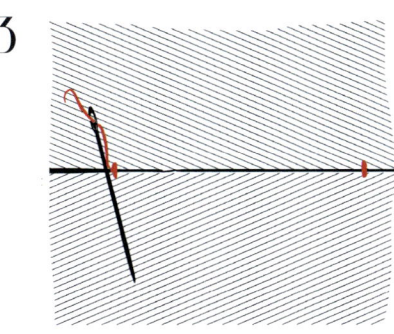

REPLACING A ZIP

Zips can fail but it doesn't render the whole garment unwearable. This task is not for the faint-hearted but if you take your time, it's a great one to be able to do yourself. The zip on the right is the most common in high street garments so the one you'll face most often. I would always carry out this zip replacement first before moving on to trickier trousers or jeans.

- Threaded needle (a double thread is better here for durability)
- Snips or scissors
- A new zip
- Pins
- Another threaded needle for basting (contrasting colour, etc.)

BUYING A NEW ZIP

When buying a replacement zip it is best to remove the old zip and find the exact same size and type rather than trying to guess. Before removing with a stitch ripper, I mark where the zip disappeared behind the fabric and also photograph it so I can use it as a guide for my new zip's placement as well as stitching. These photos will be your guide so make sure you take images both inside and out!

1   After the original zip is removed, it can be a little messy and hard to work on the garment. Clean up and steam press the area around the zip to ensure she is immaculate and ready to go. No loose threads and lovely straight edges. This will make the whole process a lot easier.

------

2   With the zip closed, pin it into place so that it corresponds to the photos you took earlier.

Once happy, use your basting stitch to temporarily sew the zip into the garment. Double check it can open and close smoothly in this position and then give it a steam and press. Avoid the teeth if they are plastic.

This is the perfect time to try on the garment and make sure the zip is sitting correctly and that the garment is functioning as normal.

------

3   Looking good? Now is the time to go in with your correct thread and sew using the basic/straight stitch. Follow your photos for the placement and stitch length. Backstitch to start and finish for optimum security

Once done pull out the basting stitch etc. and voilà, your new zip is installed. Give her one more press and you are good to go.

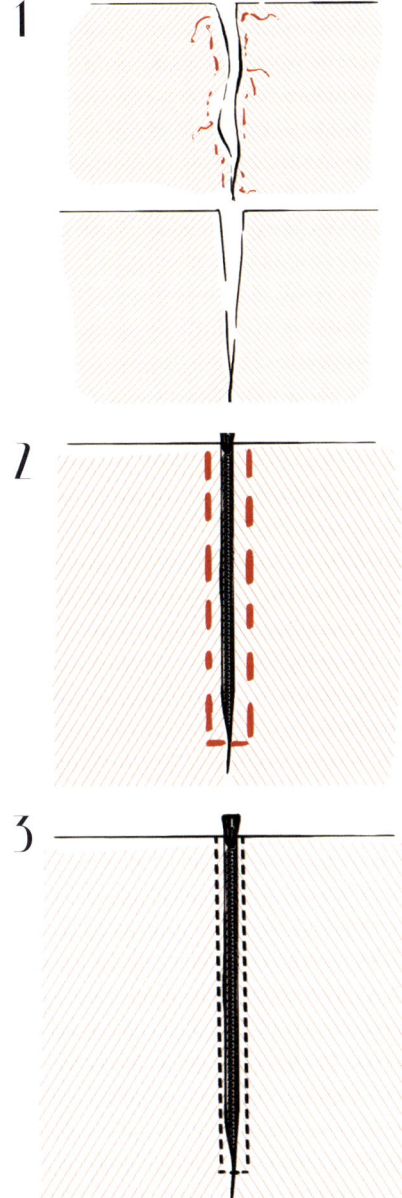

SEWING ON A BUTTON

This is another easy fix that can save a fave!

- Threaded needle (a double thread is better here for durability, knot her for speed, but you'll also be starting with some back stitching BB)
- An unthreaded needle. This will make sense I promise!
- Snips or scissors
- New button(s)
- Tailor's chalk

Buttons can loosen or fall off for many reasons. In cheaply made clothing, buttons fail due to rushed production or too little thread. In more expensive clothing, it can be down to wear and tear or it could be due to repeated stress in one area of the garment. Whatever the reason, the button is letting you know she would LOVE some extra care and attention and that its original attachment was not fit for purpose. Here are the ways I sew back on buttons to make sure they stay put for a long time so I can continue to shimmy in peace.

There are two main categories of buttons:

SEW THROUGH BUTTONS:

The holes, usually two or four, are facing you. These are normally found in thinner fabrics.

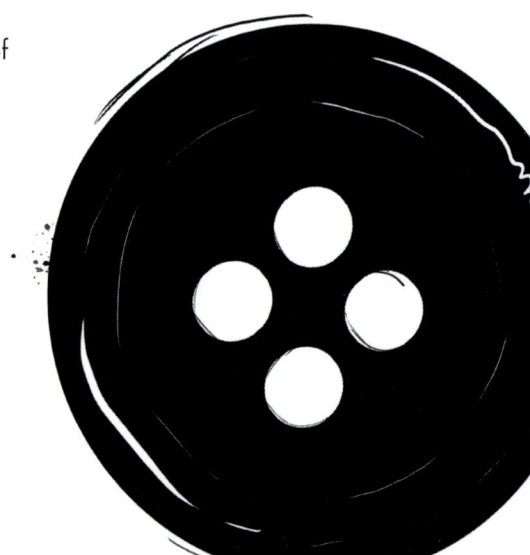

SHANK BUTTONS: these are better for thicker fabrics and are more likely to be found in coats, denim, outerwear, etc. They allow the thicker fabric some room to sit under it.

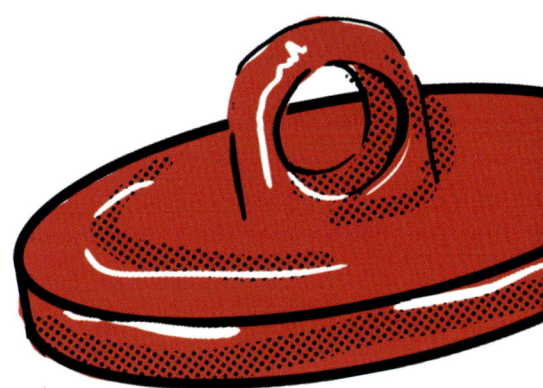

VITAL PREPARATION

Whichever one you are sewing, there is some vital prep first. When a button loosens or comes off, it will usually leave some dishevelment behind. This needs to be sorted to create a lovely patch on which you can work:

- Using a tailor's chalk or a very light dot of a regular pencil, mark where the original button was. You want to make sure the new button is perfectly aligned with its corresponding hole.
- Remove all the old threads completely. They will only get in your way later.
- Now press and stream, ensuring you don't remove the mark you created. This will allow the fibres to reset and any wear will settle down in most fabrics.
- Check if the other button threads appear as two lines or an X as you'll need to copy this pattern on yours.

SEW THROUGH

1. Anchor your thread on the inside, making sure you come out exactly where you need the button to sit.

---

2. In order to protect the fabric damaged by the old button, and to act as a visual guide, sew an 'X' smaller than your button on to the fabric.

---

3. Pop your button over the 'X' and then your spare needle on top. Sewing over this needle will help you to create enough leeway to make a shank around the threads later. This means the new button will be super long lasting.

---

4. Sew your first stitch, coming from the underneath, through the first button hole over the needle and then into the next. If your button needs an X, sew diagonal to diagonal; parallel is top to bottom or left to right (whichever matches the other buttons).

---

5. I like to repeat this five times for shirting and up to eight for an over layer. Keep your stitching tight and neat and end with your thread under the button but still on the outside of the garment. Then pull the spare needle out.

---

6. Wrap the thread around the stitches under the button and this will create a shank. My magic number of times here is five. Then bring your needle through to the back and tie off.

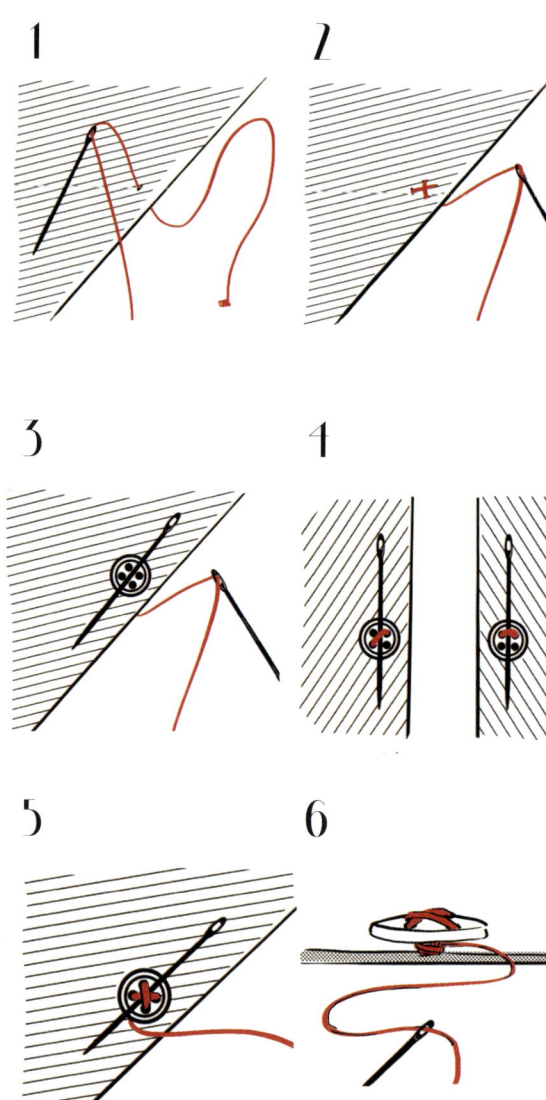

SHANK BUTTON

1. For a shank button, you'll follow many of the same steps, but you'll be sewing one hole under the button.

2. Once you have her sewn five to eight times, depending on the thickness of the fabric and size of the button, you can finish in the same way at the back.

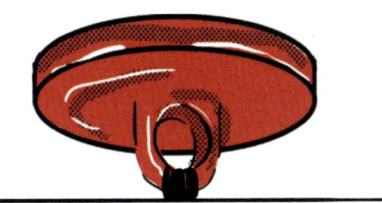

SEWING ON A HOOK AND EYE

A big issue with a lot of modern clothing is that zips keep falling. This is usually down to there being nothing to keep the zip tape at the top together, a stage skipped to save costs.

Usually, you would have an adequate fastening above the zip to prevent it from slipping open.

To create your own, you'll need:

- Hook and eye
- Needle and thread, double trouble here and a knot, please
- Tailor's chalk

A NOTE HERE: This is a fast fashion fix, usually you will have some glorious room above the top of the zip to place your

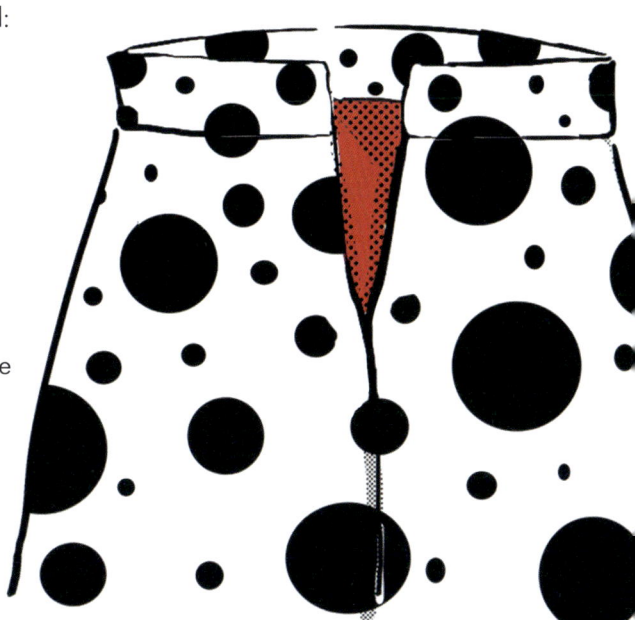

hook and eye but in some cheaply made garments there is none. This means you have to sew right onto the zip tape. Do not fear, if it keeps you wearing the garment for longer, it's worth it.

1. Zip your zip right up. Place your closed hook and eye above the zip head, near the top of the garment. Once happy with placement, mark the position with tailor's chalk, as per the image.

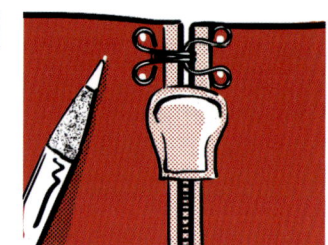

2. Open back up the zip and begin with the hook. Sew loops around her shaft first (around 4 to 5 loops here). Make sure your stitches only catch the zip tape and don't come through on the exterior of the garment.

   Then sew her looped ends. Enough to cover each so much that they cannot lift from the fabric.

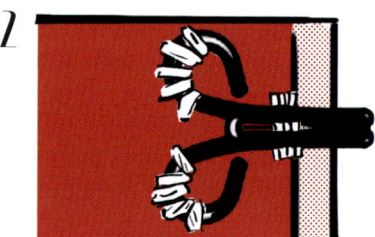

3. Now it's time for the 'eye'. She just needs her loops sew down, but be sure she is in the right place as you sew.

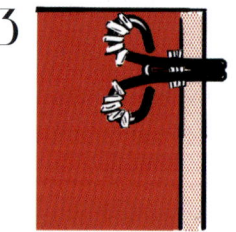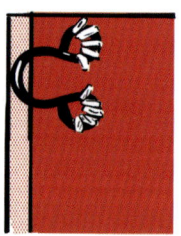

DRAWSTRINGS

Rushed production and less attention to detail can mean that many drawstring garments are not fit for purpose and end up being decarded prematurely. With the sharp rise in cheap loungewear, this has become a major issue on the high street.

HOW TO FIX IT

If a drawstring end disappears inside the waistband and you cannot massage it back through the channel, it's an easy fix.

Pull the entire string out (I know, I know). You're going to rethread it from scratch but trust me it is worth the effort and can be done quite quickly.

WHAT YOU'LL NEED

- As large a safety pin as can fit through the drawstring holes (when closed).
- Patience and maybe a couple of your favourite songs playing.

Attach the safety pin to one end of the drawstring and slide it in through one hole. Start to feed the pin and drawstring through the waistband, coaxing the safety pin with your fingers as it drags the drawstring along with it.

Using a safety pin is perfect as it will hold onto the drawstring, be smooth enough to slip through fabrics and not cause any damage due to its rounded, smooth shape.

HOW TO PREVENT IT

If this happens often with a garment, consider a few stitches to tighten the hole it sits in and a knot at the end of the drawstring. If the ends of the drawstring are a feature, you can pop it in a bow for washing.

Now you have a kit to die for and have learned some of best sewing basics that relate to modern clothing ... let's dip in to some tszujs you can carry out yourself. If your main thrill in life is a makeover, this one is for you.

12 Make Me Over

THERE MAY BE times you do not wish to part with a garment but would love to give it a new lease of life. It may not need a repair or a heavy alteration, just a little edit to make it more you. Our wardrobes tend to have items that we absolutely love many elements of, but they are missing that little something to catch it up with the rest of what we are wearing or how we want to wear it.

The following tips are super simple and easy to do but they are tips that can help lengthen the life of a garment. Be wary of any quick clothing makeover tips and hacks that lower the integrity of the garment, make it less suitable for wearing and washing or render it useless after one outing. The whole point of a tszuj is to make something more fabulous. It shouldn't reduce its quality.

To take full advantage of this chapter, my advice would be to pull out anything that you feel is of good quality, fab but worn looking or that you find super enjoyable to wear but it needs a little *je ne sais quoi*. You can then match them up to a section and plan your tszuj!

FABRIC RENEWAL

This first tip is the easiest. If you notice that a garment has little hard balls on the fabric that are making it look aged and worn, this means it is suffering from pilling. This is easy to sort and the difference that removing these balls can make is stunning!

DEBOBBLERS: Battery-operated, handheld devices. These are better for sweats and tighter knits. Work in circular motions.

RAZORS: A simple razor (one you'd use on your legs) can be good if it's a very dense weave like a wool trouser. Be gentle and work in lines.

PILLING COMB: These are better for very woolly knits as they remove fewer fibres than a debobbler and just lift the top layer to neaten. They also allow you to comb the whole garment with ease.

To prevent further pilling, make sure you are turning the garment inside out when washing and also washing less frequently. It is also wise to not wash with harsher fabrics as this may be causing the pilling in the first place.

Removing pilling can bounce a garment back to life but don't do it more than once a season as you are reducing the amount of fibres in the garment.

DYEING

With more and more people opting for natural fibres and avoiding synthetics, dyeing is set to be a permanent fixture in our futures. This is not only because dyeing naturals is so easy, but also

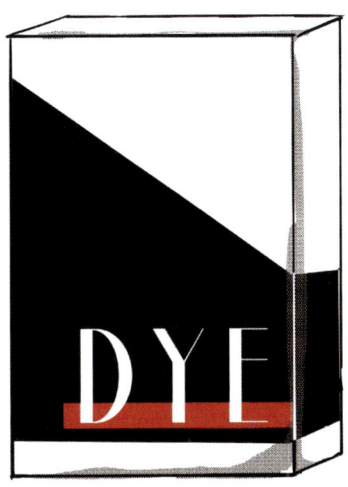

because natural fibres tend to fade a little quicker and need a top-up from time to time.

ASSESSMENT

Always check the label of both the dye product and the garment. You want to make sure the temperature and composition guidelines match.

These girls can hack it all:

- Cotton
- Linen
- Hemp
- Viscose (although technically a synthetic, it is porous enough by nature to take on dye)
- Denim

These can be tricky:

- **SILK:** Can sometimes be so delicate that it can pill a little.
- **WOOL:** Be careful with hot temps as she can be harmed.
- **SYNTHETICS:** When we think about how synthetics are made, it will be obvious that they will be very difficult to dye. This is down to them needing a lot of heat to be able to take on colour. That said, there are some dye brands and some synthetics that can take on some colour. Usually, these recommend a stove-top dye method and use other additional products like vinegar and salt.
- **BLENDS:** When there is a mix of fibres, there will be a different outcome. Most synthetics will not take on the dye at all or as well as the natural. For this reason, most brands say if there is over 20 per cent synthetic, not to dye unless it's a very slight change you are after.

COLOUR

Colour-wise, it is always easier to dye something darker. Don't forget that if a garment has a dye already this will have some say in the overall outcome. It's a bit like mixing paint. If you wish the garment to go lighter, many dye brands have a product that helps you to strip the original dye and then redye after.

The bottom line is to get to know what outcome you want and the brand guidance for this. It is rarely a case of one batch of dye in the machine and you're ready to go. This is usually only the case for faded dyes that you want to top up as opposed to a colour change.

Note the colour guide on the packs as it will tell you the weight of garments you can dye with that pack and the anticipated colour. Many brands will need a lot of packs for a few garments. The weight is usually measured in kilos. A pair of jeans can be 1kg, for example, so get to know your load. If this info is not present, it may be a big risk.

PRO TIPS

PREPARATION: Always make sure the garment is stain and dirt-free. A freshly washed garment will ensure that the dyes can be absorbed properly. No fabric softener please! This includes deodorant and grease stains; pop to page 224 to learn how to remove these first as they can leave patchy marks.

METHOD: Once you have the product and the garment in harmony, you'll be able to crack on nicely. Many people find machine washing a lot less strenuous than stove-top dyeing and it can use less water if you are doing many items at once, as well as be less damaging to surfaces and skin.

DRYING: Always prepare your drying area. Garments should be air-dried without heat. Although the machine should rinse them enough if the instructions are followed to a tee, you never know what could still have some dye on it and drip onto a carpet or flooring. For this reason, I recommend an outdoor dry where possible or over a covered surface. Don't be tempted to hang over a bath without protecting it first. Some old baths will stain badly.

POST-DYE: If using a machine, remember to empty it as soon as the load is finished. Then immediately follow the aftercare advice on how to cleanse the machine of the product.

REPLACING BUTTONS

Changing up the buttons on a garment can give it a whole new look. This works especially well on shirting and coats. Getting it right couldn't be easier. It's best to keep to the same size as the existing buttons not just for the aesthetics but because otherwise you would need to alter the buttonholes. Measure across the diameter to get the right size.

BUYING BUTTONS

Buying new buttons is a joy! They are so easy to pick up online once you know the measurement and amount you are after. My top tip here is to buy second-hand or vintage. Older buttons are usually much better quality and branded buttons can be a cost-effective way to tszuj up a garment. Be sure to buy a couple of spares just in case!

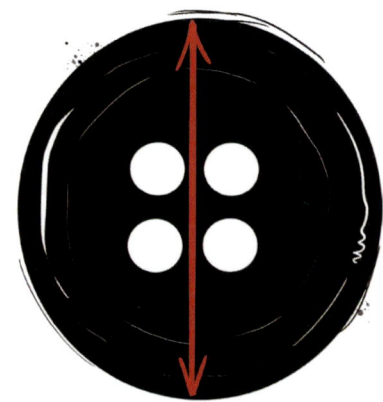

METALLICS: If you want to make a garment more dressy, elevate the look with gold or similar pop of luxe. This can be great for transforming shirts. Dyeing a white shirt black and adding gold and black enamel buttons (or perhaps a bright pink with gold buttons) can give it a whole new lease of life.

TONAL: If you want to tone down a garment for a more laid-back look, get buttons in the exact same shade. The better the quality, the more luxurious this look.

A BOHO GAL?: Look for wooden or tortoiseshell buttons.

UTILITY QUEEN?: Go for buttons designed for workwear and it will bring any garment to your taste level.

COATS: Buttons are like door handles. Swapping them out can create a whole new vibe. If you want to feel like you have a new winter coat and there are exposed buttons, have a look at what else you can get in the same size. When it comes to coats, black on brights can give a mod look, tonal is more modern, and for the late 80s/early 90s, metallic or high shine is a buzz.

CHANGING LENGTHS

Changing hem lengths on a trouser, skirt or sleeve of a top that you love is a stunning way to get even more wear out of them. Hems are one of the most important parts of trends as they tend to anchor the overall style. Raising or lowering a hem can change a garment dramatically and it can also mean you will wear it more. The hem tutorial on page 278 will show you how to sew your new hem length but things to remember are:

- Pinning is the first step to getting your desired length with no commitment. Play around!
- Once happy, give the hem a light press so you can see how the length looks properly on you. Pin excess fabric higher up the leg/arm/body for now, the main thing here is not to cut until you are sure you're happy.
- If the hem is quite flowy or heavy, then you should baste before cutting. This will allow you to see the fall of the garment at the new length in all its glory.
- When you have your desired length, remember you need an adequate hem allowance to turn up and you also need to be able to turn the raw edge under to keep it secure.

- If you have fabric to work with, copy the original hem allowance. If in doubt, hems are usually 3cm in depth.

JEANS

I have jeans for years and years that I feel get better with more wear but the only thing that makes them feel dated is the hem length. Denim doesn't always have to have a top stitch along the bottom. Hand sewing the hem up inside with a blind stitch can give a more formal look as it is a clean finish at the bottom. This also means you don't have to cut the denim and simply have a longer hem allowance if you feel you will need to change them again. I often remove the stitches entirely and wash and hem at another length. It means one pair of jeans can be changed as much as I like over time.

One top tip here is that jeans are so structured you can actually just use bobby pins to trial the length and push up and down as desired. It's a quick way to trial a new hem length with no pinning.

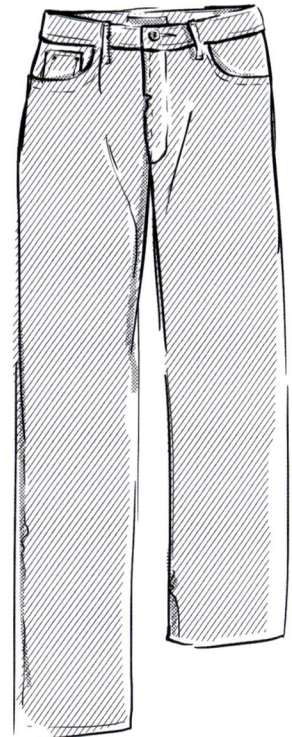

WE ARE GATHERED HERE

Gathers/frills are a great way to tszuj up a garment. This can be to a skirt, dress, cuffs, tops of pockets, around the ends of collars, you get the gist.

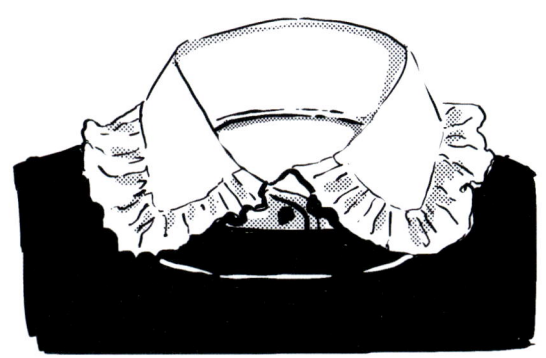

THE FRILL: A ready-made trim or ribbon is best as the edges will not fray. However, if you are using a strip of cut fabric, you'll need to finish the edges. Simply do a double-turned hem to tuck any raw edges out of harm's way. Don't forget to press before you sew for a crisp finish!

LENGTH: The fabric (or trim) that you are attaching should be at least 2.5 times the length of the hem you are attaching it to. This will give you enough to create a gloriously full frill. If you want a flatter frill you can always shorten it later. If you want fuller ... go mad.

You will need:

- Threaded needle (make it a double length of thread for strength and tie the two ends in a knot – like a balloon)
- Fabric (finished edges, please!) trim or ribbon pressed and ready to sew
- Snips or scissors
- Pins

NOTES

APPLICATION: You can be as adventurous as you like here; a massive ruffle to the end of a mini or pair of evening gloves is always

a welcome sight. Or, perhaps a simple contrasting ribbon along a collar. Chic.

SEWING THE FRILL: Choose to work left to right or right to left. Whichever is comfier for you. As a *ciotóg*, I tend to go left to right for example.

SIZE: Consider the size of your gathers before you begin to sew. If you want full and bouncy, remember to make your stitches long. Short stitches will give you flatter, ruching-style gather. A wee trial is always handy if you are unsure.

CREATING A FRILL

Now, it is time to consider the size of your gathers. If you want big, do longer stitches, thinner, go shorter. Do a wee trial if you are unsure as it's an easy stitch to remove.

1. Press your fabric so she is ready to be worked with.

2. You'll be using a running stitch. It's like a basic stitch but with a twist: her stitches are as long as the gaps in between them. This allows for gathering once sewn.

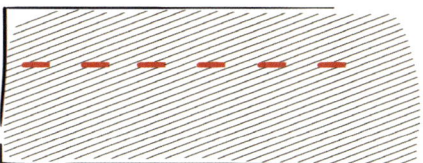

3. Anchor your thread as normal near the top of the fabric. Now do a double backstitch. We need this end of the stitch line to be super secure, so this backstitch is vital!

4. Sew a straight running stitch the whole way across.

5. Once you have the full stitch line done, hold the needle and gently push the fabric back towards the anchor. If it is a long piece or tough fabric, go back to the start and pull in stages, gently.

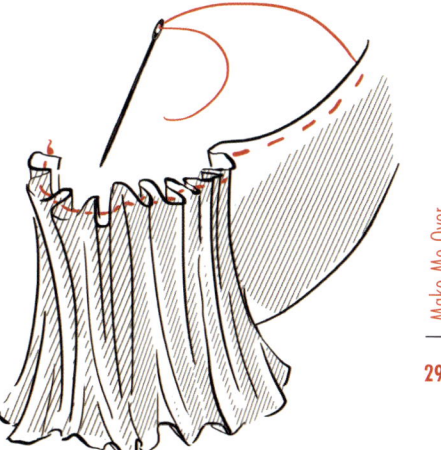

6. You should start to see a beautiful frill appear. Space it out as you see fit.

7. Once happy, use a pin to hold the last gather in place and double check the full frill fits to your desired hem. If you are too short or too long, this this is the time to adjust!

8. All good? Do a triple backstitch and then tie off as normal.

ATTACHING THE FRILL

1. Pin the frill into place before you sew. I like to pin in quarters first to ensure everything is sitting where it should. If you have a particularly enthusiastic ruffle (divine), a basting stitch will help you massively in place of pins.

2. Sew the frill in to place using the slip stitch on page 281.

3. You can then finish the frill by sewing the ends together with a basic stitch.

UPCYCLE EVENTS

Upcycling and sewing events, classes and courses are a brilliant way to transform clothing under some guidance. They often have machines and supplies, which can be super if you don't have your own. Usually, these are centred around transforming one type of piece – say a pair of jeans – into something else or adding embellishments or decorations of some kind.

In general, when it comes to clothing makeovers, you want something that will last. There are a lot of online hacks and snappy ways to create a look but don't forget to think of how the garment will need to be cared for and if it will need to be hand-washed, etc. Sometimes it is better to give it to someone you know will wear the garment many times instead of committing it to a shorter life.

Until next time

Garment Goddess,

We have come to the end and, while I am sad to part ways into the night, I am simply delighted to have been on this journey with you.

When I was creating this little gem, I wanted to share the secrets, tips, tricks and lesser-known sides to garment production to be able put the power back in your hands. My aim was to clear up the common grey areas and help empower us in something that plays such a big role in daily life.

I hope you have enjoyed this book and within her pages have found some pause for thought and useful tips, and had a ball. She is here for you to dip in and out of any time you need her, and she will always have your back.

Bonne chance bebe,

L

Acknowledgements

You would not be holding this book in those gorgeous hands if it wasn't for some people very dear to me. I'll start with my husband Shane. Your support, love and superhuman patience kept me going through the long days and late nights. Thank you for every meal you placed on my desk and every word of encouragement you gave me. I love you.

Fiona Murphy will murder me for this, but it will be worth it. Thank you for believing I could write not one book but three and giving me the confidence and guidance to do so. Your advice and time have always been so appreciated. I am so grateful for the friendship that has blossomed since we first worked together on *Gaff Goddess*.

To Richard, Louise, Kim, Joe, Aiden and the rest of you icons. Thank you for always for being there when I needed to talk something through and helping me to tweak the pages gently. Those moments of support are what make the process of writing a book so much easier. The martinis during the down time helped too ...

Thank you to the team at Gill. A big thank you to my family and dear in-laws for their support throughout the process, always checking in and pushing me along.

Lastly, a thank you to you, reader. I hope she's been a good one.

L

x

INDEX

acrylic 18, 123–4
airing clothes outdoors 161–2, 164
allergies 14
alterations 143–5
   see also dressmakers; makeovers; sewing; tailors
bicarbonate of soda 162, 225
blends/mixes 38, 39, 46, 124, 126, 187, 292
brands
   cashmere and 38
   customer service 60
   fit models and 54–5
   in-house designers 65
   long-staple cotton, use of 27
   margins and 50, 65
   online selling 131–2
   organic fibres and 30, 31
   polyester and 40, 41–4
   responsible accreditation 48
   sizing and 52, 54–5, 56, 59
   suppliers and 56, 65
   Tencel™ 45
   trims, cost-saving and 29
   websites, used section on 126–7
brushed loopback 119–20
buttonholes 99–101
buttons 99, 100, 261, 263
   replacing 294–5
   sew through buttons 284, 286
   sewing on 284–7
   shank buttons 285, 287
   shirt buttons 110
   types of 110, 294, 295
   vintage/second-hand 294
   washing and 168
care labels 51–2, 92, 135–6, 159–60, 163, 165–6
   preloved garments 128–9, 235
cashmere 14, 37–9, 52, 211
cellulose-derived fibres 13
changing room tips 139–45
   accessories 142–3
   alterations 143–5
   damage, assessing for 143
   fastenings 143
   fit 144–5
   hems 143–4
   pockets 142
   preparation 140
   seam finishing 145
   temperature 143
   wearing the item 141–3
charity shops 127–8
   donations of clothing 236–9
   profit and 238–9
   recycling and 239
   unsellable donations 239
clothing
   discarding 240–1
   donating 230, 235–40
   recyclable 231, 239
   repurposed 231
   resaleable 230
   selling 231–5
   used clothing, private companies and 239
clothing bins 240
coats and jackets 114–17
   buttons, replacing 294–5
   centre back seam 115
   facing 88–9
   fastenings 115
   hangers 202
   lining 91–2, 116
   pockets 115–16
   shipping, stitches for 116–17
   sleeves 114
   vintage/preloved 127–8
collars 29, 59, 109, 297
   stains/washing 169, 226
comp shopping 64–5, 66
cotton 13, 23–31
   advantages of 24–5
   blends 46, 117
   day-to-day garments 25
   dyeing 292
   extra-long staple (ELS) 27
   gaps in the weave 28–9

handfeel 28, 117
knitwear 124
long-staple 25–8, 135
organic 30–1
pilling 26, 29
production of 29–30
short-staple 26, 28, 29
sustainability 29–30
trims (cuffs/collars) 29
wash cycle 188
cotton thread 253–4
cuffs 29, 109–10, 118, 119, 125, 276

darts 93–4, 108
debobblers 291
delicates
   storage 199, 202, 203
   wash cycle 166, 188, 189
denim/denim jeans 120–3
   airing 164
   appearance 120–1
   dyeing 292
   elastane and 46, 164
   find your perfect match 121–2
   hem length 297
   metal rivets 123
   steaming 164
   washing 164, 167–8
designers, mass-production 64–6
detergents 172–80
   bio/non bio 176, 224
   brighteners 174, 176
   builders 175
   cool wash claim 176
   dosing 183–5
   dyes added to 173
   eco-detergents 178–9
   enzymes 174–5, 176
   fragrance 173–4
   liquids 177
   pods 177, 183–4
   powders 177
   surfactants 175, 176
drawstrings 288–9
dresses 113–14
dressmakers 62–4
   garments, examining/critiquing 65–6
   pattern cutting and 62–3, 106–7
   shopping and 63–4
   see also alterations; makeovers; sewing; tailors
dry-cleaning 163, 166, 207, 208–11, 228
   see also hand-washing; laundry
drying clothes 193–6
dyes/dyeing 291–4
   cashmere 39
   colour 293
   cotton 29, 30
   denim 122
      indigo 122
   linen 33
   natural fibres 16, 37, 39
   pro tips 293–4
   stains caused by dye 217–18, 227–8
   synthetics 21
   wash temperature 189
   wool 37, 39

eco wash cycle 187
eco-detergents 178–9
eco-washing bags 171–2
Egyptian cotton 27
environment
   cotton production and 29–30
   natural fibres and 15, 16
   rayon and 21–2
   synthetic fibres and 20, 40
   viscose production and 44
etui 262

fabric 12–13
   composition 10, 135
   fast fashion and 11, 16
fabric softeners 180–5, 222
fabric weight 85–6
facing 86–90
   checking 89–90
   coats and jackets 88–90
   reasons for using 87–8
   stitching line 90
fast fashion
   darts 94
   fabrics 11, 16
   online shopping and 132
   overconsumption 230
   pleated trousers 113
   polyester 40
   prints, patterns and stripes 104
   quality of 61–2
   seams 77
   shirts, button direction on 101
   sizing, effects on 55–6
   stripes 106
   vintage/preloved market 130
   washing 191
fastenings 115, 143, 148, 203–4
   online shopping and 135
   vintage/preloved garments 129, 130
   see also buttons; hook and eye; zips
fibres 10
   see also natural fibres; synthetic fibres

fit issues 56
fit models 54–5
flax 13, 31
footwear, effect/impact of 140, 147

garment assessment
　fashion 66, 104–6
　finish 66–84
　form 66, 84–96
　function 66, 97–104
garment design 106–7
garment finish 66–84
　batch check 67
　hems 82–4
　seams 73–82
　stitching 67–73
garment form 84–96
　darts 93–4
　facing 86–90
　lining 90–3
　sleeves 94–6
　weight (of fabric) 85–6
garment function 66, 97–104
　buttons/buttonholes 99–102
　pockets 97–9
　zips 102–4
gathers/frills 297–300
Global Organic Textile Standard (GOTS) 31
Google 128, 133, 135
greenwashing 45, 46, 178
GSM (grams per square metre) 85
gym kits/sportswear 41, 169, 221–3

hand-washing 163, 166, 188, 191, 209, 301
hand-made items 67, 82
hangers 201–3, 210
hemp 13, 292

hems 82–4
　altering 143–4, 149
　blind/invisible 83–4, 113, 278–80
　bound hem 83
　details and 144
　double fold 83
　lengths, changing 296–7
　prints, effect on hem 144
　seam finish 144
　synthetic fabrics, needle holes in 144
　T-shirts 118
　turn and stitch 82
　vintage/preloved garments 118, 130
　visible hem stitches 82–3, 144
hook and eye 104, 108, 168, 287–8

jeans 54–5, 123, 137, 140, 199
　see also denim jeans

knitwear 123–6
　acrylic 123–4
　construction 124–6
　cotton 124, 163
　faux knit/cut and sew 124–5
　fibre 123–4
　lanolin in wool knits 163
　merino wool 124
　overlocking and 125
　specialist brands 125–6
　storage 200
　synthetic 163
　true knit 124, 125–6, 162
　washing 162–3, 188
　wool 123

labels
　sizing 52–3
　see also care labels
lace 188, 199
lambs' wool 35
landfill 15, 20, 40, 158, 172, 236
　avoiding/reducing 153, 240, 241
laundry 155–96
　cycle selection 185–9
　drying 193–6
　energy and water 156–7
　fast fashion and 191
　microplastic shedding 156, 157
　natural fibres, impact of 15
　step 1: undress and assess 160–4
　step 2: line up the load 165–7
　step 3: preparing the load 167–70
　step 4: loading 170–1
　step 5: dosing 183–5
　stress on garments 156, 157–8
　wash tests 159–60
　see also dry-cleaning; hand-washing; odours; stains
linen 13, 31–3
　characteristics 31–2
　creasing/wrinkling 32
　dyes/dyeing 33, 292
　handfeel 32
　merino/linen blend 124
　natural undyed form 33
　storage 32, 199
　sustainability 33
lining 90–3, 107, 116
　assessment 92–3

care label 92
composition 92
garments, function for 90–1
polyester lining 91–2
wearers, function for 91–2
loopback 119–20
Lycra 19, 122
lyocell 45–6

makeovers 290–301
buttons, replacing 294–5
dyeing 291–4
fabric renewal 291
gathers/frills 297–300
lengths, changing 296–7
upcycle events 300–1
see also alterations; dressmakers; sewing; tailors
mass production 84, 107
mass-production designers 64–6
measuring/measurements 57–60
flat measuring 59–60, 234
menswear 58–9
size charts 57–8
sizing 52–3
womenswear 58
merino wool 35–6, 117, 124
microplastics 20, 22, 43, 157, 171–2, 188
modal 45
moths 129–30, 211–15
cold and 213
heat/hot wash and 213
pheromone traps 214
prevention 213–15

repellents 214
steam and 213
what to do/treatment 212–13

natural fabrics 13
organic 48
responsible production 48
washing 167
natural fibres 12, 13, 14–16
absorbency 14–15, 221, 224
allergies 14
biodegradable 15
breathability 14, 221, 224
cellulose derived 13
comfort 14
durability 15
dyeing 291–2
high-quality connotations 16
keratin in animal-based fibres 211, 212
minimal laundry impact 15
production, ease of 15–16
protein queens 14
sustainability 15
necklines, neck tape and 88, 118
needles 248–52
ballpoint 251
beading 251
betweens 250
calyx eye/easy thread 250
chenille 251
darners 252
leather 251
sharps 250
tapestry 252

threading 271–2
nylon 18

occasion wear 32, 45, 127, 128, 170
storage 206, 208
odours
eliminating 161–2, 164, 170, 180, 222
fabric softeners and 182
gym kits and 221–3
spritzing and 169, 223
steam/steaming and 170
vinegar and 180
see also hand-washing; laundry; stains
online shopping 131–3
advantages 131
before you check out 137–8
care label 135–6
delivery time 137
fabric composition 135
fast fashion 132
fastenings and function 135
flat lay of the garment 134
images 133–5
information 135–7
length of garment 136
necklines/waistlines, shots of 136
negative aspects 132
poses, images and 134
preloved garments 138
return policy 137
similar items, search for 138
sizing and silhouettes 137
source of garments 136
sustainability 137

zoom option 134
organic fabrics 48
    certification 31
    cotton 30–1
    Global Organic Textile
        Standard (GOTS) 31

pattern cutting, basic blocks
    62, 63, 106–7
petrochemicals 17
pilling 26, 29, 37, 39
pilling comb 291
Pima (cotton) 27
pockets 97–9
    assessment 98–9, 142
    ciotógs and 115
    in coats and jackets
        115–16
    external pockets 115, 116
    flap pockets 115–16
    interior breast pockets
        115
    openings, reinforced 98,
        112
    patch pockets 115
    pocket bags 98, 115, 116
    sewn-up pockets 98
    size 98
    ticket pocket 99
    torn pocket bags, sewing
        280–1
    in trousers 112
    washing, empty pockets
        before 169
polyester 17, 18, 40–4
    advantages 40–1
    aesthetic 41–2
    appearance 43
    characteristics 42–3
    environment and 40
    fast fashion and 40
    function 42
    longevity 42
    performance 41, 42

recycled 45, 135
repairing 43
sportswear 41, 42
sustainability 43–4
polyester lining 91–2
polyester thread 254–5
polymers 12, 17
pop fasteners 115
prices/pricing 49–51
prints, patterns and stripes
    104–6
protein naturals 14, 163

quality 15, 16, 36, 50, 54,
    153
    cashmere and 38, 39
    cotton and 24, 25, 28,
        29
    linen and 32, 33
    polyester and 41, 42,
        43
    poor quality 5, 11, 12,
        20, 61–2

Radziwill, Carole 54
rayon 21–2, 44–6
razors 291
recycled fibres 47–8
recycled polyester 45, 135
recycling 231, 239
    clothing bins and 240

sales/sale prices 50–1
SBS zips 103
Sea Island cotton 27
seams 73–82
    alterations and 145
    bound seams 79–80
    closed seams 79
    double stitched 78–9,
        118
    fast-fashion approach
        77
    flat felled seams 81–2

french seams 80
hanger appeal 77
importance of 74–5
open seams 75
overlocked 75, 76, 77,
    118, 125
raw edge 75
repairing split seams 277
seam allowance 73
seam finishing 145
serged 75, 76, 77
side seams, puckering in
    72–3
in T-shirts 118
vintage/preloved
    garments 130
welt seam 78
semi-synthetics 21–2
sewing 149
    basic stitches 273–6
    basting/tacking stitch
        275–6
    buttons, sewing on
        284–7
    drawstrings 288–9
    hems 143–4, 149,
        278–80
    herringbone stitch 280
    hook and eye, sewing on
        287–8
    invisible stitches 276,
        278–80
    pocket bags, torn 280–1
    pressing and 270
    repairs 277–89
    scissors, sharpening 270
    seams, burst 277
    slip stitch 280–1
    thread, tips and tricks
        267–9
    threaders 272
    threading a needle
        271–2
    zip, replacing 282–3

see also alterations;
  dressmakers;
  makeovers; tailors
sewing kits 246–5
  button jar 261–2
  etui 262
  magnet 260
  measuring tapes 257–8
  needle types 250–2
  needles 248–52
  pin cushion 259–60
  pins 258–60
  preowned tools 247–8
  sewing box 260–1
  shears 256–7
  snips 255–6
  thread 252–5
  tools 247
  travel sewing kit 262–4
  wall-hanging sewing kit 264–5
sheep's wool 34–5
shirts 109–11
  buttonholes 100–1
  buttons 110, 294, 295
  collar and cuffs 109
  cuff placket 109–10
  finish 110
  hanger loops 111
  storage 203–4
  yoke 111
shopping 62–6
  buying less 47, 153–4
  buying well 8–9
  cotton garments 28–30
  overconsumption 229, 230
  sales 50–1
  see also changing room tips; comp shopping
shoulders/armholes 72
silk 14, 163, 176, 188, 199, 211, 292
sizing 52–3

fast fashion, effects of 55–6
fit issues 56
fit models 54–5
  gold seal sample 55
  grading 54
  measurements 53
  size 12 54–5
skirts 107–8
sleeves
  drop sleeves 96, 118
  raglan sleeves 95–6
  set-in sleeves 94–5
  two-piece sleeves 95, 114
Spandex 19, 122
SPI (stitch per inch) 68–9
stains 216–28
  armpit stains 220–5
  blood stains 226–7
  categories of 217, 218
  collar stains 226
  deodorants/ antiperspirants 223–4
  dyes 217, 218, 227–8
  fresh stains 219
  greasy food stains 226
  long-term sweat stains 225
  oils 217, 218
  pretreatment 169, 187, 190, 217, 218
  proteins 217, 218
  set-in stains 219
  spritzing 169, 187, 190, 218, 223, 224
  sweat shields 224–5
  sweat stains 220–5
  tannins 217, 218
  see also dry-cleaning; hand-washing; laundry; odours
static/static cling 181

steam/steaming 161, 164, 170, 210–11, 213
stitching 67–73
  errors 70
  gaps 69
  investigation of 69–73
  loose threads 70–1
  puckering 70, 72–3
  SPI (stitch per inch) 68–9
  stitch length 68–9
  uniformity 69
storage
  delicates 199
  floor storage 205–6
  folding 199, 200
  hangers 201–3
  hanging 198–201, 203–4
  hanging bags 206–7
  hanging loops 200–1
  knitwear 200
  occasion wear 206, 208
  off-season items 204–8
  plastic garment bags 207, 209
  pre-storage 197–8
  pressed 199
  storage bags 206, 209
  storage system 198
  tailoring and suiting 199
  vacuum bags 207–8
  wovens and non-wovens 198
Supima (cotton) 27
sustainability 33, 39, 43–4, 46, 137, 153
sweat shields 224–5
sweat stains 220–5
sweaters 119–20
synthetic fabrics
  blends 46
  characteristics 19–20
  dyeing 292

fabric softeners and 222
needle holes in 144
production 20–1
types of 17–19
washing 167, 187, 221–2
synthetic fibres 12, 13, 15

T-shirts 117–18, 199
tailors 145–9
  see also alterations; dressmakers; makeovers; sewing
Tencel™ 45, 46
thread 252–5, 267–9
travel sewing kit 262–4
trousers 111–13, 199, 202

upcycle events 300–1

vacuum bags 207–8
Velcro 115, 168, 204
vinegar 170, 179–80
  moth larvae and 213
  odours, removing 180, 222–3
  softening and 180
  spritz (50:50 vinegar/water) 169, 223
  stains, prewash treatment of 169, 225
  vinegar rinse 170, 180
vintage/preloved garments 126–7
  care of 128–30, 235
  cashmere 39
  charity shops 127–8
  damage 129
  fastenings 130
  flat measuring 59–60
  hems 130
  inside 129
  issues 129
  labels 128, 235

lambswool 35
moths 129–30
occasion wear 127
online shopping 138
outerwear 127–8
quality of 129
seams 128, 130
selling 127, 231–5
sizing 127
viscose 44–5, 292

wall-hanging sewing kit 264–5
wash cycles
  cool washes 190
  cottons 188
  cycle selection 185–7
  delicates 188
  eco wash 187
  fast wash 189
  hot wash 190
  machine cleaning 190
  mixes 187
  synthetics 187
  temperature 186, 189
  warm wash 190
washing machines
  cycle selection 185–9
  dirty marks on clothes 192
  drawers/compartments 184–5, 192
  dyeing and 293–4
  garment damage 192
  maintenance 191–2
  smelly drum 192
Westwood, Vivienne 34
womenswear measurements 58
wool 14, 33–9, 211
  advantages/uses 33–4
  cashmere 37–9
  dyes/dyeing 37, 39, 292

knitwear 123
luxury wools 37
pilling 37
quality 36
sustainability 39
types of 34–6
waterproof characteristic 37
wool garments, lining 92
woollen (short-staple wool) 35
worsted (long-staple wool) 35

yarns
  cashmere 38
  cotton 25–6, 28, 29, 117
  creation of 12, 17, 21
  synthetic 123
  warp and weft 121
  wool 35, 36, 37
YKK zips 102–3

zips 102–4, 108, 114, 148, 168, 204
  hook and eye, sewing on 287–8
  replacing 282–3